STRAFBATALLION

STRAFBATALLION
HITLER'S PENAL BATTALIONS

WALTER S. ZAPOTOCZNY JR.

FONTHILL

For the survivors

Fonthill Media Language Policy

Fonthill Media publishes in the international English language market. One language edition is published worldwide. As there are minor differences in spelling and presentation, especially with regard to American English and British English, a policy is necessary to define which form of English to use. The Fonthill Policy is to use the form of English native to the author. Walter S. Zapotoczny Jr. was born and educated in the United States; therefore American English has been adopted in this publication.

Fonthill Media Limited
Fonthill Media LLC
www.fonthillmedia.com
office@fonthillmedia.com

First published in the United Kingdom and the United States of America 2017

British Library Cataloguing in Publication Data:
A catalogue record for this book is available from the British Library

Copyright © Walter S. Zapotoczny Jr. 2017

ISBN 978-1-78155-647-4

Typeset in 10pt on 13pt Sabon
Printed and bound in England

Preface

Condemned to prison sentences, the men who became members of Hitler's penal battalions had an opportunity to have their sentences reduced by service at the front. Not only were these soldiers considered criminals, but their families were also tainted by the men's actions and words. For many, the dangerous combat missions were better than the horrific conditions they faced in the military prisons. While gathering material for this book, I realized that the story of the Strafbattalions had to be told within the larger context of the German penal system and the increasing need for manpower, as World War II progressed. Therefore, many pages are dedicated to an understanding of the evolution of the Nazi criminal justice system and the military's interpretation and implementation of that system.

Soldiers were transferred from penal custody to parole and pardon combat units that were used to supplement regular military units. While many records of the penal units did not survive the war, the military organization of the Third Reich and the German Army groups listed in the appendices give us an idea of larger organizations that the Strafbattalions became part of.

Many soldiers took advantage of the opportunity to repent for their crimes and served on the front heroically. Others could not and continued criminal activities, committing atrocities on innocent civilians. While others were transferred back to prisons or executed for their crimes.

This book is the story of the men who were caught up in ideas of National Socialism and became the pawns of its policies.

CONTENTS

Introduction

The toughest measures are necessary to maintain discipline in the troops, to suppress cowardice, and to give members of the Wehrmacht, who had blundered one time, the opportunity for parole.

Adolf Hitler
December 21, 1940

Penal military organizations are military units consisting of convicted individuals mobilized for military service. To understand the Strafbattalion, we have to look at the German military penal system as a whole and the requirements for more and more manpower as the war went on. The Strafbattalions were an extension of that penal system. These units were not exclusive to the German military. This approach was regarded as a form punishment or discipline in place of imprisonment or capital punishment for many governments.

The Napoleonic era of warfare, for example, saw the first dedicated penal units. They were first envisioned as large armies formed of recruits who often suffered from disciplinary trouble.[1] Soldiers who refused to face the enemy were seen as damaging to the army, bringing dishonor to the nation. The development of penal battalions was seen as a way of punishing individuals and keeping other soldiers in line. In order to better utilize national manpower during wartime, many nations conscripted criminals into penal battalions *in lieu* of imprisoning them. These penal military units were treated with little regard by the regular military and were often placed in compromising situations, such as being used in suicide missions.[2] In his article, *French Penal Regiment Organization*, François Lo Presti observed:

The French Empire in particular was notable for employing penal military units during the wars of the coalition [1792–1815], especially during the later years of the conflicts as manpower became limited. The *Régiment pénal de l'Île de Ré* (132nd Infantry Regiment), was formed in 1811 and was composed almost entirely of criminals and other societal undesirables, would see action during the later years of the Napoleonic Wars.[3]

Following the Napoleonic era, conscripted armies were disbanded and large-scale warfare ended. As a result, this lead to the decline of the penal battalion system in continental Europe. However, the system continued in overseas colonies, with the French as the primary employers of penal battalions. In 1832, Louis Philippe I formed the "Battalions of Light Infantry of Africa" for the purpose of expanding the French colonial empire.[4] The Battalion fought in the French conquest of Algeria and during the Crimean War. The French also used military units they termed as "companies of the excluded," which were stationed at Aïn Séfra in Southern Algeria, situated in the Saharan Atlas Mountains, 45 kilometers east of the border with Morocco. These penal units consisted of convicts who were judged unworthy to carry weapons and who were condemned to five years or more of hard labour.[5]

In 1843, during the various Italian unification conflicts (1815–1871), the "Redshirts" recruited convicts and revolutionaries from prisons into penal battalions known as *Battaglioni della imprigionato* (Battalions of the Imprisoned). In April 1859, during the Second War of Italian Independence, the Piedmontese army, strongly supported by the French, found that it needed to use all available manpower resources. Therefore, it was decided to use convicts in May of that year. The *Battaglione dei Cacciatori Franchi* (Battalion of the Franks Hunters) became the home for the soldiers who had committed offenses mild enough to be confined to the regiment but not so serious as to require being sent to a military prison. Service in the *Battaglione dei Cacciatori Franchi*, which could last many years, was designed to reward the soldiers if they behaved well and to reward them by allowing them to move up from one class to another.[6]

Shtrafbats were Soviet penal battalions that fought on the Eastern Front in World War II. Joseph Stalin greatly increased their number in July 1942 with his Order Number 227. After the panicked routs of the first year of combat with Germany, the order was a desperate effort to re-instill discipline. The order, which became known as the "Not One Step Back" order, established severe punishments, including the death sentence, for unlawful retreats.[7]

The first Russian *Shtrafbats* were originally designed for 800 men. Penal companies were also authorized, consisting of between 150 and 200 men per company. In addition to the battalions already serving with the Russian armies, other battalions, subordinated to Army Groups, were established. The first penal battalion deployed under the new policy was sent to the Stalingrad Front on August 22, 1942, shortly before German troops reached the Volga River. It consisted of 929 dishonored officers convicted under Stalin's Order Number 227. They were demoted to the lowest enlisted rank and assigned to the penal battalion. After three days of assaults against the Germans, only 300 were alive.[8]

During the American Civil War, captured Confederate soldiers sometimes recanted the rebellion, swore allegiance to the Union, and became "Galvanized Yankees." Approximately 5,600 former Confederate soldiers enlisted in the United States Volunteers, organized into six regiments between January 1864 and November 1866. Of those, more than 250 began their service as Union soldiers, were captured in battle by the Confederates, and then enlisted in prison to join a regiment of the Confederate States Army. They surrendered to Union forces in December 1864 and were held by the United States as deserters, but were saved from prosecution by being enlisted in the 5th and 6th U.S. Volunteers. An additional 800 former Confederates served in volunteer regiments raised by the states, forming ten companies. Four of those companies saw combat in the western theatre against the Confederate Army. Two served on the western frontier, and one became an independent company of U.S. Volunteers, serving in Minnesota.[9]

Confederate recruitment of Union prisoners of war was authorized by Confederate Secretary of War James A. Seddon on September 30, 1864, after inquiries from General Braxton Bragg to recruit foreign-born prisoners. Seddon had, as early as March 1863, granted discretionary permission to commanders including General John Pemberton to recruit prisoners, but few, if any, were actually enlisted. A concerted recruiting effort began on October 12 and continued to the end of the war. At least four Confederate units were recruited, including three units of regulars in the Provisional Army of the Confederate States.[10]

The British Royal African Corps was composed of military offenders from various regiments pardoned on condition of life-service in Africa and the West Indies. Military service for life overseas and banishment from England forever were conditions of service. Such an assignment to a regiment in the then West Indies or Africa during 1809–1822 also can be thought to be analogous to a sentence of death. For troops in such tropical areas, the chances of death from disease were magnitudes greater than becoming a fatality from combat operations. Soldiers of that period serving in tropical climates died in droves, primarily from yellow fever and malaria. Of course, there was no possibility of return to England, even though they survived military service.[11]

The Military Police oversaw the Ottoman Army penal units. These were soldiers under punishment by wearing a fez with the tassel cut off. Prisoners of war or rebels were often fed into existing punishment systems without being formally sentenced. Peter the Great, for example, made use of Turkish, Tartar, Swedish, Finnish, Estonian, and Latvian prisoners, sending them to labor alongside convicts as part of the failed attempt to colonize the Black Sea port of Azov.[12]

With Adolf Hitler moving Germany closer to war in 1938, the Nazi Government issued a decree for the purpose of suppressing any activity opposed to the Wehrmacht (German Armed Forces) or the Nazi regime (see Appendix I for a brief description of the military organization of the Third Reich).

Wehrkraftzersetzung (subversion) or undermining military morale is a term from German military law established in the Third Reich. The crime of *Zersetzung der Wehrkraft* (seduction of the war effort) was included in the anti-sedition decree. Commonly called *Wehrkraftzersetzung*, the term is variously translated as "subversion of the war effort," "undermining military morale," and "sedition and defeatism."[13]

Paragraphs already in the military penal code were consolidated and redefined, creating the new crime, which carried the death penalty. In 1939, a second decree was issued that extended the crime to civilians.[14]

Any criticism of the political or military leadership and the Nazi form of government or dispiriting statements, such as doubt about the eventual victory of Germany, were punishable by death or long sentences in military prisons or concentration camps. If the soldier was fortunate, he could face deployment to the field or to a probationary unit. Conscientious objectors in particular were frequently convicted of undermining military morale in addition to other charges. This was done to minimize the potential of negative influence on others, even when the refusal of military service had not been made public. Many civilians were also convicted of subversion by military courts.[15]

The term "undermining military force" was established in law by the Wartime Special Penal Code or KSSVO on August 17, 1938. It criminalized all criticism, dissent, and behavior opposed to the Nazi's political and military leadership, particularly within the Wehrmacht's military justice system. The definition of the KSSVO was equivalent to the Treachery Act of 1934 but escalated the crime. Critical comments by soldiers violating the Treachery Act had previously been punished only with a prison term, but the KSSVO added the death penalty, allowing for a prison term only in minor cases.[16]

With the introduction of the Wartime Regulations for Criminal Procedures, those accused under the law were also deprived of the right to appeal, further weakening their position at trial. The extent of the military judge's discretion and the degree of arbitrariness involved are indicated in a 1942 statement by admiral and chief medical officer in the Kriegsmarine, Alfred Fikentscher. Speaking before military lawyers, he said:

> … similar circumstances exist with subversive remarks, which may be seen as violations of the Treachery Act. Protracted submission [of documents] to the Minister of Justice to order a criminal prosecution is unnecessary if you approach the statement as undermining the military, which will be possible in almost every case.[17]

In the later stages of the war, the Wehrmacht and Nazi leadership were deeply afraid of 1918-like events during the German Revolution when uprising of workers, sailors, and soldiers spread throughout Germany. The regulations created by the Wehrmacht as they prepared for World War II served as an instrument of terror in an effort to maintain the soldiers' "will to continue" through the threat of severe penalties for themselves and their families. The concept of *Sippenhaft* (Guilt by Association) is described in Chapter 10. Every act of resistance was to be suppressed so that a repeat of the "stab-in-the-back" legend, promoted by Hitler, was to be prevented. At the beginning of 1943, the jurisdiction for the Wartime Regulations for Criminal Procedures was transferred to the Nazi People's Court, though minor cases could be sent to the special courts that were originally instituted for political crimes. As a rule, the People's Court imposed the death penalty. Section 5 of the KSSVO reads:

> Whoever openly challenges or incites others to refuse to fulfil their duty to serve in the German armed forces or their allies, or otherwise openly tries to self-assertively put up a fight to cripple or subvert the will of the German people or their allies … will be sentenced to death for undermining the military.[18]

The word "openly" offered room for interpretation, so that even comments made within a person's own family could be used by relatives against the accused. As a means to more comprehensively control the military and civilian population, the indistinct wording of the regulation made it possible to criminalize every type of criticism, also by civilians, deliberately encouraging denunciation. The November 1, 1944 decree from the head of the National Socialist Secret Service of the Luftwaffe (Air Force) illustrates that "undermining the war effort" in the Third Reich was by no means a trivial offense:

> It has long been self-evident that whoever expresses doubt about the Führer, criticizes him and his actions, spreads disparaging news or vilifies him, is without honor and worthy of death. Neither standing nor rank, nor personal circumstances or other grounds can exculpate such a case. In the most difficult, deciding period of the war, whoever expresses doubt about the final victory and thereby causes others to waver, has likewise forfeited his life![19]

Among others, examples of subversion given were as follows:

1. Remarks in opposition to Nazi ideology.
2. Doubt about the legitimacy of the struggle for survival imposed on us.
3. Dissemination of news about battle fatigue and German soldiers deserting.
4. Doubt about military reports.
5. Cultivating private contact with prisoners of war.
6. Disparaging that important weapon in war: German propaganda.
7. Discussing contingencies in the event of defeat.

8. The assertion, that bolshevism is not so bad or that the democracy of our western neighbors could be contemplated.[20]

Defeatist remarks were not prosecuted under military law, but were tried in "accelerated trials," such as in the case of Norbert Engel, then a masseuse and physiotherapist. He was sentenced to death after expressing his regret to a nurse over the failure of the July 20, 1944 plot to assassinate Hitler. He said: "If it had succeeded, the war would have been over in five days and we'd have been able to go home." Engel escaped execution by fleeing to the Netherlands.[21]

The introduction of the Wartime Special Penal Code marked a new stage in the persecution of the Nazi's political opponents. Many thousands of them were killed. According to Wehrmacht criminal statistics, by June 30, 1944, there had been 14,262 convictions for subversion. However, German military historian Manfred Messerschmidt says the number of convictions was likely to have been closer to 30,000. As the war dragged on, criticism increased and the number of convictions and proportion of death sentences steadily increased.

As a consequence of the way the regulation was constructed, a conviction generally came from a denunciation by associates, though some convictions came from comments in letters or slogans written on walls. A potential accuser could hardly be certain that during the course of the investigation, he too would not also be denounced. The fact that every soldier was informed about the consequences of using banned speech may have limited the number of denunciations.

The law as it stood, vague and tyrannical as it was, did not prohibit conscientious objection. A quote from Doctor Günther Vollmer, a Ministerial Director at the Reich Ministry of Justice, read:

No longer tolerable and fundamentally worthy of death are remarks of the following kind: The war is lost; Germany or the Führer picked a fight and senselessly or frivolously started the war and must lose it; the NSDAP should or will relinquish power and, like the Italian model, make way for the understanding of peace; a military dictatorship must be established and will be able to forge peace, one must work slowly in order to bring about the conclusion; an intrusion of bolshevism would not be as bad as the propaganda paints it, and will only harm the leading National Socialists; the English or the Americans will stop bolshevism at the German border; urging by word of mouth or letters to the front to throw down their guns or turn back; the Führer is sick, incompetent, a butcher, etc.[22]

The Wehrmacht legal system had no allowances for conscientious objection. Instead, the military grouped conscientious objectors into the category of subversion, the group that also included deserters, chronic shirkers, and other malcontents. Defendants accused of being conscientious objectors were not allowed to state their moral or political reasoning for their actions during their trials. According to Lauren Faulkner Rossi, this had made it somewhat difficult to identify specific instances of conscientious objection within the Third Reich (with the notable exception, Jehovah's Witnesses were a special case in that they were much easier to identify and were the largest social bloc of subversion). Article 48 of the military penal code had affirmed that German's duty to obey superseded any needs of individual conscience, religious or otherwise.[23]

The punishments for subversion in both military and civilian courts was quite severe and often became more brutal as the fortunes of war turned against Germany. Yet the harsh attitude of the Third Reich's legal system towards objectors was often quite severe from the beginning. Punishments for this offense could range from military discipline, a sentence into a concentration camp or penal unit, or execution.[24] In the latter case, military tribunals gave out 112 death sentences for subversion during the first year of the war alone, and passed out approximately 23,000 death sentences for desertion by 1945, of which about 15,000 were carried out.[25]

For its part, much of the *Wehrmacht's* military leadership approved of the harsh penalties for subversion. Even officers with little love for either Hitler or the Nazis took it as a matter of pride that their units did not suffer a "humiliating collapse" as in 1918. As a result, a number of subversion were segregated from allegedly "healthy" units and placed either in Strafbattalion units for reform or otherwise punished.[26] The attitude of *Wehrmacht* jurists was that individuals brought up on subversion charges were somehow mentally deficient or otherwise lost their nerves and such defeatism could spread into their comrades.[26]

Before the concept of penal units was implemented by the German military, the common method of treating offenses by service members was by court martial and punishment, either by incarceration or dismissal from the service. In the post-World War I period (1919–1933), separate courts martial, including the *Reichsmilitärgericht* (RMG—Court of Justice), were abolished by Article 106 of the Weimar Constitution, but were revived by the Nazi government. After they seized power, the Nazis enacted a special law on May 12, 1933. The *Reichskriegsgericht* (RKG—Reich War Tribunal) was established as the high court of the German Armed Forces by another directive, which took effect on October 1, 1936.[27]

During the time of National Socialism, the Reich War Tribunal was the highest military court in Germany. In accordance with Section 14 of the Ordinance on Military Criminal Proceedings, the RKG was responsible for offenses such as high treason, state treason, and war treason, as long as these persons were not located in the operational area or belonged to a conscription force, which was directly under the control of the commander-in-chief of an army group. The Reich War Tribunal was also responsible for all criminal proceedings against general or admiral rank officers.[28]

For serious cases of subversion under Section 5 of the Special War Criminal Code, the Reich War Tribunal was the first and last stop.[29] Therefore, religiously motivated conscientious objectors fell into the Tribunal's jurisdiction. The President of the RKG could confirm or annul judgments of court judges, unless Hitler, as Supreme Judge of the Wehrmacht, reversed it. In the period between August 1939 and February 7, 1945, the Reich War Tribunal filed 1,189 death sentences, including 313 for high treason, ninety-six for state treason, twenty-four for war treason, 340 for espionage, and 251 for refusal of military service. A total of 1,049 of these death sentences were carried out.[30]

The Reich War Tribunal almost always imposed the death penalty on grounds of refusal of military service for religious reasons. These judgments concerned primarily Jehovah's Witnesses and Reform Adventists.[31] After numerous interventions by religious leaders, the RKG decided to grant the possibility of a revocation. In this case, a term of imprisonment of three to four years was imposed, to be served after the war.

In a ruling of April 2, 1940, the Reich War Tribunal had extensively extended the meaning of the term "public" to private conversations, so that any defeatist statement could be regarded as undermining military force.[32]

With the arms build-up in Germany and continued warfare, the number of Wehrmacht courts martial increased to over 1,000, prompting Hitler to order Field Marshal Wilhelm Keitel (chief of the *Oberkommando der Wehrmacht* (OKW—Supreme Command of the Armed Forces) to issue a directive on May 13, 1941, giving any Wehrmacht officer the authority to execute accused civilians in the Barbarossa area of Operation and the Eastern Front without trial. Against the laws of war, the official repeal of criminal prosecution led to widespread hostage-taking, mass executions, burning, and looting by German forces.

Since 1934, every division of the German Army had a process for conducting courts martial. After the occupation of Poland, the German High Command believed that a fast judicial process would be a more valuable deterrent. They wished to begin a system that allowed speedy trials to be performed. In November 1939, a law was passed that permitted a court martial held in the field to hear urgent charges of offences committed in action. Named "drumhead trials" or "flying court martial," every commander of a regiment could decide to either refer the case to the court or could convene a drumhead trial when somebody was accused of a crime. The term is said to originate from the use of a drumhead as an improvised writing table. The drumhead trial could be executed immediately. With the beginning of the year 1944, the High Command formed a special police, the High Command Military Police, which were in charge of special drumhead trials composed of motorized judges.[33]

An example of this was the summary trial of five officers found guilty of failing to prevent the Allies from capturing the Ludendorff Bridge during the Battle of Remagen on March 7, 1945. On the direct order from Adolf Hitler,

Lieutenant General Rudolf Hübner tried Major Hans Scheller, Captain Willi Bratge, Lieutenant Karl Heinz Peters, Major Herbert Strobel, and Major August Kraft. Hübner, who had no legal experience, acted as both prosecutor and judge. He conducted extremely brief show trials, during which he harangued the defendants for their alleged command failures and then pronounced sentence. All of the officers were sentenced to death except for Bratge, who had been captured, the others were taken to a nearby woods within twenty-four hours and executed with a shot to the back of the neck and buried where they fell.[34] Overall, the Nazi military justice system led to about 2.5 million trials with members of the armed forces, and about 1.5 million soldiers were sentenced.

The period of military rearmament preceding World War II caused renewed interest in the concept of penal military units. In May 1935, the German Wehrmacht instituted a new policy under German conscription law that stated soldiers who were deemed disruptive to military discipline but were otherwise "worthy of service" would be sent to military penal units. Criminals were also conscripted into penal units in exchange for lighter sentences or as a form of a stay of execution.

These units, referred to as "special departments," were overseen by the German military police. Prior to World War II, there were nine Strafbattalions within the Wehrmacht. The primary role of Strafbattalion was to provide front-line support. As the war progressed, the size of Strafbattalion companies dramatically increased due to changes in German military policy. Under such policies, any soldier who had a death sentence commuted for retreat was automatically reassigned to a penal unit, greatly increasing the number of soldiers available to the Strafbattalion.

The records of Strafbattalion were mixed. A combination of criminals, political prisoners, and undisciplined soldiers made up the Strafbattalion. The units often required harsh measures to be imposed for unit cohesion to be maintained. Strafbattalions were often ordered to undertake high-risk missions on the front line, with soldiers being coached to regain their lost honor by fighting. Certain penal military units, such as the 36th Waffen Grenadier Division of the SS, gained a reputation as being brutal towards civilian populations and POWs, and were employed as anti-partisan troops due to the fear they inspired. Other units, most notably the 999th Light Africa Division, suffered from poor morale and saw soldiers desert the Wehrmacht to join resistance groups.[35] From the beginning of their service, soldiers had certain duties and rights.

Every German soldier, upon induction, was compelled to affirm his legally established military obligation by means of the following oath:

> I swear by God this holy oath that I will render unconditional obedience to the Führer of Germany and of her people, Adolf Hitler, the Supreme Commander of the Armed Forces, and that, as a brave soldier, I will be prepared to stake my life for this oath at any time.

If, because of an oversight, the oath had not been administered to a soldier, he was held to be in the same position as though he had sworn it; the oath is regarded only as the affirmation of his inherent legal duty.

The German system of military discipline was rigorous, and excesses were severely punished. In principle, absolute and unquestioning obedience towards superiors was required. However, since the summer of 1944, when the Army came under the political influence of the Nazi Party, new orders were issued providing that disloyal superiors not only need not be obeyed, but also in emergencies may be liquidated by their own men. Officers who did not lead their men into combat or showed other signs of cowardice or who, for any reason, mutilate themselves were normally condemned to death. Divisional commanders and other high-ranking combat officers were specifically ordered to set an example of leadership in the front lines; this explains the high casualty rate among German generals. Traditionally, German superior officers were addressed only indirectly, in the third person, as "*Herr* Major is absolutely right." Hitler, however, was addressed directly as "My Leader." Therefore, the Nazis made use of the direct form of address toward superior officers at first optional, then compulsory. Superior officers and non-commissioned officers were addressed as "Mr." ("*Herr*") followed by their rank; in the Waffen SS, however, only by their rank, "*Herr Leutnant!*"

Originally, a distinction was made between the regular military salute and the German salutation (*Deutscher Grass*) which consists of saying "*Heil Hitler!*" with the right arm outstretched. In August 1944, the latter type of salute was made compulsory throughout. Everyone saluted his own superiors as well as others entitled to a salute according to the following general rules:

> Every officer is the superior of all lower-ranking officers and all enlisted men; every non-commissioned officer is the superior of all privates; every non-commissioned officer in one of the first three grades is the superior of lower-grade non-commissioned officers in his own unit. There is no general rank superiority otherwise among non-commissioned officers or among the various grades of privates; however, all members of the Armed Forces were obliged to greet one another as a matter of military etiquette.

Members of the Armed Forces were forbidden to associate with foreigners even if they are racially related. Marriages between soldiers and non-German women were subject to approval, which was given only after a very thorough investigation. The offspring of such marriages were considered to be German. In the Waffen SS, such marriages were entirely probated for German personnel.

Men who severely and repeatedly violated military discipline, if not to an extent that warranted a death sentence, were transferred to correction battalions for probationary period and given arduous and dangerous assignments. If incorrigible, they were then turned over to the police for extreme punishment, or transferred to the SS or Gestapo.

Honor was considered the soldier's highest possession. Except in extreme case, he may be given the opportunity to redeem himself for a dishonorable action by a heroic dead in battle or, in milder cases, by exceptionally brave and meritorious service in the lowest grade of private to which he was reduced from his former rank. However, there also existed a rigid personal honor code for officers. Under its provisions, they were obligated to defend their own personal honor as well as the good name of their wives by every possible means. They were held to account for violations committed by themselves or their wives. According to the German conception, special honor rules applied to officers and those civilians who were socially their equals. These rules provide in extreme cases for settlement by duel with pistols until one of the two parties was fully incapacitated.

This was a leftover from feudal times, before Hitler's assumption of power. It is significant that under Hitler, dueling of officers was legalized in cases where all efforts at settlement by an officers' court of honor (appointed by a regimental or higher commander) failed. However, for duels between two officers, but not between an officer and a civilian, a decision had to first be obtained from the Commander-in-Chief of the Army. Their medieval conception of honor had a strong influence on the mentality and actions of many German officers. An officer was obligated to react to deliberate insults instantaneously, in a positive and masterly fashion, and to protect other officers from becoming the object of public disgrace. In the SS, qualified enlisted men (those who carried a dagger) were subject to the same honor rules as officers, being obligated to defend their honor by force of arms.

The opening of the officer's career to the common German man of the people was a revolutionary change in the German social system brought about by Hitler. It had created an entirely different type of relationship among the ranks than existed in the armies of Imperial Germany. No one could become an officer without being a certified Nazi, even if not a member of the Party, and without being considered capable of inspiring his men with the Nazi spirit. Thus, the social mingling between officers and men in off-duty hours, which had been encouraged by the Nazis to some extent, appears to have had a strong propagandist purpose. A sincere personal interest of the officer in his men was encouraged, the all-important requirement being that he must have their confidence. In case of death, the soldier's next of kin received their first notification through a personal letter from his company commander, which was handed to them by the local leader of the Nazi Party.

Traditionally, all German military personnel were barred from all political activities including the right to vote. Hitler, when introducing general conscription, maintained this tradition in order to obtain the full support of the military and decreed that membership in the Nazi Party and all political activities would be dormant during the period of any man's active service. In the later stages of the war, however, serious reverses and the increasing danger of sagging morale caused the official introduction of politics into the German Armed Forces. This occurred progressively from the latter part of 1943 on, by appointment of National-Socialist guidance on all staffs, the organization of political meetings, and other efforts at raising morale, as well as through the merciless terrorization of wavering officers and soldiers by the strong men of the Waffen SS.

When Hitler reintroduced general conscription in 1935, the greatest possible care was taken to create a strong military force without disrupting the economic life of the nation. Men were registered by annual classes, and during the years before the war, those of the older classes were called only in small groups to attend training exercises of limited duration. Even for the younger classes, all feasible arrangements were made for the deferment of students and of those engaged in necessary occupations. Men accepted for active service were called to duty by individual letter rather than by public announcement for their annual class. This system was continued in the gradual mobilization that preceded the outbreak of the war in such a way that the wartime Army could be built up organically and the normal course of life was not seriously upset.

As long as the war was conducted on a limited scale, the Armed Forces were very liberal in granting occupational and medical discharges. As the war progressed and grew in scope and casualties mounted, it became necessary to recall many of these men and eventually to reach increasingly into both the older and the younger age groups. After Germany changed from the offensive to the defensive in 1943, it became both possible and necessary to transfer an increasing number of Air Force and Naval personnel to the Army, to bolster voluntary enlistment in the Waffen SS and to commit communication units to regular combat against partisans and regular enemy forces.

The increasingly heavy losses of the Russian campaign forced Hitler to cancel his order exempting last sons of decimated families and fathers of large families from front-line combat duty. Prisons and concentration camps were combed for men who could be used in penal combat units with the inducement of possible later reinstatement of their civic rights.[36]

A study of transformation of the German penal system affords us an understanding of the very system that created the Strafbattalions.

1

The Nazi Penal System

In 1945, Frederick Hoefer wrote two articles about the Nazi penal system for the Journal of Criminal Law & Criminology. In the articles, Hoefer describes certain aspects of the administration of criminal justice in Germany under the Nazis. The following are some excerpts from those articles.

The penal law of both the Hohenzollern Empire and the Weimar Republic was codified in the Criminal Code of 1871 and the Code of Criminal Procedure of 1877. The Criminal Code of 1871 was essentially a product of the penal jurisprudence of the classical school. Its legal definitions, distinctions, and other technical matters may be traced to Napoleon's Code Penal of 1810. However, the "deterrent" philosophy and rather cruel punishments of the French Code had been eliminated by the humanitarian jurisprudence of the nineteenth century. For those features, the classical jurists had substituted a rather lenient variety of retribution. The penalties were mostly simple imprisonment (paragraph 16; from one day to five years); imprisonment with hard labor (paragraph 14-15; from fifteen years to life), and fines from three Reich Marks to 10,000 Reich Marks (paragraph 27ff). The death penalty was provided for murder only and was executed by decapitation (paragraph 14).

For the protection of the innocent, paragraph 2 laid down the doctrine of *nulla poena sine lege* (no punishment without law), and prohibited retroactive punishment. This was repeated in Article 116 of the Weimar constitution.

Among the Fundamental Rights of Citizens recognized by the Weimar constitution, the following were particularly important for the administration of criminal justice and were supplemented by appropriate statutory law: Equality of all citizens before the Law (Article 109); freedom from illegal arrest (Article 114) and from illegal search and seizure (Article 115); inviolable secrecy of all communications by mail, telegraph or telephone (Article 117); freedom of speech and freedom of the press (Article 118); freedom of assembly (Article 123); and freedom to organize clubs and associations (Article 124).[1]

The Weimar Republic made definite progress along the lines of individualized correctional treatment. Rehabilitation rather than mere punitive measures were stressed in the Juvenile Welfare Law of 1922, the Juvenile Court Law of 1923, and the Federal Prison Rules of 1923. The penal legislation of the Hitler government since 1933 may be summarized under the following aspects:

1. Abolition of all constitutional guarantees for the freedom of innocent citizens Legislation by government decrees.
2. Creation of new and hitherto unknown criminal offenses in order to promote political, racial and religious persecution.
3. Increase in the severity of punishment; increased use of the death penalty.
4. Creation of new punishments.
5. Dualism of legal and extra- legal punishment.

On February 28, 1933, in the first days of the Nazi government, a presidential decree abolished the most important civil rights of the Constitution, namely: freedom from unlawful arrest, search and seizure; inviolability of mail, telegraph and telephone; freedom of speech; freedom of the press; freedom of assembly; freedom to organize; inviolability of private property.

Ostensibly, these civil rights were only temporarily suspended as an emergency measure, but they have never been re-established.

The constitutional prohibition of unlawful punishment was violated by ex post facto laws and finally abolished by a decree of June 28, 1935. This decree recognized punishment *ex post facto* as a general principle of the criminal code. Likewise it abolished the doctrine of *nulla poena sine lege* (no penalty without a law); for it permitted the punishment of acts offending the "sound feeling of the people" even though no existing law was violated.[2]

The totalitarian state tolerates neither a legislative power nor an independent judiciary as they are understood in constitutional government. Accordingly, law is no longer made by the legislature; it emanates directly from the executive power. This was accomplished at first by presidential "emergency decrees," based on Article 48 of the Constitution; soon, however, a more convenient device was found by simply delegating all legislative power to the Cabinet. A good example of how this integration of government powers operates was the famous blood purge of June 30, 1934. Having murdered probably more than 1,000 political opponents in a few days, Hitler declared that he had acted as the "Supreme Lord of the Law," and a decree signed by Hitler declared that all government measures taken in this matter were legal. Substantive penal law was changed by a number of decrees threatening the most severe punishment against political, racial, and religious minorities.

The Law on Treason was codified in a decree of April 24, 1934, replacing paragraph 80–93 of the old criminal code. Almost all activities of opposition groups were punishable by death, the death penalty being either mandatory or alternative with imprisonment and hard labor for life or for not more than fifteen years. The penalties applied to: preparation of treason (new paragraph 83), such as any work with non-Nazi political organizations (underground work); the establishment or continuation of such organizations; acts of sabotage; anti-Nazi radio broadcasts; printing, circulation or smuggling into Germany of forbidden literature; likewise not only the betrayal of state secrets but also the attempt to discover such secrets (paragraph 90).

The forging of state documents was punishable with imprisonment at hard labor. This provision probably made it possible for the government to issue a *dementi* (an official denial of a published statement) in case a genuine document should be smuggled out of Germany. Under this law preparation for high treason had been found in cases in which the accused had received anti-Nazi leaflets from someone and had neglected to turn them over to the police; likewise when the accused had a discussion with a person opposed to Nazism without making an immediate denunciation to the Gestapo.[3]

Virtually all public and private criticism of the government by the spoken word was prohibited and made punishable by imprisonment up to five years by the decrees of March 21, 1933 and December 20, 1934, the latter known as the so-called "Law against treacherous criticism" of the government. The official wording of this law, as published in the RGB1, spoke only of untrue statements, but the authentic interpretation, given by the government, did not permit the defendant any proof that his statement was true.

It was believed that as many as 80 percent of all political trials in 1934–38 were based on this law. It was especially applied against ministers of the gospel, who had spoken against the government's interference in church matters. The famous Pastor Niemoeller was tried in 1938 under this law. Less prominent victims of the same law may be found among old women and others who were guilty of grumbling against the government.

Among the notorious anti-Semitic manifestations in the administration of justice, the so-called "Law for the protection of German blood and honor" of September 15, 1935, deserves a prominent place. This law created the new criminal offense of race defilement. It prohibited all marriages between Jews and Aryans under penalty of imprisonment with hard labor up to fifteen years. The same penalty was provided for extramarital sexual intercourse between members of these two racial groups. Jews were not permitted to employ Aryan female domestic help under forty-five years of age, this offense being punishable with imprisonment up to one year and with fines. The same law also punished German Jews for showing the Swastika flag, probably an infrequent offense. Another decree of the same day deprived all German Jews of German citizenship. The connection between the two decrees is obvious; both were manifestations of racial persecution in the field of law.

The legislative use of the death penalty has enormously increased. This penalty for numerous new categories of treason provided mandatory death penalty for kidnapping, violation of economic regulations, highway robbery through automobile traps, espionage in peacetime, theft and burglary in areas under military law, theft of metal pieces from scrap collections, acts of violence perpetrated with a weapon, and so forth. Possible death penalty was also threatened for listening to foreign broadcasts, black market operations, undermining the military strength of the nation, etc.[4]

The laws concerning imprisonment have similarly become more severe. This was done in three different ways: the penal laws provided for longer terms of imprisonment; often for life terms; the prison regime was made more severe; and last but not least, imprisonment was followed by preventive or protective custody for an indefinite time.

The government had introduced several new punishments. Most important among these were the so-called "preventive custody" and "protective custody." Both were legal devices enabling the government to imprison individuals for indefinite periods of time; however they served different purposes and should not be confused with each other.

Preventive custody was introduced by the "Law against dangerous habitual criminals," of November 24, 1933. This law is comparable to the New York 'Baumes Law' against recidivistic offenders, but is far more severe than the latter and gives more arbitrary power to the courts and other government authorities. Under this law, any person who is convicted of a criminal offense for the third time, will not only be given a prison term of many years, but will, after the expiration of his term, be placed in preventive custody for an indefinite time. Although the law does not call this a punishment, it is in reality a most severe one. The available German literature indicates that it was carried out in practically the same fashion as regular imprisonment with hard labor. It was always for an indefinite time. The release from this "custody" was always a conditional release; it could be revoked at any time without trial or any other legal guarantees.

Among other preventive measures, the same law also introduced the castration of sex offenders. In this connection it should be remembered that race defilement as described above was a sex offense in Germany. Moreover, the religious persecutions against Catholic priests, monks and nuns had frequently taken the form of sex trials. Accordingly it is evident that the innocent as well as the guilty may live in fear of this "preventive measure."[5]

Protective custody was no legal institution at all, but was just a name for imprisonment by the Gestapo. There were virtually no laws governing this subject, and no court of justice had anything to do with it. It will be sufficient to say here that the Gestapo had the power to arrest, imprison or execute any individual without giving any explanation to anyone. Its actions were expressly exempted from judicial review. It was also authorized to imprison the accused who had been acquitted in criminal court or who had served his sentence. The words "protective custody" were based on the theory that the victim was a heinous offender who was to be protected against the wrath of the people, no matter whether such wrath existed or not. In other words, the ground for imprisonment was entirely fictitious. In reality, the victim was either a political suspect or a potential witness from whom the secret police was trying to extort certain information.

The Nazi government had thus created a peculiar duplicity of legal and extra-legal punishment. Under the existing laws, the various regular and special courts may try and sentence the innocent as well as the guilty under certain legal charges. However, this was not sufficient for a true regime of terror. Therefore, there was another, independent system of punishments, operated by the Gestapo, which was completely exempt from law. Its actions are solely dictated by political expediency.

This duplicity of legal and illegal action was deeply rooted in the history of National Socialism. Long before Hitler came into power, his party had a double policy. Legally it took its place as an organized political party under the Weimar Republic, was represented in the Parliament, published newspapers and propaganda literature, etc. Illegally it used the Storm Troops and Special Guards armies for purposes of terror, planned the overthrow of the government by force, caused street riots and committed assassinations. After coming into power, this old duplicity was preserved in a system of both legal and illegal administration. Lastly this shows that law as such was irrelevant for tyrants and was used by them merely as one of several tools of power.[6]

Prior to 1933, the judicial administration in Germany was regulated by the Federal laws of 1877 and 1924. Jurisdiction in civil and criminal law suits belonged mostly to the several states, but the federal law prescribed general principles for judicial independence, for the organization and hierarchy of state courts and the distribution of business between higher and lower courts. The federal government had only a few tribunals; most important among these was the Supreme Court in Leipzig. This court was the highest tribunal of Germany. It decided all matters of federal law as a court of revision, i.e., upon errors in the interpretation of law by the state courts. The Supreme Court also had original jurisdiction in all cases of treason, for impeachment of members of the federal government and in matters concerning litigation between different state governments or between state and federal government.

The judicial hierarchy in each state as well as in the Reich was centralized in a state (or federal) ministry of justice. Each ministry of justice was headed by a cabinet minister. All his subordinates were civil service men. In each state the ministry of justice was the highest authority for the organization and administration of courts. It controlled the appointment and retirement of judges, subject to federal and state law. However, it had no right to interfere with judicial decisions, the latter being within the sphere of judicial independence.

The ministry of justice also appointed and controlled all public prosecutors, the latter being subjected to its orders in all matters. Likewise, most prisons in Germany were under the control of state ministries of justice, especially after 1918.

The judicial personnel in all states represented an ancient bureaucracy, famous for its efficiency and moral integrity. All judges and prosecuting attorneys received their appointments through a century-old civil service system. Every judicial officer was a university graduate, trained in the law, who had gone through a several years' apprenticeship in the civil service. Before receiving a judicial appointment, he had to pass several rigorous examinations, usually followed by several more years' service as a temporary judge.

After receiving a permanent appointment, the individual judge was theoretically independent in all legal matters. He was more or less obliged to follow the principles laid down by the Supreme Court in the interpretation of law, but he would not tolerate interference from the executive branch of government in any law suit. His tenure of office was for life, subject to retirement at a certain age. He could not be removed from office except for having committed a serious offense and only through the action of a special, independent tribunal (paragraph 68 GVG, Weimar Constitution Article 104).[7]

Nevertheless, judicial independence was limited in certain ways. If a judge belonged to an opposition party or was otherwise refractory, the Ministry of Justice could refuse to promote him to a higher rank or to grant his application for a transfer to a different city; he could thus be 'frozen' in an insignificant position or in an undesirable location. When Hitler came into power in 1933, one of his first objects was to break the independence of the judiciary. This was done by removing all anti-Nazi judges, abolishing all guarantees for the tenure of judicial offices, and changing the civil service system gradually into a system of political appointments.

The first step in this direction was the famous decree of April 7, 1933, ironically called the "Law for the Restoration of Civil Service." This decree removed from office all judicial officers of Jewish or non-Aryan extraction, all judicial officers who had been members of liberal or socialist parties or other democratic organizations, or all those who were likewise politically unreliable. They were replaced by loyal National Socialists, and henceforth all judicial appointments required membership in the National Socialist Party or its affiliated organizations. The Civil Service Law of 1937 required a personal oath of loyalty to Hitler and made all judicial officers removable for political causes.

The political control over the judiciary was strengthened by the federalization of all state governments in 1934; all courts became federal courts and subject to control from Berlin. In the first years of Nazi government, the higher courts still showed a certain degree of independence; this was especially true in the famous Reichstag's fire trial in 1933 when the Supreme Court in Leipzig refused to convict certain Communist leaders for the alleged burning of the Reichstag building, the accused being obviously innocent.

In order to prevent similar occurrences in the future, the government removed all political offenses from the jurisdiction of the Supreme Court and the regular courts, and created special tribunals of a "Star Chamber-type" (any tribunal, committee, or the like, which proceeds by arbitrary or unfair methods) for treason and other political crimes.[8] Major cases were brought before the People's Court, others before special courts. Only the most loyal representatives of the Nazi movement were appointed to these courts. There was no appeal against their sentences.

Even the Reich's Ministry of Justice was not given full power in matters of the judiciary. This central authority soon began to receive orders from the Propaganda Ministry in all matters concerning political trials. Moreover, the Gestapo was permitted to interfere in all these cases. While a geographical centralization took place, there developed thus what may be called a functional decentralization. The latter was increased through the creation of military courts and party tribunals, each absorbing a certain quota of cases. As a result of these developments, the old judiciary was deprived of the last shred of independent power and was turned into a body of government agents, controlled by political authorities and functioning as an instrument of despotism.[9]

Both under the Hohenzollern Empire and the Weimar Republic, public safety was almost exclusively a matter of state and municipal administration. The German states maintained highly efficient, technically trained police forces; especially the police of Prussia was well known for its clean, intelligent administration. Through its very efficiency, it constituted a potential menace to political freedom, but a system of administrative courts protected the individual citizen against abuses of governmental power; moreover, the regular courts of justice had jurisdiction over violations of civil and criminal law committed by public officials.

When the National Socialist party came into power, its leaders immediately made plans to obtain absolute control of the police system and to meld it into an instrument of political oppression and terror. For this purpose they removed the existing constitutional guarantees of freedom. This, however, was not sufficient; for they had to overcome the attitude of the police forces that had been trained under liberal government to use intelligent methods rather than brutality; these policemen were largely indifferent or even hostile to the Nazi state.

Accordingly, the government started a purge of the police forces, eliminating all non-Aryans, former liberals and other 'politically unreliable' elements. Since even this purge was not sufficient to bring about the desired changes, a special political police organization had to be created that would be absolutely ruthless and entirely loyal to the Nazi government. This was done by Göring, the new President of the Ministers of Prussia, who established the secret state police; abbreviated Gestapo by a decree of April 26, 1933.[10] Another decree of November 30, 1933 made it a police and solely responsible to the President of the Ministers him. It was exempted from the control of regular or administrative courts. Its function was to hunt down and crush every form of opposition to the government. For this purpose it had unlimited powers to arrest, imprison, and kill political suspects and to search and confiscate their property. Its victims had no right to a judicial hearing and were completely at its mercy.

After having assisted Hitler and Göring in the blood purge of June 30, 1934, the powers of the Gestapo were increased and its organization became more elaborate. Officially it remained a branch of the Prussian government, responsible to Göring, but actually it began to function as a federal agency when Himmler, Reich leader of the SS, was put in charge in 1934. Himmler combined the forces of the SS and Gestapo officers were given high rank in the SS force while every soldier in the SS was also a potential agent of the Gestapo. In other words, the Gestapo officers were the brains of this combined organization while SS guardsmen acted as their subordinates. They had to do the actual man-hunting, killing, and torturing of prisoners. The SS was also left in charge of the concentration camps for political prisoners. The Gestapo was officially responsible for these matters but more or less limited itself to giving the orders and supervising these activities.

The status of the Gestapo as a government agency was officially defined and its powers were further enlarged by decrees of the Reich and Prussia in 1936.

Two Prussian decrees of February 10, 1936, maintained the formal status of the Gestapo as a state agency. Its official task was the repression of all subversive activities, investigation of all matters of political importance, and the giving of information and recommendations to the state government. Its central bureau was the state secret police office in Berlin. Its official chief was the [minister in charge] Göring, but its deputy chief, Himmler, was the actual man in command.[11] Under this central bureau, thirty-five Gestapo bureaus were functioning in conjunction with the regular administrative district authorities of the state.

The Gestapo was authorized to take measures for the entire territory of Prussia, to give orders to all state and municipal authorities, and to request information from all these. Apart from those requests, all state and local police authorities had to report automatically all matters of political interest to the Gestapo.

The Reich's decree of June 17, 1936 went even further. The federalization of state police forces, which had actually begun in 1934, was now officially sanctioned by creating the new office of a Chief of Police for all Germany. This office was combined with that of the Chief of Police of Prussia, Deputy Chief of the Gestapo, and Reich's leader of the SS. Needless to say, all of these offices were combined in the person of Himmler. While officially subordinate to the governments of the Reich and Prussia, he was made actually independent and omnipotent; he became directly and solely responsible to the Führer.

This decree completed the centralization of the German police forces, thus creating what is probably the most powerful instrument of political oppression in the history of Europe. It was operated with the most refined scientific methods as well as with the utmost brutality. It had efficiently checked every bit of opposition inside Germany. It also kept under control the population of all territories conquered since 1939. The highest Nazi party leaders and Army generals had to fear the Gestapo as much as the humble citizen

Although the Gestapo was authorized and able to do away quickly with every political opponent, the Nazi government still maintained its political tribunals, the People's Court and the Special Courts. It even staged political trials sometimes in the regular criminal courts. This was done solely for purposes of propaganda. Actions by the Gestapo was necessarily secret. Therefore the Government had to resort to a public trial whenever it desired to give a particular impression to public opinion. Cases that were to serve this purpose were carefully selected and prepared by the Ministry of Justice under specific instructions from the Propaganda Ministry, and all newspaper reporting on these matters were supervised by the Propaganda Ministry and by the Press Bureau in the Ministry of Justice. Vice versa, all trials that might reflect unfavorably on the government or the Nazi party, were held in absolute secrecy.[12]

One of the more interesting political cases was the trial against Pastor Niemoeller, the head of the Protestant Confessional Church which refused to submit to government dictation in matters of religious doctrine. Hitler himself had ordered his arrest and trial and personally demanded that the pastor be severely punished. Niemoeller, however, had been very careful in avoiding direct criticism of the government. When speaking from the pulpit, he had given accurate reports on the arrest and imprisonment of Protestant clergymen by the Gestapo and on other matters important to the Church. Thus, for instance, in February 1937, he had discussed the death of an imprisoned clergyman, officially described as suicide; he avoided raising the question whether the government had committed murder. Accordingly, it was difficult to find a legal pretext for a trial and sentence. As he defended himself skillfully and the case was beginning to arouse more sympathy for the victim than the government desired, the order for a public trial was cancelled and a trial, lasting only a few hours, was held in secrecy on March 1, 1938. The Special Court in Berlin found Niemoeller guilty of violating the Treachery Act and of incitement from the pulpit. He was sentenced to seven months imprisonment. The Court considered this sentence as served by more than seven months detention awaiting trial, and ordered the discharge of the prisoner. However, before leaving the courtroom, Niemoeller was seized by the Gestapo and taken to a concentration camp. He was released. According to Edith Roper, the Gestapo asked Niemoeller to sign a statement acknowledging his guilt and voluntarily relinquishing his pulpit. If he had signed it, this statement would have been given the widest publicity, thus making up for the lost publicity effect of the trial. The pastor, however, refused to give his signature and therefore had to remain a prisoner.[13]

Prison administration under the Weimar Republic was that of a civilized, progressive country, somewhat handicapped by legal and financial problems. All prisons belonged to the several states, and most of them were under the state ministries of justice, thus having the advantage of centralized administrative control.

Prussia, the largest state, had, in 1928, forty-five state prisons for convicted criminals, each with a capacity for 700 inmates; it had three large institutions exclusively for detention awaiting trial; there were about nine hundred local jails, most of which would not admit more than fifty inmates; these figures do not include mere police lockups. The size and distribution of the greater state prisons was favorable for good administration; they were large enough to warrant the employment of professional personnel, but not too large for individualized treatment of inmates. The local jails were inferior as might be expected, but the supervision of the state authorities prevented the worst of those evils that are commonly found in a decentralized administration.

State ministries of justice mostly exercised their control through district prison boards which were coordinated with the district courts of appeal in each state. Prussia had thirteen districts of this nature.

The administration of the state prisons was conducted in a progressive spirit, under the Federal Prison Rules of 1923 which stressed the social rehabilitation of offenders. The poor economic situation of the post-war years did not permit large scale reforms of all institutions, but the governments of most states did as much as they were able to do. Some remarkable experimental institutions were conducted in Prussia, Thuringia, Hamburg, and elsewhere.

The fundamental problem of prison personnel was attacked in a courageous spirit. Prison wardens were usually appointed from the ranks of lawyers, judges, physicians, clergymen or administrative officials. The more important states, including Prussia and Bavaria, provided for a training period through probationary appointments or appointments in an assistant capacity. The custodial force mostly came from the ranks of discharged military personnel.[14] Considerable efforts were made to educate custodial officers through in-service training; here, too, probationary appointments were made, and the permanent civil service appointments were given after successful training.

The professional personnel consisted traditionally of physicians, clergymen and teachers. The more progressive states under the Republic modernized this branch by adding psychiatrists and social case workers; Saxony and Thuringia were leading in this introduction of prison social work.

The Federal Prison Rules of 1923 introduced a progressive grade system. Prisoners earned their promotion to higher grades and increased privileges through good conduct. Several fine experiments in prison self- government were made in Prussia and Thuringia. There were numerous private social agencies for the aid of released prisoners.

In 1933, these promising developments were abruptly stopped by the National Socialist government. Rehabilitation was no longer favored; intelligent understanding of the individual prisoner was replaced by severe, repressive methods of mass treatment.

The ranks of prison personnel were purged as in all other branches of the government. The most important prison reformers, such as Gentz in Prussia, Frede and Krebs in Thuringia, and Koch in Hamburg, were removed. All experiments in prisoners' self-government were immediately abandoned. Social work was reduced to insignificance, and about six hundred private prisoners' aid societies were disbanded. Prison education and recreational activities were mostly given up.

They were replaced by goose-stepping and pseudo-military drill, even in women's prisons. The prisoners' privileges, such as receiving visitors, writing letters, or making complaints were reduced to an absolute minimum. Some of the old prison wardens who had kept their positions tried to escape the extremes of the new regime by remaining personally fair to their inmates. They were able to prevent that extreme cruelty which characterized the Gestapo's concentration camps. But they were effectively prevented from continuing any constructive efforts.[15]

While the treatment became generally more severe, it should be noted that many victims of political and religious persecution were incarcerated in the regular prisons. Political trials, including those against religious and racial minorities, usually ended with a stiff prison term, later to be followed by incarceration in concentration camps. One Protestant sect, the 'Bible Researchers,' was totally prohibited by the government and most of its members imprisoned. Many fine, upright citizens were thus branded as criminals and languished in penal institutions.

Beside the regular prisons, the Hitler government maintained an independent system of institutions for political prisoners, members of religious and racial minorities, and other victims. These are the concentration camps. The first camps in 1933 were run by the SA (Storm Troopers). Since 1934 the SS had taken their place. The supervision of all camps was in the hands of the Gestapo, probably since 1934; officially, since 1936.

Various procedures had been observed in the arrest and imprisonment of victims. Political suspects had been arrested and questioned by the Gestapo after suffering cruel physical tortures in connection with questioning. Many were dispatched to concentration camps without trial. Others were sentenced by regular or special courts to certain prison terms and were taken to concentration camps as soon as the term of imprisonment had been served.

Again others were thus imprisoned after having been acquitted in criminal court. In 1938 and 1939, during the mass persecution of Jewish citizens, the victims were arrested wholesale on the street or in their home, and were imprisoned without further formalities.

The duration of the incarceration was entirely indefinite, at the pleasure of the Gestapo, It ends either with the victim's death or with a conditional release which was always revocable.

The treatment suffered by the prisoners was of the utmost cruelty. Long work hours in stone quarries, road building, cultivating wastelands and so forth, were supplemented by pseudo- military drill under the most sadistic drill-masters. While thus occupied, prisoners were kept with insufficient food and insufficient clothing, often without sanitary facilities, sometimes without drinking water. Their shelters were overcrowded and unsanitary, Medical attention was refused to most of them. Moreover, they were systematically flogged, beaten and tortured while the most ingenious methods of humiliation were used. It should be borne in mind that these prisoners included middle-aged and elderly individuals many of whom were totally unfamiliar with manual labor. Among the victims were some of the most prominent citizens; former liberal statesmen, members of parliament, writers, scholars, clergymen, physicians, attorneys and well- known businessmen and members of the military. The death of prisoners from exhaustion, injuries, disease or suicide was a matter of routine, not to mention those who were shot, purportedly "while trying to escape."

German newspapers were strictly forbidden to report any of these atrocities. All released prisoners were threatened with instant death in case they told anyone about the treatment they had received. Thus, an element of mystery was added to that of organized terror.

The immediate responsibility for these conditions rested with Himmler and his Gestapo and SS henchmen. However, there is no doubt that Hitler himself and his friends such as Frick, Göring, Hess, Goebbels, and others have been fully aware of what was going on and gave their approval. All phases of penal administration in Germany had deteriorated under the totalitarian regime.

The great humanitarian and scientific ideas of the nineteenth and twentieth century as well as the penal philosophy of the enlightened age have been discarded; in her theories Germany has gone straight back to the seventeenth century. The same is true in the field of penal legislation. Penal law has regained the quality of utmost severity which it had three hundred years ago. Principles of political, racial, and religious persecution have been embodied in laws that can be compared only to corresponding laws of the seventeenth and earlier centuries. The barbarities of the Middle Ages and of the great religious wars have returned in these statutes.

In the administrative and judicial fields, one of the best modem civil service systems has been destroyed. All government personnel, including that of the judiciary, has become a mere tool of political oppression.

With hypocritical deference to the traditional German sense of law and justice, the government left certain outward forms of legal procedure intact. However, the existing legal agencies had been supplemented by others that were outside the law. Thus a system of "Star Chamber" tribunals had been added to the regular Courts of Law; both of these courts and the regular police have become subordinate to the Gestapo. Concentration camps have been added to the regular prisons. The government had thus constructed a dualistic system of legal and extra-legal institutions. Matters of the greatest importance, especially political matters, were handled by extra-legal agencies. The old, legal authorities have been maintained for propaganda purposes and for minor matters.

There is no doubt that this utterly unjust, tyrannical system of government was out of harmony with political and legal traditions that have previously existed for centuries in Germany as well as in other civilized countries.

This was the judicial system and conditions that spawned the Nazi military penal system and the creation of the Wehrmacht's penal organizations.[16]

2

The Creation of Penal Units

In 1939, the Wehrmacht was pleased with the success of deferring sentences for soldiers assigned to the front during the invasion of Poland. They considered the practice of this to be a great success.[1] On September 30, 1939, therefore, the Supreme Command of the Armed Forces (OKW) issued a directive that authorized military commanders, who had been authorized to function as a court, to consider changing their initial order on how punishment of soldiers would be executed. From that day forward, the court had the authority to parole an inmate after the partial conclusion of the sentence or order a prisoner transported to a Wehrmacht penal camp if the prisoner had behaved badly during confinement. The court also received the power to parole penal camp inmates or to relocate them to a military prison for the completion of their sentence.[2] An OKW clarification on the parole system, dated January 13, 1940, stated that parole should be used "so as not to give the dishonorable and cowards incentive to avoid service at the front by committing a punishable offense."[3]

In order to make it perfectly clear to field commanders, the 7th Implementation Ordinance for the Wartime Judicial Procedure Code of May 18, 1940 was circulated at the start of the German invasion of France and the Low Countries. This gave the fields commanders the maximum latitude in managing their soldiers. The Ordinance listed the following actions available to court when rendering a sentence:

1. Partial or complete suspension of the sentence for serving at the front.
2. Immediate and full completion of the sentence.
3. Transfer to a Wehrmacht penal camp.[4]

A large number of men were paroled for service at the front by the Wehrmacht during the French campaign. A total of 2,762 prisoners were released from detention by the military judicial authorities for service in the offensive in the West. Of the 2,762, the percent of soldiers that remained free after proving themselves in combat was 93.6 percent while only 6.4 percent (or 177) soldiers had their paroles revoked. The Wehrmacht offered these statistics as additional justification of the parole system.[5]

The possibility of parole for service at the front was not possible by the end of the French campaign. After the armistice was signed with the Vichy regime on June 22, 1940, conviction meant incarceration for soldiers. With hundreds of soldiers sitting in their cells, the Wehrmacht prison system commandant complained that many prisoners who had committed minor offenses, or a one-time blunder, expressed the desire to prove their worth but had no opportunity to do so. As the military prisons filled up, the Wehrmacht once again began considering parole for service at the front.[6]

In a memorandum dated September 18, 1940, Rudolph Lehmann, chief of the Armed Forces Legal Division, wrote about the problem. While the Führer insisted that all means be taken to maintain discipline, Lehmann promoted an approach based on the Polish and French campaigns. Lehmann wrote:

> … it was crucial not to destroy the lives of the many men who had blundered once but were otherwise orderly and thereby usable soldiers. The system of front-parole accomplished this. But, the possibility of parole should exist even for soldiers whose units were not engaged at the front. The Wehrmacht has been forced in the war to use unusual means for securing discipline. It is its duty to find balance for this harshness, that is, through new and difficult ways.[7]

As a solution, Lehmann proposed the creation of special parole units. After the OKW legal division consulted with the OKW and the *Oberkommando des Heeres* (OKH—Supreme High Command of the German Army) regarding the proper size of the planned parole units, the OKW legal division approached Hitler with the plan for paroling convicted soldiers whose units were not engaged at the front, especially those who might simply have committed a one-time blunder. On December 21, 1940, Hitler ordered the creation of special parole units. The Führer's directive, the Suspension of the Execution of Punishments for the Purpose of Parole, stressed: "The toughest measures are necessary to maintain discipline in the troops, to suppress cowardice, and to give members of the Wehrmacht, who had blundered one time the opportunity for parole."[8]

On April 5, 1941, the OKW published its initial conditions, stipulating that soldiers meeting certain criteria could be released for service in the new parole battalions after partial atonement of their sentence. The remainder of the sentence would be deferred until after the war. The seven criteria initially established were as follows:

1. The convicted must have conducted himself flawlessly until the time of the crime for which he was condemned and he could be legally punished previously only very in significantly.

2. The crime must represent a one-time blunder and could not have its cause in a deficiency of character.
3. The convicted must have the sincere intention to prove himself against the enemy and must express this intention in a formal petition for parole.
4. The convicted must be a member of the armed forces or liable for military service or fit for employment as a soldier.
5. The convicted must be fit for employment in an infantry battalion.
6. The remainder of the punishment must amount to at least six months.
7. Prisoners serving punishments in a civilian penal institution and prisoners in penal battalions of the Wehrmacht must pass a one-month fitness examination at a Wehrmacht prison.[9]

Service in the new penal units would be considered as honored service according to Hitler 's initial instructions.[10] The OKW demanded strict but accurate treatment of the soldiers, emphasizing that battalion members were to be handled with good judgement but also with total fairness. In addition, battalion commanders were to refrain from revealing any shameful information about a parolee's punishment, especially before the group. An important aspect of the program was promoting and strengthening the sense of honor among the battalion members.

On February 17, 1941, OKH issued a directive requiring that upon the confirmation of a verdict, the decision was to be made deciding whether a soldier would be eligible for parole after the partial completion of the sentence or whether the prisoner should be released to a regular unit or to a parole battalion. Soldiers receiving simple prison sentences could be sent directly to a parole battalion. Wehrmacht penal camp inmates and soldiers serving sentences had to pass a one-month fitness examination at the Torgau prison complex near Berlin before they could be transferred to a parole battalion.[11]

According to Hans-Peter Klausch, the month-long examination boiled down to hard work, drill, and physical endurance. "One gets the impression from reading the evaluation reports," states Klausch, "that a certain mental or character deficiency could be compensated for by strength and daring recklessness." Klausch's observation describes a penal system devoted to mobilizing hardened fighters, individuals suitable for integration into the force, not necessarily the ideal German soldier.[12]

According to Klausch, the harsh treatment went further than just instilling discipline. The program was based on the military's desire for soldiers with a feeling of invincibility, self-confidence, and superiority over their opponent. Once they passed the test, the soldiers who had been treated like animals found a fresh sense of courage and hope.[13]

In 1941, about 24 percent of the prisoners tested at Torgau prison complex failed the exam and were returned to the appropriate penal facility. Most were returned to Emsland concentration camp located in Lower Saxony, Germany. The camp was used to house soldiers sentenced to penal sentences. The selection process was significantly affected after the losses in the winter of 1941–1942. The fitness exam failure rate dropped to about 10 percent, while the success rate steadily increased as the need for manpower increased; however, it never reached 100 percent as the soldiers coming from the Emsland camp were not in the best of physical or mental condition. As need for manpower increased, the military was increasingly agreeable to reactivating soldiers who were being punished for common offenses, rather than soldiers who violated discipline. The military considered cowardice and desertion to be more odious crimes than rape, theft, and murder. To be considered for parole, the soldier only had to have the capacity and the will to fight. Crimes that did not affect the war effort were overlooked, while anything that was perceived to hinder the war effort was much more serious.[14]

While there was no specific policy for rewarding their service, soldiers could earn a reassignment to a regular unit if their behavior was flawless and they performed in an outstanding manner in combat. A point system was developed that measured operational readiness, conduct, and bravery. A large number of points could be earned by volunteering for dangerous missions such as reconnaissance patrols. Those volunteering for such hazardous duties had a good chance for an early transfer, if they were not killed or captured first. The point system promoted the image of the daredevil who was constantly prepared. On April 3, 1945, an evaluation by the battalion staff of parolee "G," a former naval officer with Infantry Battalion 500, read:

> "G" proved himself to be extremely brave in the most difficult military engagement. During the Russian counterattack on 9 December 1944, he remained with his detachment despite his wound and did not allow the connection to the companies to be severed in spite of a furious bombardment. Also, in a subsequent fighting retreat through East Slovakia, "G" was always engaged with the enemy and through his relentless action was a constant example to his comrades. And even when the enemy's ranks broke through during a huge armoured assault, "G" did not retreat but participated in the defensive battle with rifles and hand grenades.[15]

If a parolee failed to conduct himself in a perfect manner, the court could order him back to a penal institution for the completion of his sentence. For extreme failure, the parolee could find himself transferred to a Wehrmacht penal camp, which were considered the worst form of punishment. The subjects were usually given a formal warning prior to their transfer.[16]

Other than relieving overburdened prisons, no urgent desires existed when Hitler created the order for the parole battalions in December 1940. The decision to create the parole battalions was based in practical military planning. The need for manpower, as the Wehrmacht planned for the assault on the Soviet Union (Operation Barbarossa), was paramount. Planning for Operation Barbarossa was ordered by Hitler three days before he issued his directive creating parole battalions. The need for reserves and soldiers of all types was recognized by Hitler and the military as the war expanded into the Balkans and further east. In February and March 1941, the OKW began preparing for the creation of parole battalions. As the need for soldiers increased, the selection criteria used by the Wehrmacht steadily decreased. By the winter of 1942, the only selection criteria was whether the parolee could be useful to the unit. He had only to be mentally and physically fit for service with the infantry and to exhibit during his custody that he had the honorable will to atone for his crime through model performance and good conduct with the unit.[17]

By 1944, the requirement that soldiers had at least six months left in their sentences was dropped. This action opened up the parole battalions to anyone who was sentenced. By the end of the war, the only criteria remaining was fitness for combat, and this was overlooked in many cases. By 1944, there were almost 1,000 parolees in penal battalions.

While many researchers believe that a death sentence awaited soldiers who served in parole battalions and the members were nothing more than cannon fodder, Hans-Peter Klausch believes differently. According to Klausch, based on the rigorous selection criteria and basic requirements for the parolees to be considered for service in the parole battalions, many battalions possessed an almost elite quality.[18] Wehrmacht leadership considered them to be valuable in the fight against the Russians. They received very important high-risk missions that inevitably produced high casualty rates. As manpower shortages resulted in the Wehrmacht drastically reducing the selection criteria, by the end of the war, the elite qualities of the battalions began to disappear as the ranks grew with true criminals and soldiers who were unfit for combat.

It is difficult to determine the exact number of men who served in the parole battalions since few documents related to the battalions survived the war. High casualties caused high turnover rates, making it even more difficult to gain an accurate count of participants. Used continually at the front as advanced parties and shock troops, the units needed constant replacements. Some scholars estimate that the death rate reached 50 percent in the parole battalions. Three of the parole battalions disappeared without any trace in the final weeks of the war, with documents simply listing them as "destroyed in battle."[18] Even though the actual numbers are not quantifiable, the parole battalions played an important role in the Wehrmacht's attempt to maintain the "military community" through deterrence and to mobilize manpower.

Postponing sentences for service at the front in regular units and service in the parole battalions was planned to discourage those hoping to avoid the danger of combat by committing crimes and to guarantee that the troops were not deprived of necessary personnel. After the *blitzkrieg* (lightning war) in Russia at the end of 1941 failed, the government considered the parole system insufficient for the requirements of the Wehrmacht. As the high losses in the east and the extension of the war into 1942 took their toll, the Wehrmacht looked to new methods for mobilizing prisoners for military service. Hitler decided that the continuing conflict against the Soviet Union required the mobilization of every available soldier. Hitler demanded that more possibilities for parolees to serve at the front after the failures in Russia. Hitler ordered that individuals convicted for crimes that had their cause in carelessness or youthful indiscretion were to be paroled immediately and become replacements for the Eastern Front. Units that had served as means of punishment were directed to train inferior soldiers to become productive soldiers for the war effort.[19]

Losses on the Eastern Front in April 1942 exceeded 300,000. By December of that year, the Wehrmacht required 625,000 replacements. A diary entry made at the end of 1941 by the Army's Chief of the General Staff General Franz Holder reflected the seriousness of the reserve situation:

> Conversation with [General] Bock: Guderian reports that the condition of the troops is so critical that he does not know how he is supposed to fend off an enemy attack. A crisis of trust of a serious nature in the troops. Declining battle strength of the infantry! In the rear, all available forces were assembled.... The Army Group needs people![20]

A study written by the OKW Command Staff in the spring of 1942 stated: "Without resort to the class of 1923 and without resort to key defense industry personnel, no reserves are available." Faced with this crisis, the Wehrmacht made decisive changes in how legally imposed punishments would be executed. On April 2, 1942, Hitler signed a directive stating the following:

> The execution of sentences during the war must be adapted as soon as possible to the changing requirements of the military situation. Measures cannot be adhered to that proved effective under other circumstances. The possibilities for parole on the eastern front must be used much more than hitherto ... many convicted soldiers will not be able to be employed with the fighting troops immediately and some not at all. Unstable elements that count on this must be denied any incentive, through the intensification and gradation of punishments, to evade operations at the front because they are atoning a prison sentence. For this purpose, field penal battalions must be established immediately and mobilized for the hardest labor under dangerous circumstances as close as possible to the fighting troops.[21]

The OKW produced a new order (Ordinance for the Execution of Punishments) on April 14, 1942. The order translated Hitler's directive into action. Parole as service at the front had top priority. In order to satisfy Hitler's requirements, the OKW created the first three field penal battalions. The penal battalions were created to provide manpower to the front as well as punishment other than imprisonment. In theory, the parolees freed up active soldiers for combat elsewhere.

The OKW ordered the military's existing penal camps converted into field penal camps as the New Ordinance for the Execution of Punishments was created. The field penal camps, like the field penal battalions, would be given dangerous missions at the front. The camps became the center of the new graduated penal system of the Wehrmacht.[22]

Section 104 of the Wartime Judicial Procedure Code was created as a deterrent against the commission of crimes in order to avoid combat. Many commanders were skeptical about accepting criminals in their units. They feared that these "bad" soldiers would have negative effect on their units. Commanders need continuous replacements, but they were also worried about combat effectiveness. The Wehrmacht believed that by mobilizing manpower for use in the field, but in separate self-contained penal units, they could satisfy the requirements of Section 104 of the Wartime Judicial Procedure Code and the commanders' apprehensions about maintaining discipline. Commanders now had more punishment alternatives at their disposal. If a soldier conformed to the regime and performed well, he could receive less harsh punishment. On the other hand, if he did not conform, he could be moved up in the punishment ladder. If the soldier failed completely, he could be dismissed from service and handed over to the SS or the Gestapo.[23]

The Nazi regime established fifteen penal camps in the Emsland area, in the north-western edge of the German Reich, between 1933 and 1938. The Emsland camps were made up of concentration camps, prison camps, and military POW camps. The Emsland camps held inmates and prisoners from all over Europe. Since the beginning of the war, the Reich Ministry of Justice increasingly interned former German soldiers in the northern camps. They had been declared unworthy of military service and removed from the Wehrmacht. They were detained, meaning that the time spent there would not be taken into account as part of their prison sentence, which was to officially begin only after the war was over. Between 25,000 and 30,000 people convicted before military courts were held in the camps. About 5,000 to 6,000 prisoners were transferred by the Wehrmacht military court system to the Torgau Military prison at Fort Zinna.[24]

During the pre-war years, the creation of large camps had been one of the major innovations in Nazi prison policy. The Emsland camp was the largest prison camp and was reserved for male prisoners. The majority of the inmates in the Emsland camp were Germans sentenced by military and civilian courts as "war offenders." By the end of March 1941, 6,400 of the 8,100 Emsland inmates were considered "war offenders." They were to be held at Emsland until the war was over and only then would their imprisonment officially begin.[25]

The inmates in the Emsland camp faced extreme conditions. Life was already extremely hard in the first years of the war, and conditions declined rapidly as the war went on. Inmates were forced to carry out extremely exhausting labor, while their rations became smaller and smaller. Many prisoners were so hungry that they ate grass, leaves, bones, and potato peelings.[26] As a result of the extreme conditions, hard labor, brutal treatment, and less than adequate rations, the camp witnessed a dramatic increase in illness. In March 1941, the camp doctor reported that sometimes well over 10 percent of inmates were so sick and weak that they could not work. The cases of tuberculosis was much higher than before the war, and between 1940 and 1941, the number of inmates taken to the hospital with dysentery almost doubled.[27] More and more inmates collapsed with colds, edema, pneumonia, or exhaustion. More prisoners died in the Emsland camp than in any other German penal institution. According to official numbers, around 1,330 prisoners died between 1940 and 1941.[28]

The Military Penal Code was used by the German military courts extensively during the war. Not counting Navy and Air Force courts, there were over 1,000 military courts operating at the front and in almost all larger German cities. From the start, the courts handed down sentences very rapidly.

Over 30,000 members of the Wehrmacht were sentenced to death by military courts. A number of judgments openly referred to 1918. One Navy judge stated: "In determining the punishment I take into account whether the defendant could be considered a revolutionary type or not. I make sure that 1918 will not be repeated. I exterminate revolutionary types."[29]

Soldiers sentenced to imprisonment in a penitentiary by German military courts were branded "unworthy of military service," kicked out of the Army and handed over as "war offenders" to the prison service (this practice only changed in autumn 1944, when these men were taken straight to new probation forces or to concentration camps). By spring 1941, the Army had already transferred some 3,500 men, sentenced to imprisonment in a penitentiary by military courts, to the legal system. According to Army guidelines, these ex-soldiers had to receive especially harsh punishment. It did not take long for the legal authorities to decide that the Emsland camp best fitted the bill. The exhausting work, the violent disciplinary sanctions, and the guards' brutality guaranteed that the imprisonment would be as painful as possible. Consequently, the vast majority of Army offenders turned over to the prison service were taken to Emsland—a total of more than 20,000 men throughout the entire war, according to one estimate. The majority had been convicted for offences against military discipline. Men sentenced for desertion, for being absent without leave, and for "sedition" made up well over half of the ex-soldiers taken to the Emsland camp.[30]

The military authorities were clearly happy with the way these ex-soldiers were maltreated in Emsland. "Imprisonment in this camp," the Navy High Command noted, "seemed much more effective than in other penal institutions."[31]

Initially, the former soldiers taken to the Emsland camp had little hope of getting out before the war was over, but this soon changed.[32] Soldiers who wanted to escape front-line fighting now knew that the most likely outcome was either a death sentence or a period of brutal imprisonment followed by a return to the front in a potentially even more exposed position.[33]

Prison officials in the Emsland camp played a significant role in the creation of probation units, as they were charged with examining potential candidates among the imprisoned ex-soldiers. Only those men judged fit to return to the front were to be selected. Strict selection was considered vital to keep out trouble-makers and to prevent a repeat of 1918. The official requirements for an ex-soldier to be sent back to the Army included that the inmate had behaved well, had only minor convictions, had no serious deficiencies of character, and was physically and mentally fit for military service. According to the guidelines, the prisoner also had to volunteer. This rule was later relaxed. The fact that prisoners did volunteer is a testament to the appalling conditions in the Emsland camp. The prisoners were so desperate to escape that they actually preferred fighting at the front.[34]

The primary destination for convicted soldiers was now the field penal battalions and field penal camps. These camps and battalions effectively replaced the Wehrmacht prisons. Soldiers were only sentenced to prisons in exceptional cases.

The OKW instructed all commanding officers functioning as a court to abide by the new Ordinance for the Execution of Punishments. After April 1942, nearly 40 percent of soldiers convicted to minor prison sentences were sent directly to field penal battalions. About 2 percent of the soldiers were sent to the Wehrmacht penal camps for non-compliance with the requirements of the field penal units. The creation of the field penal battalions and the conversion of the penal camps into field units were intended as a deterrent, but also served the increasing manpower requirements. Several Nazi supporters truly gained pleasure from the fact that criminals might no more be "preserved" in prisons as the nation's youths risked their lives at the front.[35]

The Wehrmacht penal camps served the same function as the disciplinary units served before the war. Beginning in April 1942, most of the Wehrmacht's unruly soldiers were placed in the field penal camps. The penal camps were directly subordinated to the prison commandant and represented the highest form of punishment that a soldier could receive without being turned over to the SS or Gestapo. With the April 1942 changes in the execution of punishments, the OKW ordered the existing Wehrmacht penal camps converted into field penal camps and their detainees transferred to the new units, regardless of their fitness rating. Every Army group on the Eastern Front had a field penal camp at its disposal by 1943. Unruly soldiers sentenced to prison or penal servitude could be sent to the field penal camps. Just as in the former penal camps, time served in the field penal camps during the war was not credited to the prisoner's account. The inmates were required to perform heavy work in operational areas. They worked without weapons on clearing mines, retrieving corpses, and constructed field emplacements. In addition to heavy work, the soldiers had to perform formal military drill and training. Franz Seidler writes about the formal military training: "It consisted as a rule of formal military training and battle simulations and differed in no way from the barracks square exercises of basic training."[36]

While the incorporation of drills and education was intended as punishment, they did prepare the soldiers for eventual service at the front. The normal workday lasted twelve to fourteen hours and at least four hours on Sundays and holidays. The punishing routine and reduced rations quickly led to hunger, exhaustion, and the gradual deterioration of the inmates' physical and mental health. Suicide was allegedly a daily event in the military's version of the civilian concentration camp. The guards treated the inmates as cowards, weaklings, and parasites. According to one contemporary account, the guards' behavior bordered on sadism.[37]

An inmate's stay in a field penal camp could be ended if he exhibited good conduct. This meant a transfer to a field penal battalion or a parole battalion. Those who were deemed as incapable of education were dismissed from service and turned over to either civilian police for internment in a concentration camp, the SS, or the Gestapo. According to the original OKH implementation order:

> … the field penal camps are designed to exercise a lasting deterrent on the unstable elements in the troops and to counteract decisively the incentive to avoid one's duty by incurring a prison sentence. For this reason, the chances of survival for penal camp inmates is intended to be no better than the chances for the regular troops.[38]

As the war situation deteriorated, translating Hitler's decision to adapt punishments, the OKW'S April 1942 New Ordinance for the Execution of Punishments provided for the creation of the field penal battalions. The ordinance of April 14, 1942 included the following specifications for the battalions in Section I, Paragraph 3:

> For the execution of punishment in the field penal battalions comes in to consideration: Wehrmacht prisoners, except those who will be dismissed from detention in the near future because of visible improvement (with

the remainder of the punishment perhaps up to six months)—specifically: cowards (for example, those convicted of desertion) serious cases of absence without leave, and subversion of fighting power), and those repeatedly and strikingly punished) as well as those punished for other intentionally dishonorable offenses.[39]

There were issues of personnel management related to the formation of the new units. A 1942 memorandum summarizes the purpose of the field penal camps and penal battalions in the following text of a circular published in the fall of 1942. It clearly explains the objectives of the Wehrmacht's newest penal institutions:

1. Atonement and Deterrent Doctrine. Through the severity of the punishment it must be brought strikingly and clearly to the consciousness of prisoners or the penal camp inmates respectively that they have transgressed severely, and for this, they have brought upon themselves and must punishment in the form of the deprivation of freedom of the most varied type. The knowledge of this severity must deter others from committing similar crimes. Only if this knowledge actually comes to the consciousness of wider circles will the punishment fulfil its purpose.
2. Improvement and Educational Doctrine. It must be clear to prisoners and penal camp inmates that they can "ascend" with good conduct; that is, they can earn alleviation and privileges, which promotes them so far that they can be proposed for parole with the regular troops, or transfer from a penal camp for the orderly execution of the punishment. But they must first of all feel the full severity of the punishment... Every alleviation of suffering presumes an especial merit of the prisoners or penal camp inmates through flawless conduct and good performance.
3. Work Doctrine. The work is not the punishment; much more the circumstances and burdens under which it must be carried out should deter the prisoners or penal camp in mates respectively and all the people in general. A different interpretation would degrade the work of the front fighters, which in part is just as hard and difficult. For this work, which the prisoners carry out in the interest of the whole as important to the war effort and which supplies a criterion for his performance evaluation, the inmates must be kept physically and mentally fresh and fit for work through suitable measures.[40]

Strafbattalion is the common term for penal units created from prisoner during the World War II in all branches of the German Armed Forces. The word *Bewährungsbataillone* (Probation Battalions) is often used interchangeably. Soldiers and civilian criminals sentenced to these units were generally poorly armed and required to undertake dangerous high-casualty missions.

Strafbattalion were operated and administered by the German military police. By 1943, the course of World War II had turned against Nazi Germany. Due to military losses and the need to maintain discipline by example, the German High Command ordered that further punishment units should be formed from the thousands of Wehrmacht military prisoners held in its military prison. These Strafbattalion were then used to conduct dangerous operations (sometimes akin to suicide missions) for the Army, such as clearing minefields, assaulting difficult objectives, and defending positions against overwhelming attacking forces. They were also made to do manual hard labor in front-line locations building and repairing military infrastructure and defenses.

Prisoners that survived their missions would be deemed fit to fight and returned to the field with the rights of a combat soldier. Although Strafbattalions were mainly used on the Eastern Front, some were sent to the Ardennes on the Western Front during the last major German offensive in December 1944.

The Strafbattalions were developed from the *Sonderabteilungen* (special departments) that existed in pre-war Nazi Germany. Initially, Nazi policy was to rebuild the armed forces by keeping potential troublemakers away from the troops and removing any destructive elements from military service. However, on May 21, 1935, Adolf Hitler decreed that under the new Nazi Defense Act, any conscript who was deemed unfit for military service because of subversive activity would be arrested. However, soldiers who were deemed disruptive to military discipline, but were otherwise worthy of service would be sent to military battalion.[41]

These units were designed to change attitudes toward state and national policy while instilling a sense of duty, honor, and purpose. These goals were to be achieved through harsh discipline and punishments, extensive indoctrination programs, and restrictions on home leave. Troops who conformed were eventually transferred to regular units. However, those who continued to show indiscipline or opposed the military were transferred to concentration camps. Before World War II, there were Strafbattalion battalions within the Wehrmacht in Nazi Germany. According to estimates, between 3,000 and 6,000 Wehrmacht personnel passed through these special departments. A total of 320 "incorrigible pests" were transported to concentration camps.

Yet with the outbreak of war in 1939, the *Sonderabteilungen* were disbanded. They were replaced with the *Feld-Sonder Battalion* (Special Field Battalion) under the control of the Field Police. As the duration of the war increased, the need for more military personnel grew accordingly. The OKW directed military tribunals to send incarcerated members of the Wehrmacht as well as subversives to probation battalions at the front.[42]

The Classification and Organization of Penal Units

Parole Units

1. Special employment units:
   A. Series 500 and other special battalions under the orders of the OKW.
   B. Units numbered 361 or basic infantry units deployed in North Africa.
   C. Battalions of the Luftwaffe and Kriegsmarine for special use made up of minor offenses against discipline.
   D. SS Special troops of assault created from disciplinary companies.

2. Formations composed of second-class soldiers (unworthy):
   A. Units numbered 999 and deployed in Africa plus units of the Fortresses 999 Africa Fortification Group.
   B. Forced labour in probation assigned to the Todt organization for construction on the front.[1]

Second-Class Soldiers

The second-class soldier was deprived of his rank, decorations, and honors and was considered unworthy to carry a weapon in the defense of Germany. The less fortunate of the German military prisoners were sent to Armed Forces punishment camps in Emsland in the north-western part of Germany and at Esterwegen and Bürgermoor concentration camps near Papenburg. Since their creation in 1933 and serving as a center of detentions by the SA for the enemies of the regime, these camps were subsequently reserved for the political prisoners of the Communist Party and the Socialist Party, the usual criminals, Jews, religious objectors, military delinquents, and, after 1939, Allied POWs. In the harsh disciplinary environment of the Waffen SS in particular and the Wehrmacht in general, profound distinction was made between the penalties that fell within the classification of delinquents and those relating to the classification of offender and criminal. The offenders were minor disciplinary cases while the latter were much larger and renamed second-class soldiers.

Depending on the extent of the offense committed, and at the discretion of the commander, these men could be denied their rank and decorations, denied mail and packets, prohibited from writing at home, and refused leave. According to the importance and gravity of the offense, the soldier of the concerned was generally stamped "no decoration, medal or authorized promotion."[2]

Probation Units

At the beginning of the war, prison sentences were suspended for the duration of the war. This was to prevent the troops from escaping personnel and the fact that criminals were oppressed before the start of the war. The place of offenders, whose offense was suspended, was basically the front. There they should prove themselves. Since many units of the Wehrmacht were unitary units, a probation could not take place, whereby the penalty itself lost its meaning. In the nine-month campaign after the French campaign, immediate punishment was ordered for most offenders. This should at least partially serve longer custodial sentences. However, the practice robbed the troops of disproportionately many soldiers, since thousands were in prison. As a result, the armed forces were filled with soldiers and battalions. Many of these soldiers felt their punishments were unfair, as comrades were much less punished during the campaigns. For this reason, a probationary group was created, in which soldiers of all parts of the Wehrmacht should be given the opportunity to prove themselves at the front. The punishment for probation could be exercised both in the grave way and by the direct execution of the court's decision. It had seven prerequisites:

1. The condemned man had to have led himself perfectly, except for the deed for which he was condemned.
2. The offense had to be a one-time derailment and should not be based on character deficiencies.
3. The condemned had to have the honest will to prove himself before the enemy and to express this will in a written application for probation.
4. The convicted person had to be a defendant or a conscript or to be employed as a soldier.
5. The sentence had to be at least 6 months.
6. The convict had to be capable of being used in an infantry battalion.
7. Convicts whose sentence was executed in a civilian penitentiary, and prisoners in the detention centers of the Wehrmacht had to pass a month-long examination as a convict of the Wehrmacht.[3]

In the course of the war, the prerequisites for parole were reduced further and further. After all, a soldier had to be physically and mentally fit for infantry. On April 1, 1941 the Infantry Battalion z.b.V. 500 was set up as the first test unit by the Military District Command IX in Meiningen. The members of the battalion wore the white collar mirrors of the infantry. In the basic leadership of December 21, 1940, it was expressly stated that the service in the probationary group was honorary service like any other military service and that the unit had in no way the character of a criminal group. In the case of promotions, a more stringent standard should be applied, since the punishment imposed on probation already represented an award. Orders were not awarded, only the storm badge, the wounded badge, and the war memorial badge were authorized. There was only a chance for vacation after service at the front.

As early as 1941, the battalions 540, 550, 560, and 561 were deployed in the east. They consisted of reinforced grenadier battalions with three armored companies, a machine-gun company, a staff company, a huntsman's train, a parachute train, and a pioneer's train. Up to the end of the war, about 82,000 soldiers had served in the 500 battalions. At least thirteen officers of the permanent staff were awarded the Knight's Cross.[4]

These units were supplied and treated nearly as normal units but used for special, dangerous missions. Usually, these soldiers had to make their probation in their field unit and were transferred to these *Zur Besonderen Verwendung* (z.b.V.—Special Purpose Infantry Battalions) when their unit was not at the front or saw no actions where the soldiers could stand the test. The units were normally used as Army groups instead of being part of a division or lower unit. The below battalions consisted of soldiers who were condemned to probation.

Infantry Battalion z.b.V. 291 and 292

These units were formed in September 1944. It ended the war with the 19th Army. The 19th Army occupied southern France from the LXXXIII Army Corps and defended southern France, the Vosges Mountains, Alsace, Baden and southern Württemberg during the Allied invasion of southern France and other large Allied military operations that had as their goal the liberation of southern France and the invasion of southern Germany. During Operation Dragoon, the 19th Army was trapped in an enormous encirclement, suffering 7,000 killed or missing, 20,000 wounded, 130,000–140,000 captured and was largely destroyed as a fighting force. However, its headquarters survived intact, retreated northwards and participated in the defense of the Rhine River. After Operation Dragoon, the 19th Army was recreated with poorly trained conscripts and tasked with defending the west bank of the Rhine, and the city of Strasbourg. The 19th Army was again encircled and largely destroyed during the battle for the Colmar Pocket in January and February 1945.

Once again its headquarters survived capture and was rebuilt largely from *Volkssturm* (the national militia established during the last months of World War II) and hastily trained replacement troops in early 1945. With many of its best men and junior leaders dead or captured, the 19th Army's effectiveness was seriously impaired and it proved unable to parry the thrusts of its constant foe, the French First Army. Split by deep French Armoured thrusts into Baden, the Black Forest, and Württemberg, the 19th Army was destroyed in the area of Stuttgart and Münsingen in late April 1945, with remnants of the army surrendering as late as May 8, 1945.[5]

Infantry Battalion z.b.V. 491

The infantry battalion z.b.V. 491 was established according by the merger of the Luftwaffe Hunter battalions 1, 2, and 10, which were transferred simultaneously to the Army, and the Special Company z.b.V. 1 at the Army Group North with three protective companies and a heavy company. The battalion was subordinate to Army Group Northland and was deployed with the X Army Corps. From January 25, 1945, the battalion became part of the Army Group Kurland.

Army Group Kurland had been encircled by the Red Army on the east coast at Memel on October 20, 1944, in Courland. On January 24, 1945, the Red Army entered the 4th Kurland battle. The attacks on both sides of Prekuln, followed by further attacks between Frauenburg and Tukkum, showed the new Russian tactics to attack at several points simultaneously, thereby destroying the opponent's reserves. The 30th Infantry Division and the SS Division Nordland defended the center of gravity. The positions on the Vartaya had to be abandoned. After dedicating reserves, further Russian attacks against the 205th and 215th Infantry Division at Frauenburg, as well as the 122nd Infantry Division, emerged. The violent attacks quieted on both sides in snow and mud after many losses. The 5th Kurland battle began on February 20, 1945, with fierce Russian artillery fire as well as battleship attacks on the German positions. The subsequent heavy battles did not bring any significant success for the Russian attackers. Only the village of Džūkste was lost. The thawing weather, which began on March 11, turned all the dirt roads into mud and hindered any movement. The 6th Kurland battle lasted from March 18 to March 31, 1945. It did not bring any territorial gains to the Red Army, and it was the last battle of the Kurland until the end of the war. Army Group Kurland went into Russian captivity on May 8, 1945. Parts of the Army group were evacuated westwards across the Baltic Sea. The replacement for the battalion was carried out by the 500th Infantry Replacement Battalion.[6]

Note: Special Companies were brought on line to replace the Probation Camps. The Special Companies 1, 2, and 3 were established by order LV43 Number 1667 on August 6, 1943. All members were demoted to the rank of private and were assigned dangerous work on the front line without weapons for three to six months.

Infantry Battalion z.b.V. 500

The Infantry Battalion z.b.V. 500 was formed on April 1, 1941, in Meiningen, in the Military District IX. The battalion was divided into three rifle companies with twelve officers, eighty-four non-commissioned officers, and fifteen men. Five officers and fifty-one men were envisaged for the battalion staff. The battalion was the first of a series of probation units of the Wehrmacht. The battalion was ready for operation on June 1, 1941. At the beginning of the Eastern Campaign, the LII Army Corps in the 17th Army in Galicia, and under harsh circumstances, used the battalion as a fighting force under difficult conditions. Some features of the battalion consisted of up to 80 percent degraded officers and non-commissioned officers. In October 1941, the battalion stood near Kharkov and in the Caucasus in 1942. In 1943, it was used in the Kuban. From July 23, 1943, the battalion was placed under the command of the 13th Tank Division. In the later stages of the fighting west of Krimskaya, the battalion was deployed as a corps reserve in the third line of the 98th Infantry Division. In September, it was deployed at Melitopol and Zaporozhye. In 1944, the battalion was deployed at Nikolaev, and at Lviv and then in the Carpathians in July. In 1945, it fought in the High Tatras in Moravia and lastly with the 1st Tank Army. The replacement of the battalion was initially carried out by the replacement company 500. From October 1941, the task of the infantry replacement was one of the missions of this battalion.[7]

Infantry Replacement Battalion 500

The infantry replacement battalion 500 was set up on October 1, 1941, in Fulda, in the Military District IX. The battalion under division 159 was the replacement for the battalions of the Wehrmacht. The battalion came from the 500th Infantry Replacement Company, which had been formed in June 1941 as the part of the 500th probation force established by the Decree of December 21, 1940, from soldiers of the Wehrmacht Prisons. From September 23, 1942, the battalion was under the command of the 409th Division. On December 1, 1942, the battalion was transferred to the General Government District, where it was divided. This resulted in an infantry training battalion 500 with five companies in Skierniewieze and a replacement battalion in Tomaszow. In April 1943, the battalion handed over a fifth companies to the Landes Bau Battalion 17. In August 1943, the battalion made contributions to the Construction Battalion 999. In 1944, the staff of the Grenadier Replacement and Training Regiment 500 was expanded and transferred with the battalions to the Protectorate of Bohemia and Moravia to Brno and Olomouc. After the move, the regiment was subordinated to the commander-in-chief of Prague. In March 1945, the regiment was mobilized with the 1st to 4th Battalions and a spare battalion, and distributed to the Army Group Center. The replacement provision for the unit was carried out by the Land Protection and Replacement Battalion 17 in Frankfurt am Main, in the Military District IX. The replacement battalion also replaced the following Infantry battalions: z.b.V. 491; Z.b.V. 500; Z.b.V. 540; Z.b.V. 550; Z.b.V. 560; and Z.b.V. 561.[8]

Infantry Battalion z.b.V. 540

The Infantry Battalion 540 was formed on December 1, 1941 in Fulda, in Military District IX. The battalion was set up with three armored companies, a machine-gun company, a staff company, a huntsman's train, a parachute train, and a pioneer train. The battalion was part of the Wünnenberg group of the SS police division in 1942, involved in the encirclement of the 2nd Russian Shock Army under Lieutenant General Vlasov. In August, September, and November 1942, the battalion was deployed under the 1st Army Corps. On October 15, 1942, the battalion was renamed the 540th Grenadier Battalion. Until January 22, 1943, the battalion was installed in the bridgehead of Grusino. The section of the battalion was extended by a distance of 1.5 kilometers south on the west bank of the Volkhov River. After a hasty detachment on the night of January 23, 1943, the battalion was replaced by the XXVI Army Corps. On the night of January 24, 1943, the battalion completely relieved its forces in the east section of Ssinjawino. Here, the strengthened 3rd Company under the leadership of First Lieutenant Wolff and to the right of it, the reinforced 1st Company under First Lieutenant Feuchter, was used. One-third of the fighting strength initially remained as a reserve in Ssinjawino. In the course of the January 24, 1943, the 3rd Company carried out counterattacks against the Russian forces. On the evening of January 24, 1943, the main area was occupied as planned.

On the night of January 25, 1943, several attacks were repealed on the left wing of the battalion. On January 25, 1943, two Russian tanks broke through on the left flank. A third tank came to Ssinjawino and two of the tanks were put out of action by men of the 4th Company. Daily frontal attacks, with strong artillery and air force support, were repulsed. On January 25, 1943, the commander of the battalion took over the entire area of Ssinjawino. Half of the 1st Company, with parts of the 4th Company under First Lieutenant Tetzner, took over the left wing and detached the completely weakened SS police units. In the evening, the last remaining battalion's sixty men, who had remained as reserves in Grusino, arrived. On the night of January 26, a number of attempted attacks on the left wing of the 3rd Company were rejected. On the night of January 27, a number of attacks on the left wing of the 3rd Company were immediately reversed in a counterattack. The battalion section in the north-west was taken over by the 1st Battalion of the 45th Grenadier Regiment.

On the night of January 28, 1943, those killed were brought back for the first time, the ammunition was sorted and stacked, and preparations for normal defense and position were made. The Russian attacked again, and the fire was even heavier than in the past few days. The 45th Grenadier Regiment took over the entire section. On January 29, mass raids against the battalion were carried out with the strongest fire on the main area and the command posts. All attacks were repulsed under very high enemy losses. The losses of the battalion were now also high. A ski pioneer company of the 45th Grenadier Regiment was subordinated and deployed on the left wing of the battalion.

On January 30, 1943, the Russian continued its mass encroachments on the entire front. They continued advancing with stronger forces early in the morning at the ski company.

Before the fight ended, the Russians broke through on the west on the early morning of January 331, 1943. They penetrated to Ssinjawino and blocked the battalion command post. In the evening, the remains of the battalion were finally withdrawn to Tschudovo. During these seven days of deployment, the battalion had 112 killed, 321 wounded, and thirty-four missing. The replacement of the battalion was performed by the 500 Infantry Replacement Battalion. The following is a list of the penalties committed by the battalion members as of February 18, 1943:

8—for desertion
20—for unauthorized travel
4—for cowardice before the enemy
8—for decomposition of the Wehrmacht
13—for attack on a superior
5—for lack of commitment
8—for not waking up
3—for abuse of the service
54—for theft of property
5—for fornication between men
6—other moral acts
1—for drunkenness
10—for other offense

These figures contain eleven members of the Kriegsmarine and twenty-six members of the Luftwaffe. At the end of January 1944, the battalion was then deployed under the 61st Infantry Division. The battalion surrendered in 1945 to the 18th U.S. Army in the Courland Peninsula.[9]

Infantry Battalion z.b.V. 550

This unit was formed in October 1942 from the re-designation of Infantry Battalion 550 z.b.V. It was stationed on the central sector of the Eastern Front and retreated through Poland before ending the war in East Prussia with the 3rd Tank Army. During the Soviet counteroffensive, the 3rd Tank Army fought its way out of an encirclement and later fought at Tekino, the Duna, and Vitebsk. In March 1944, the 3rd Tank Army took part in the forced assembly and deportation of Russian civilians in the Borisov area. The civilians were deported to Germany for use as forced labor. The Army later retreated through Lithuania and Courland, fighting in the Battle of Memel in late 1944.

In February 1945, the 3rd Tank Army was one of the armies that made up the new Army Group Vistula. On March 10, 1945, General Hasso-Eccard von Manteuffel was made the commander of the 3rd Tank Army, which was assigned to defend the banks of the Oder River, north of the Seelow Heights, thus hampering Soviet access to Western Pomerania and Berlin. They then faced an overwhelming Soviet attack launched by General Rokossovsky's 2nd Belorussian Front during the Battle of Berlin. On April 25, the Soviets broke through 3rd Tank Army's line around the bridgehead south of Stettin and crossed the Randow Swamp. Following the defeat at Stettin, the 3rd Tank Army was forced to retreat into the region of Mecklenburg—the headquarters of 3rd Tank Army. Manteuffel made negotiations with British generals including Field Marshall Bernard Montgomery at Hagenow on May 3, 1945 so that he, with 300,000 German soldiers, would surrender to the British rather than Soviet forces.[10]

Infantry Battalion z.b.V. 560

This unit was formed in October 1942 from the re-designation of Infantry Battalion 560 z.b.V. It was stationed on the southern sector of the Eastern Front and retreated through Poland before ending the war in East Prussia with the 4th Army. From 1943 on, as Army Group Center was in full retreat, the 4th Army also had to move its troops backwards. The Red Army's campaign of autumn 1943, Operation Suvorov (also known as the 'battle of the highways'), saw the 4th Army pushed back towards Orsha. Between October and the first week of December, the Russians had tried four times to take Orsha and had been beaten off in furious battles by 4th Army.

In 1944, the 4th Army was holding defensive positions east of Orsha and Mogilev in the Belorussian SSR, occupying a bulging 40×128-kilometre bridgehead east of the Dnepr River. Few units were able to escape westwards. After the battles in the rest of the summer, the Army required complete rebuilding. During late 1944–45, the 4th Army, now under the command of Friedrich Hoßbach, was tasked with holding the borders of East Prussia. The replacement for the battalion was carried out by the 500th Infantry Replacement Battalion.[11]

Infantry Battalion z.b.V. 561

The unit was established in Skierniewicze on January 13, 1943. The battalion was built with three armored companies, a machine-gun company, a staff company, a huntsman's train, a parachute train, and a pioneer's train. In January 1944, the battalion was renamed the Grenadier Battalion 561 z.b.V. The battalion was subordinated to Army Group Northland and stood at Lake Ladoga in 1943. At the beginning of 1944, the battalion was north of Novgorod under the XXXVIII Army Corps. The Russian breakthrough came and the battalion was pushed south, where it was placed under the command of the Combat Group Apelt. It was used as a blocking organization on both sides of Motorovo, with front to the north. In December 1944, the battalion was deployed at Pampali. Here the battalion suffered heavy losses. The battalion was destroyed by the U.S. 18th Army on the Courland Peninsula. The replacement of the battalion was performed by the 500th Infantry Replacement Battalion.[12]

Infantry Battalion 609 z.b.V.

No information is available about this unit.

999 Units

The organizations with the number 999 had a completely different background. In these units were, defenseless, so called dismissed brethren and prisoners. Homosexuals, traitors, gypsies, and Jews were excluded. With these units, it should be achieved that condemned criminals were not safely seated in the rear areas, while at the front, the soldiers died. First, these men were grouped together in Africa Brigade 999 and deployed in Africa. After the loss of Africa, the battalions were deployed on all front sections. The men were employed in the infantry battalions, in battalions, or other units with the number 999, depending on physical and mental disposition. The estimates, how many 999 there were, are far apart, ranging from 25,000 to 40,000 men. There were no soldiers who had come directly from the concentration camp to the 999s. The 999 units were made up of men seen as not worthy to serve, so they were not condemned in a court. The men included men assigned there for political reasons but also many others.[13]

999 Light Africa Division (also known as 999 Africa Division)

The division was formed from the Africa Brigade 999.

Note: See Chapter 7 for Order of Battle and Operational History.

Reinforced Africa-Regiment 361

The reinforced Africa Regiment 361 was created on June 15, 1941. The regiment was made up of former foreign-legionaries, who had not been in Germany before, and second-class soldiers. The staff and the 1st Battalion of the regiment were placed on the Baumholder camp, in the XII Army zone. The 2nd Battalion was set up in Rheine, in Military District VI. The regiment received an Artillery Division 361 with three batteries. On July 23, 1941, the regiment received an anti-aircraft company from the 1st Anti-Aircraft Defense Battalion 613. The regiment was transferred to Africa. There, the regiment of the 90th Lightweight Africa Division was subordinated. On April 1, 1942, the regiment was renamed to a Light Infantry Regiment 361. On June 28, 1942, the Regiment was expanded by an 11th Heavy Infantry Company. On July 22, 1942, the Regiment was named Protection Regiment 361. The regiment continued to be subordinated to the 90th Light Africa Division. On July 27, 1942, the Regiment was renamed 361th Panzer Grenadier Regiment, Light Africa Division. The Infantry Replacement Battalion Rheine was responsible for the replacement of the regiment.[14]

Africa Protection Regiment (Motorized) 961

The Africa Rifle Regiment 961 was formed on October 12, 1942 at the military training area Heuber, located in Military District V. The regiment was made from two battalions, a pioneer company, and an artillery division. The regiment was transferred to the north of France after the establishment of the Africa Brigade in 999. On February 18, 1943, the artillery division of the Regiment formed the 1st Division of the Artillery Regiment 999. On that day, the 1st Battalion of the Africa Protection Regiment 963 entered as the 3rd Battalion to the regiment. Also in February 1943, the pioneer company was given the formation of the 1st Company of the Pioneer Battalion 999. From March 1943, the regiment was relocated to Africa. The 3rd Battalion remained behind in Europe. There the regiment of the new 999th light African division was subordinated. The regiment was destroyed in May 1943 in Tunis. On June 1, 1943, the 3rd Battalion formed the 1st Fortress Infantry Battalion 999. During their short history and despite the fact that they were penal units, they committed themselves fairly well. Ordinary ranks were not permitted to wear the national eagle, collar patches, or cockade on their uniform, nor were they allowed to wear the traditional Army belt with the national eagle displayed on them.[15]

Africa Protection Regiment (Motorized) 962

The Africa Rifle Regiment 962 was formed on October 30, 1942, at the military training area Heuberg, in the Military District V. The regiment was made from two battalions, a pioneer company, and an artillery division. The regiment was transferred to the north of France after the establishment of the Africa Brigade in 999. On February 5, 1943, the Artillery Division of the Regiment formed the Second Division of the Artillery Regiment of 999. On this day, the 2nd Battalion of the Africa Rifle Regiment 963 entered as the 3rd Battalion to the regiment. Also in February 1943, the pioneer company was given the formation of the 2nd Company of the pioneer battalion 999. From March 1943, the regiment was relocated to Africa. There the regiment of the new 999th light African division was subordinated. The 3rd Battalion remained behind in Europe. The mass regiment was destroyed in May 1943 at Tunis. The 3rd Battalion formed on June 1, 1943 the 2nd Fortress Infantry Battalion 999. The Replacement Battalion 999 was responsible for the replacement of the regiment.[16]

Africa Protection Regiment (Motorized) 963

The Africa-Rifle Regiment 963 was formed on January 8, 1943, at the military training area Heuberg, in the Military District V. The regiment was first made up of a battalion and a pioneer company. On January 27, 1943, an artillery division was set up for the regiment. On February 3, 1943, the Second Battalion was also set up. The entire regiment was subordinated to the 999th Light Division of Africa. On February 23, 1943, the regiment was dissolved. The Artillery Division of the Regiment formed the 3rd Division of the Artillery Regiment 999. The 1st Battalion of the Regiment formed the 3rd Battalion of the Rifle Regiment 961. The 2nd Battalion formed the 3rd Battalion of the Rifle Regiment 962. The Pioneer Company was used to form the 3rd Company of the Pioneer Battalion 999. However, the units were no longer moved to Africa.

This regiment was set up with three battalions, and again subordinated to the 999th Light Division of Africa. The field usability was to be established by June 1, 1943. From May 14, 1943, the regiment became an Army group. The regiment was transferred to Greece. On June 10, 1943, the regiment was dissolved. The staff formed the staff of the Fortress Infantry Regiment 963. The 1st Battalion of the Regiment formed the 3rd Fortress Infantry Battalion 999. The 2nd Battalion of the regiment formed the 4th Infantry Battalion 999. The 3rd Battalion of the Regiment formed the 5th Fortress Infantry Battalion 999. The replacement battalion 999 was responsible for the replacement of the two regiments.[17]

Pioneer Battalion 999

The battalion was set up on February 15, 1943. The battalion was created with three companies from the pioneer companies of the Africa Rifle Regiments 961, 962, and 963. The battalion of the Africa Division 999 was subordinated. Under this configuration, the battalion was deployed at Tunis.

The battalion was also destroyed there in May 1943. The third company of the battalion, which had not been sent to Africa, was renamed to Pioneer Company 999 in Rhodes. The replacement for the battalion came from the replacement battalion 999 in Heuberg, Wehrkreis V.[18]

The Artillery Regiment 999

The unit was set up in Africa on February 18, 1943. The regiment was set up with three sections. The three artillery divisions of the Africa Shooters Regiments 961, 962, and 963 were deployed. After the establishment, the regiment of the Africa Division 999 was subordinated. The mass of the regiment was used under this configuration in Africa. On February 25, 1943, the staff of the 3rd Division with the previous 3rd, 6th, and 9th Batteries renamed the 4th (Heavy) Division. The 1st and 2nd Divisions of the Regiment were destroyed in May 1943 near Tunis in Africa. The remaining regiment consisted only of two divisions (3 and 4). The 3rd Division of the Regiment was renamed in the spring 1945 in Croatia and subordinated to the Army Artillery Division 645. The 4th Division of the Regiment remained and served in Greece until the end of the war with the Rhodes Division. The substitute battalion 999, later replacement brigade 999, was responsible for the replacement of the regiment.[19]

Replacement Battalion 999

The replacement battalion 999 was set up on February 14, 1943, at the military training place Heuberg, Military District V, as a replacement unit for the penal units. It was disbanded in September 1944.

Initially, the battalion was divided into two gunmen training companies, a 3rd Artillery Training Battery, a 4th Mixed Company, and a 5th News Training Company. On April 6, 1943, the battalion was extended to become a replacement and training battalion. On December 10, 1943, the battalion was relocated to the military camp Baumholder in Military District XII. Here the battalion was also designated as a substitute brigade 999. In September 1944, the brigade was dissolved. It formed the Special Battalion 999 (as building groups): 1/999, which was last used in Koblenz; 2/999, which was last used in Mainz, also Military District XII; and 3/999 and 4/999, which were used on the Oberrhein. All battalions were set up for four companies each.[20]

Panzer Enlightenment Division 999

Set up on February 18, 1943, on the troops' training camp, Heuberg, on conditionally defendants as a probation group. The division consisted of three companies, and was part of the 999th Light Africa Division.[22]

News Division 999

Set up on February 13, 1943 from News Company 999 for the 999th Light Division of Africa. Destroyed in Tunis in 1943. Newly set up at the 15th Panzergrenadier Division, and on March 21, 1944, renamed News Division 33.[23]

Commitment Battalion 999

The unit was formed in September 1944 from the disbanded Replacement Battalion 999 and was used for construction work.[24]

Construction Battalion 999

The Landesbau Battalion z.b.V. 999 was set up on August 10, 1943, in the Ruhr district, in Military District VI. The battalion was then deployed in the Ruhr area under the commander of the Land Construction Troop 3 in Essen. On October 11, 1943, the battalion was renamed the Landesbau Pioneer Battalion 999. On December 1, 1943 the battalion was then renamed the Post Pioneer Battalion I/999. In the process, the 5th and 6th Company had deployed the 2nd Battalion of the Pioneer Battalion II/999 to the Baumholder camp, in the XII Military District. From January 13, 1944, the battalion was placed at the disposal of the field army and moved to the east. There, the battalion was deployed in Russia. In June 1944, the battalion was renamed the Pioneer Battalion I/999. The battalion was deployed at the beginning of 1945 under the 8th Army in Hungary. At the end of the war, the battalion served with the 6th Panzer Army in the spring of 1945. Replacement troops for the unit was the replacement brigade 999. From December 1, 1943, the building replacement Battalion 6 took over the substitute provision of the permanent staff.[25]

Light Reserve Flak Department 999

The Light Reserve Flak Department 999 was installed in April 1941 in Military District XIII with three light batteries and then used in the Bordeaux/ Royan area. The division was under the command of the staff of the Flak Regiment 86 at the 12th Flak Brigade. In July 1942, the division was renamed to Light Anti-aircraft Division 999. In 1943, it was extended to four batteries; at the end of 1944, a 5th battery was installed.[26]

Replenishment Column Division 999

The supply column division 999 was set up in the summer of 1941 in the Military District IX with seven large car columns as an army group. In 1943, the department was dissolved.[27]

Field Custody Detachments

The prisoners' detachments (*Feldstrafgefangenen abteilungen*) were introduced in 1942. It was based on the directive that prison sentences of more than three months then on should only in exceptional cases be served in the military prison. The main reasons for their establishment were the troop replacement of the armed forces due to the high loss of soldiers on the Eastern Front. Already in March 1943, there were nineteen prisoner detention centers, which were deployed without exception on the Eastern Front. By the end of the war, their number had risen to twenty-two. The detachments provided more than twice as much capacity for soldiers as the probation units.

They were larger than a normal infantry battalion, each being composed of five companies (while a regular battalion had three), but sometimes they came disarmed and were used to build bridges, reclaim mined fields, or were used in fighting in particularly dangerous areas. They were also used for mining, mowing, setting, and road construction. These units were often used in partisan contaminated areas.

The detainees received only a greatly reduced food rations. After three to nine months, the prisoner could be given direct transfer to a probation units, assuming good behavior. If they were not capable of being trained, they were transferred to the SS or Gestapo. However, by repeated sentences, for example, unauthorized travel and thefts due to the hunger, their stay could be extended.

They came from the military prisons of Glatz, Gemersheim, Anklam, Freiburg in Breisgau, and Torgau. Unit numbers 1, 2, 3, 5, 6, 7, 8, 10, 11, 12, 13, 17, 18, 20, 21, and 22 fought on the Eastern Front, and those who carried the numbers 4, 9, 14, 15, 16, and 19 were formed at the end of 1944 and employed on Western Front in the Rhineland and in the Hamburg area.[28] The Field Custody Detachments were organized as follows:

Field Custody Detachment 1

The unit was initially formed with four companies. This was changed to five companies in 1942. On April 26, 1942, Field Custody Detachment 1 was placed in Military District VIII. The division was set up by the Wehrmacht prison at Glatz as an Army group. In 1944, the detachment was deployed with the 9th Army in Central Russia. Later, the detachment was deployed with the 2nd Army. In 1945, it was a battalion of the 27th Armour Corps under the 2nd Army in West Prussia. In 1945, the 2nd Army was pivotal in the defense of East and West Prussia before finally surrendering on May 9, 1945.[29]

Field Custody Detachment 2

The unit was initially formed with four companies, but this was changed to five companies in 1942. In 1943, it was changed back to four companies. The 5th Company received its own number. Field Custody Detachment 2 was set up in the Military District XII. On May 1, 1942, the department was set up by the Wehrmacht prison at Germersheim as an Army group. In 1944, the detachment was deployed with the Army Group Center.

In June 1944, the detachment suffered heavy losses there. Later, the detachment was deployed with the 4th Army. With the 4th Army, it was in operations in East Prussia. In 1944, the 4th Army was holding defensive positions east of Orsha and Mogilev in the Belorussian area, occupying a bulging 25×80-mile bridgehead east of the Dnepr. The Soviet summer offensive of that year, Operation Bagration, commencing on June 22, proved disastrous for the Wehrmacht, including the 4th Army. It was encircled east of Minsk and lost 130,000 men in twelve days since the start of Operation Bagration. Few units were able to escape westwards.[30]

Note: See Appendix III for the Army Group Centre Order of Battle in Central Russia as of April 22, 1942.

Field Custody Detachment 3

The unit was initially formed with four companies. This was changed to five companies in 1942. Field Custody Department 3 was set up in the Military District II on May 1, 1942. The detachment was set up as an Army group by the Wehrmacht prison at Anklam. In 1944, the detachment was deployed with the Army Group North in Northern Russia. In 1944–45, it was deployed with Army Group B in the Eifel area.[31]

Note: See Appendix VI for the German Army Group B Order of Battle as of September 16, 1944.

Field Custody Detachment 4

The unit was formed on August 1, 1942, in the Military District II. The detachment was set up as an Army group by the Wehrmacht prison at Anklam. Initially, the detachment was deployed in Northern Russia. In 1944, the detachment was deployed in the West with the Army Group G at Oberrhein. Later, the detachment was deployed with the 1st Parachute Army at Niederrhein. Finally, it was deployed with the 5th Tank Army in the Eifel area.[32]

Field Custody Detachment 5

The unit was formed in the Military District XII on August 1, 1942. The detachment was set up by the Wehrmacht prison at Germersheim as an Army group. After the deployment, the detachment was deployed to the 3rd Tank Army in Central Russia. The space between Minsk and Smolensk can be viewed as an application area. In 1944, the detachment was deployed in Poland with the 4th Tank Army. Later, the detachment was deployed with the 9th Army. In January 1945, it was destroyed at Vistula. Remains of the detachment were last in Torgau.[33]

Field Custody Detachment 6
The unit was formed in the Military District V on August 1, 1942. The detachment was set up by the Wehrmacht prison at Freiburg as an Army group. After the deployment, the detachment was deployed with the 18th Army in Northern Russia. In 1944–45, the detachment was deployed with Army Group G at Oberrhein. Lastly, the detachment was deployed with Army Group Center in Silesia in 1945.[34]

Note: See Appendix VII for German Army Group G Order of Battle, October 18, 1944.

Field Custody Detachment 7
The unit was formed in the Military District VIII on September 10, 1942. The detachment was set up by the Wehrmacht prison at Glatz as an Army group. After the deployment, the staff was deployed at the Southern Army Group in Southern Russia. From September 25, 1943, the detachment was deployed with the 1st Tank Army. From January 1, 1944, the detachment was deployed with the 6th Army. In August 1944, it was destroyed with the Army Group in Southern Ukraine and then officially dissolved.[35]

Field Custody Detachment 8
The unit was formed on September 10, 1942, in the Military District II. The detachment was set up as an Army group by the Wehrmacht prison at Anklam. After the installation, the detachment was deployed to Southern Russia. In 1944–45, the detachment was deployed with Army Group A. In 1945, it was employed with Army Group Centre in Reichenberg and in the Sudetenland and in Silesia.[36]

Field Custody Detachment 9
The unit was formed in the Military District XII on September 10, 1942. The detachment was set up by the Wehrmacht prison at Germersheim as an

Army group. After the installation, the detachment was deployed to Northern Russia. In August 1943, the detachment was employed with 6th Armour Corps in action. In 1944–45, the detachment deployed in the West. At the same time, the detachment was deployed with Army Group B in the Lower Rhine and in the Eifel.[37]

Field Custody Detachment 10

The unit was formed in the Military District VIII on November 1, 1942. The detachment was set up by the Wehrmacht prison Glatz as an army group. After the installation, the detachment was deployed to Southern Russia. From December 8, 1943, the detachment was deployed with the 8th Army in Southern Russia. In August 1944, it was destroyed with the Army Group of Southern Ukraine and then officially dissolved.[38]

Field Custody Detachment 11

The unit was formed in the Military District II on November 1, 1942. The detachment was set up as an Army group by the Wehrmacht prison Anklam. After the installation, the detachment was set up in Central Russia. In 1944–45, the detachment in East Prussia was in operation. At first, it was subordinate to the 4th Army, and later to the Third Tank Army. Lastly, it was in use at Gdansk in 1945.[39]

Field Custody Detachment 12

The unit was formed on the November 1, 1942, in the Military District XII. The detachment was set up by the Wehrmacht prison Germersheim as an Army group. After the installation, the detachment was deployed to Southern Russia. In 1944–45, the detachment was deployed with Army Group South in Hungary. It was destroyed in Budapest.[40]

Field Custody Detachment 13

The unit was formed in the Military District VIII on January 5, 1943. The detachment was set up by the Wehrmacht prison Glatz as an army group. After the installation, the detachment was deployed to Central Russia. In 1944–45, it was deployed with the 2nd Army.[41]

Field Custody Detachment 14

The unit was formed in the Military District II on January 5, 1943. The detachment was set up as an Army group by the Wehrmacht prison Anklam. After the installation, the detachment was deployed to Northern Russia. In 1944–45, the detachment was deployed in the West at the Oberrhein. At first, it belonged to Army Group G, later to the 19th Army.[42]

Field Custody Detachment 15

The unit was formed in the Military District XII on January 5, 1943. The detachment was set up by the Wehrmacht prison Germersheim as an Army group. After the installation, the detachment was deployed to Central Russia. In 1944, the detachment suffered heavy losses there. In 1944–45, the detachment was deployed in the West at the Oberrhein. At first, it belonged to Army Group G, later to the 19th Army.[43]

Field Custody Detachment 16

The unit was formed in the Military District VIII on March 20, 1943. The detachment was set up by the Wehrmacht prison Glatz as an Army group. After the installation, the detachment was deployed to Southern Russia. In 1944–45, the detachment was deployed in the West. As part of the 1st Parachute Army, the detachment of was deployed to the Lower Rhine. Lastly, it was deployed with the 86th Armour Corps.[44]

Field Custody Detachment 17

The unit was formed in the Military District II on March 20, 1943. The detachment was set up as an army group by the Wehrmacht prison Anklam. After the installation, the detachment was deployed to Southern Russia. In August 1944, the detachment was destroyed by the Army Group of Southern Ukraine and then officially dissolved.[45]

Field Custody Detachment 18

The unit was formed in the Military District XII on March 20, 1943. The detachment was set up by the Wehrmacht prison Germersheim as an Army group. After the installation, the detachment was deployed to Southern Russia. In 1944, the detachment was deployed with the 8th Army. There, in the summer, the detachment took up the remains of the Field Custody Detachment 7 and the Field Custody Detachment 10. In 1944–45, the unit was deployed with Army Group South in Hungary.[46]

Field Custody Detachment 19

The unit was formed in the Military District IV on August 1, 1943. The detachment was set up as an army group. After the installation, the detachment was deployed to Northern Russia in 1944 with the 18th Army. In 1944–45, the detachment was deployed in the West. There it was deployed with the 19th Army at Oberrhein.[47]

Field Custody Detachment 20

The unit was formed in the Military District VIII on October 1, 1943. The detachment was set up by the Wehrmacht prison Glatz as an Army group. After the deployment, the detachment was deployed to Central Russia with Army Group Centre. In 1944, the detachment was deployed with the 2nd Army. In 1945, it was deployed with the North Army Group in East Prussia.[48]

Field Custody Detachment 21

The unit was formed in 1945 in the Military District IV. The detachment was set up as an Army group. After the deployment, the detachment was deployed at the South Army Group in Hungary.[49]

Field Custody Detachment 22

The unit was formed in 1945 in the Military District IV. The detachment was set up as an Army group. After the deployment, the detachment was deployed at the South Army Group in Hungary.[50]

Notes:
1. Military District II consisted of the Stettin, Köslin, and Schwerin, and included the Stettin, Potsdam (parts), Stettin, Köslin, and the Grenzmark Posen-Westpreussen as well as Frankfurt (Oder) (parts).
2. Military District IV subdivided itself into Leipzig, Chemnitz, and Dresden.
3. Military District XII embraced the then Rhine Province and Hessen-Nassau. It was divided into Koblenz and Mannheim.
4. Military District VIII consisted of Breslau, Liegnitz, and Kattowitz, and included the administrative districts of Breslau, Troppau, Liegnitz, Aussig, Kattowitz, and Opole.[51]
5. See Chapter 8 for a complete listing of the German Military Districts.

Punishment Trains

The *Strafvollstreckungszüge* (Punishment Trains) of divisions and armies consisted of soldiers condemned to prison for less than three months for specific crimes. One such division containing Punishment Trains was the 11th Tank Division. The 11th Tank Division was formed on August 1, 1940 from the 11th Protection Brigade and the Tank Regiment 15 removed from the 5th Tank Division and elements of the 231st Infantry Division, 311th Infantry Division, and 209th Infantry Division. Most of its members were from Silesia.[52] The 11th Tank Division saw action for the first time in the invasion of Yugoslavia in April 1941; passing through Bulgaria, it arrived in Belgrade and assisted in the capture of that city.

The division was then sent to the Eastern Front where it was part of the Army Group South. It participated in the Battle of Kiev and later took part in the Battle of Moscow. At the Battle of Moscow, the 11th Tank Division had its legendary encounter with Panfilov's Twenty-Eight Guardsmen.[53] The division was engaged in retreat and defensive operations after the Soviet counteroffensive in December 1941. The 11th Tank Division's advance finally came to a cease due to the strong resistance of the 8th Guards Motor Rifle Division and the 78th Rifle Division. Harsh weather conditions were also a factor.[54] The 11th Tank Division was part of Operation Case Blue from June 1942 onward, participating in the capture of Voronesh and the drive towards Stalingrad. It avoided being entrapped with the 6th Army in the city but suffered substantial losses during the winter of 1942–43.[55]

It was engaged in the failed relieve attempt on Stalingrad and then participated in the defense of Rostov, which allowed the German troops retreating from the Caucasus to escape. In July 1943, it participated in the Battle of Kursk and the defensive operations and retreat that followed the German failure. It was entrapped in the Korsun-Cherkassy Pocket in February 1944 and almost completely destroyed in the breakout of the pocket. The division was withdrawn from the front and sent to Bordeaux, France, after receiving personnel drawn from the 273rd Reserve Tank Division.[56]

After being stationed in the Toulouse area, the division was moved to a section of the Rhône in July 1944. When the Allies invaded southern France in August 1944, it was forced to retreat via the Rhône corridor, reaching Besançon. Later entering combat in Alsace, it helped in the defense of the Belfort Gap after going back to the Saar. In December 1944, the division fought as part of the Army Group G.[57]

At the beginning of the Battle of the Bulge, which it participated in, the division had 3,500 personnel, including 800 infantry. Following the failure of the German offensive, the 11th Tank Division entered combat in Saarland and Moselle and fought at Remagen with 4,000 soldiers, twenty-five tanks, and eighteen guns that still remained, but was expelled from the region by the advancing U.S. forces.[58]

It was then shifted to the southern sector of the front, with its forces stationed in and encircled in the Ruhr. The 11th Tank Division retreated south east, eventually surrendering to U.S. forces in the area around Passau on May 2, 1945.

Order of Battle as of July 1, 1942

Tank Division
    Division Headquarters Section (two light machine guns)
    61st (motorized) Mapping Section
15th Armoured Regiment
    Regimental Headquarters
    Signals Section
    Armoured Reconnaissance Section
   Regimental Band
   1 Armoured Maintenance Company
  1/2/3/15th Armoured Battalions, each with
   1 Armoured Staff Company
   1 Medium Armoured Company
   2 Light Armoured Companies
11th Tank Grenadier Brigade, with
 110th Tank Grenadier Regiments, each with
  HQ Company with
   1 Signals Platoon
   1 Anti-tank Platoon (3-50mm and 3 light machine guns)
    1 Motorcycle Section (6 light machine guns)
  2 (motorized) Infantry Battalions, each with
   1 (halftrack) Infantry Companies, each with: (3-50mm PAK 41 anti-tank guns, 34 Light machine guns, 4 heavy machine guns, 2 81-mm mortars, and 3 anti-tank rifles)
   1 (motorized) Infantry Companies, each with 18 Light machine guns, 4 heavy machine guns, 2 81-mm mortars, and 3 anti-tank rifles
   1 (motorized) Infantry Support Company, with
    1 (halftrack) Engineer Platoon (5 light machine guns)
    1 (halftrack) Anti-tank Platoon (3 50-mm anti-tank guns, 8 light machine guns, 3 28-mm anti-tank guns)
    2 Infantry Support Gun Sections (2 75-mm each)
   1 Motorized Infantry Support Section
   4 (motorized) 150-mm Infantry Support Guns

3/31st Self Propelled Flak Battalion (12 20-mm guns and 4 light machine guns)

    111th Tank Grenadier Regiments, each with

      HQ Company with 1 Signals Platoon

        1 Anti-tank Platoon (3 50-mm and 3 light machine guns)

          1 Motorcycle Section (6 light machine guns)

     2 (motorized) Infantry Battalions, each with

       3 (motorized) Infantry Companies, each with 18 Light machine guns, 4 heavy machine guns, 2 81-mm mortars, and 3 anti-tank rifles

       1 (motorized) Infantry Support Company, with

        1 Engineer Platoon (4 light machine guns)

        1 Anti-tank Platoon (3 50-mm anti-tank guns, 6 Light machine guns, 3 28-mm anti-tank guns)

          Infantry Support Gun Sections (2 75-mm each)

          1 Motorized Infantry Support Section

          4 (motorized) 150mm Infantry Support Guns

     2/59th Self Propelled Flak Battalion (12 20-mm guns and 4 light machine guns)

     61st Anti-tank Battalion

       Headquarters Section (2 light machine guns)

      608th (self propelled) Flak Company (12 20-mm and 4 light machine guns)

      2 (motorized) Anti-tank Company (9 50-mm anti-tank guns and 6 light machine guns)

     61st Motorcycle Battalion

      1 Heavy Armoured Car Company (18 37-mm and 24 light machine guns)

      2 Motorcycle Companies (2 81-mm mortars, 4 heavy machine guns, 18 light machine guns, and 3 anti-tank rifles)

      1 (motorized) Support Company, with

        1 Engineer Platoon (4 light machine guns)

        1 Anti-tank Platoon (3 50-mm anti-tank and 3 light machine guns)

        1 Anti-tank Platoon (3 28-mm anti-tank and 3 light machine guns)

        1 Infantry Support Gun Section (2 75-mm guns)

        1 Armoured Car Supply Column (3 light machine guns)

    119th Artillery Regiment

       1 (motorized) Regimental Headquarters (2 light machine guns)

       1 (motorized) Observation Company

     2 (motorized) Artillery Battalions, each with

       1 (motorized) Artillery Battalion Headquarters (2 light machine guns)

       Light Munitions Supply Column

       3 Batteries, each with (3 105-mm naval guns and 2 light machine guns)

1 (motorized) Artillery Battalion, with

    1 (motorized) Artillery Battalion Headquarters (2 light machine guns)

    2 Batteries, each with (3 150-mm heavy field howitzers and 2 light machine guns)

    1 Battery, with (3 100-mm K18 guns and 2 light machine guns)

Motorcycle Training Battalion

    1 Armoured Car Company

    1 Track Motorcycle Company

    1 Protection Company

    1 Heavy Support Company

    1 Volkswagen Company

61st Armoured Signals Battalion

    1 Armoured Radio Company (16 light machine guns)

    1 Armoured Telephone Company (6 light machine guns)

    1 Light (motorized) Signals Supply Column

209th Motorized Pioneer Battalion

    1 (halftrack) Pioneer Company (23 light machine guns and 3 anti-tank rifles)

    2 (motorized) Pioneer Companies (18 light machine guns and 3 anti-tank rifles)

    1 Motorized "K" Bridging Train (3 light machine guns)

    1 Light (motorized) Engineering Supply Column (2 light machine guns)

61st Food Service Battalion

    61st (motorized) Divisional Quartermaster Platoon

    61st (motorized) Butcher Company

    61st (motorized) Bakery Company

    61st Supply Train

    1/9th Light (motorized) Supply Columns (2 light machine guns each)

    13th and 14th Heavy (motorized) Supply Columns (2 light machine guns each)

    10/12th Heavy POL Supply Columns (2 light machine guns each)

    61st Light (motorized) Supply Company (2 light machine guns)

    1/2/3/61st (motorized) Medical Maintenance Companies

    1/2/61st (motorized) Medical Companies (2 light machine guns)

    1/2/3/61st Ambulance Columns

    61st (motorized) Military Police Platoon (2 light machine guns)

    61st (motorized) Field Post Office59

Field Special Battalions

The Field Special Battalions consisted of soldiers who had served their time but were not accepted back into in their field unit because of deficiencies in character. The "500 series" numbering system was also shared by the Army, but should not to be confused with the post-1940 500 series designated divisional units, which were also to be found resurrected in the July–August 1944 Army 28th, 29th, and 31st mobilization waves of Grenadier and Volksgrenadier formations. Some battalion-sized unit numbers of the 500 series had also been former probationary units of the Army employed on the Eastern Front and integrated into new Grenadier formations in the course of, in this case, the July–August 1944 reorganization of the Field Army.[60]

Besides the 500 series units for probation, the Army also exclusively employed 999 series designations; though the latter units were considered second-class soldiers, composed of more hardened disciplinary cases that the 500 series would normally not consider for rehabilitation.

These prisoners were, by their criminal nature, generally more treated to harsher disciplinary conditioning than of redemptive probation—that is, activities leading to restoration of rank and placement within their former units. They were, by sentence, those soldiers who had refused direct orders, had assaulted superiors, or were generally serving long terms in military jail for presumably non-military criminal or political offenses, such as rape or black-marketeering, or active resistance to the National Socialist regime.[61]

The 999 series units are most popularly known to history by way of the Light Africa Division 999. This unit was formed in Military District V in October 1942 as Africa Brigade 999. It consisted of the 961th Africa Protection Regiment, 962nd Africa Protection Regiment, and 963rd Africa Protection Regiment, all made up of the lost souls dredged from the bottom of the military prisons throughout the Reich—men stripped of rank, decorations, and dignity. The 999 Light Africa Division fought well and honorably in Tunisia, and surrendered with the remnants of the German Africa Corps in May 1943. Its 963rd Africa Protection Regiment was transferred to Greece from Sicily before ever reaching North Africa. This unit went on to become the nucleus of Sturm-Division Rhodos (440th Sturm Division Rhodos) in May 1943, with the accompanying 999 unit designations intact. After the surrender of the 999 Light Africa Division, the Divisional replacement training organization, located at its home station of Heuberg, continued to process potentially redeemable criminal and political prisoners from the various Wehrmacht stockpile for replacement positions within other Army units.[62]

Perhaps the most unfortunate of all German military prisoners of this type relegated to Armed Forces Punishment camps were to be found in the Emsland camps of north-west Germany at Esterwegen and Börgermoor near Papenburg.

These were only two of fifteen notoriously bleak camps situated in the dank peat-bog marshes surrounding the Ems River, near the Dutch border. From their inception in 1933 as SA-manned detention centers for enemies of the new regime, these camps later went on to hold Communist and Socialist Political prisoners, habitual criminals, Jews, religious objectors, military offenders, and, after 1939, Allied POWs. This was perhaps the lowest rung on the military prison hierarchy to be found in the Wehrmacht prison system, where soldiers convicted of military, political, and civil crimes were purposely sent to be ultimately broken. In fact, once a soldier-prisoner was relegated to the Esterwegen camp by the military authority, the imagined benefits of a harsh-but-fair rule of military justice evaporated, as the Esterwegen camp and its ancillary camps were administered by the Reich Justice Ministry, which made it a virtual civil penitentiary type establishment subject to all the grim brutalities and deficiencies inherent in an institution ultimately under command of Heinrich Himmler.[63]

In the harsh disciplinary environment of the Waffen SS specifically, and the German Military in general, there was a quite profound difference between the punishments accorded to the general classifications of delinquents and criminals. Delinquents were minor disciplinary cases scared into discipline by the harshness of their sentence and surroundings, while criminals were hard-core cases upon whom presumably the harshest of sentences had little effect.

In a number of cases, front-line commands disregarded official formalities in sending soldiers to the far-rear for proper military judicial discipline, and simply put disciplinary cases in pre-designated field penal prison departments which performed dangerous engineer and assault functions at the blunt edge of attacks, and anti-partisan operations—i.e. the dirty work of clearing mines, fighting partisans, and other so-called "journey-to-heaven-missions," and describes any operation with extremely high risk, although not necessarily suicidal. The term is in reference to a specific type of mission, and not a unit type, such as penal battalion, although members of penal units were often sent on these types of missions. Generally, in the ranks of the Wehrmacht, this black-humor term was understood to mean a mission where the chances of survival were practically nil. Examples were rearguard actions of small groups to cover the retreat of a larger unit by holding a position and delaying the enemy as long as possible until it usually was too late for their own withdrawal, or reconnaissance and commando raids far behind enemy lines. That is not to say that these local punishments were officially any better or worse than soldiers in a rear-area punishment camps, digging trenches or peat-bogs, cutting wood, or doing the dog construction work of the Organization Todt labor details. It can be conceivably stated that life in the dangerous environment of the front only exacerbated the punishment. Depending on the severity of the individual cases, and at the discretion of the Commanding officer, these hapless men would be stripped of rank and decorations, be refused mail and packages from home, and also the ability to write home and to take leave. Another aspect of the duty in these Army, corps, and divisional penal detachments is that, depending on the gravity of the offense, the individual soldiers pay book was usually stamped "no decorations, awards, or promotion allowed."[64]

Field Police

The *Feldgendarmerie* (Field Police) were the uniformed military police units of the armies of the Kingdom of Saxony (from 1810), the German Empire, and the Third Reich until the conclusion of World War II. From 1810 to 1812, Saxony, Württemberg, Prussia, and Bavaria founded a rural police force after the model of the Napoleonic French *Gendarmerie* (a medieval French expression meaning "armed men").

Prussian Gendarmerie staffs were well-proven infantry and cavalry companies after serving their standard service time at the Army and some Companies. Officially, they were still military personnel, equipped and paid by the Ministry of War, but in peacetime attached to the Ministry of the Interior, serving as normal or as mounted police. In case of a maneuver, mobilization, or war, 50 percent of the Gendarmerie formed the core of military police of the Army. At the outbreak of the World War I, the Field Police comprised thirty-three companies. They each had sixty men and two non-commissioned officers. By 1918, the number of companies had been expanded to 115 units. After World War I, all military police units were disbanded and no police units existed in the inter-war Weimar Republic era. Garrisons were patrolled by regular soldiers performing the duties of the military police.

When Adolf Hitler came to power in 1933, Field Police were reintroduced into the Wehrmacht. The new units received full infantry training and were given extensive police powers. A military police school was set up at Potsdam, near Berlin, to train Field Police personnel. Subjects included Criminal code, general and special police powers, reporting duties, passport and identification law, weapons drill, self-defense techniques, criminal police methodology, and general administration. All prospective candidates served at a Field Police command after the first term of examinations. Courses lasted one year and failure rates were high: in 1935, only eighty-nine soldiers graduated from an initial intake of 219 candidates. *Feldgendarmerie* were employed within Army divisions and as self-contained units under the command of an Army corps. They often worked in close cooperation with the *Geheimefeld Police* (Secret Field Police), district commanders, and SS and Police Leaders.

Field Police units were generally given occupation duties in territories directly under the control of the Wehrmacht. Their duties policing the areas behind the front lines ranged from straightforward traffic control and population control to suppression and execution of partisans and the apprehension of enemy stragglers. When combat units moved forward out of a region, the Military Police role would formally end as control was then transferred to occupation authorities under the control of the Nazi Party and SS. Yet Field Police units are known to have assisted the SS in committing war crime in occupied areas. Also, *Feldgendarmerie* units took active part in Jew hunting operations, including in Western Europe. However, by 1943, as the tide of war changed for Nazi Germany, the Field Police were given the task to maintain discipline in the Wehrmacht. Many ordinary soldiers deemed to be deserters were summarily executed by Field Police units. This earned them the negative name *Kettenhunde* (chained dogs) after the gorget they wore with their uniforms. The arbitrary and brutal policing of soldiers gave them the other nickname *Heldenklauer* (hero-snatcher) because they screened refugees and hospital transports for potential deserters with orders to kill suspected malingerers. Rear-echelon personnel would also be checked for passes that permitted them to be away from the front.[65]

The Field Police also administered the Strafbattalion, which were Wehrmacht punishment units created for soldiers convicted by court martial and sentenced to a deferred execution. During the final days of the war, as the Third Reich crumbled, recruits or soldiers who committed even the slightest infraction were sent to Strafbattalions.

The SS *Feldgendarmerie* wore the same uniform and gorget as their *Heer* counterparts but had an additional cuff title indicating they were military police. Generally, they conducted the same policing role, such as controlling rear areas, but they also conducted counter-insurgency and extermination operations with *Einsatzgruppen* against Jews, partisans, and those deemed to be enemies of the Reich. These SS units had a severe reputation for being strict enforcers of military law. Nicknamed *Kopf Hunter* (Head Hunters), they also tracked down and punished those deemed to be deserters. From 1944 onwards, former members of the Order Police serving with the Waffen SS were also given military police powers and duties. These special SS *Feldgendarmerie* were denoted by a diamond Police-eagle insignia worn on the lower sleeve.[66]

In January 1944, as the Red Army began to advance on the Eastern Front, the power of the Field Police was superseded by the creation of the Military Police Corps. Military Police Corps members were recruited from decorated, battle-hardened officers and non-commissioned officers. They had the military authority of the OKW to arrest and execute officers and soldiers from either the Wehrmacht or the SS for desertion, defeatism, and other duty violations. Every unit of the Military Police Corps had command over a flying drumhead trial/flying court martial, which was composed of three judges.

Men who had sex with other men who became known to the authorities were also subject to increasing Nazi terror during the war. Obsessed with male homosexuality, the Gestapo claimed in 1941 that there were

4 million homosexuals in Nazi Germany. The police obtained confessions from homosexuals by coercion and torture. The only way to combat homosexuality, the Gestapo thought, was to castrate homosexuals. Other institutions, including Wehrmacht doctors, wanted to cure homosexuals by giving them the opportunity to prove themselves in battle. The Luftwaffe, as well as the Wehrmacht leadership, had been concerned with homosexuality for a long time. Army psychiatrists advised the Wehrmacht leadership to take a tough stance on soldiers who had homosexual sex. In the spring of 1943, Field Marshal Keitel insisted that true homosexuals, those with a genetic disposition, were to be handed over to the civilian authorities for punishment. Those soldiers only caught in a single homosexual incident were to be put under surveillance in special punishment units. In many cases, those accused of homosexuality were handed over to the criminal police and the Gestapo and confined to concentration camps.[67]

The Field Police was under the direct control of the German High Command. A Field Police major general who was in charge of all Field Police personnel attached to the Wehrmacht. He was responsible for postings and personnel administration, monitoring the performance of the police units, allocation of tasks, traffic regulations, and training. His immediate subordinate was a staff officer attached to each *Oberkommando* Army who commanded the one or more *Feldgendarmerie* battalions attached to each Wehrmacht formation. The staff officer was responsible for maintaining order and discipline, traffic control during large-scale troop movements and maintaining transport routes. Each Field Police battalion also had support personnel such as cooks, clerks, and armorers.

A battalion was subdivided into smaller-sized troops, which were attached to each division or corps. A group, a section-sized unit, were then assigned to specific field or local commands. Field Police sections would also be temporarily assigned to special operations, such as anti-partisan duties. A typical troop attached to an Infantry or tank division would have up to three officers, forty-one non-commissioned officers and twenty enlisted men. They would operate in *Kübelwagen* (trucks and motorcycles with sidecars). These battalions were equipped with motorcycles and sidecars, *Kübelwagen*, field cars such as the Horch 4×4 and 3-ton Opel Blitz lorries and a small number of armored vehicles as a means of transport. Personal weapons consisted of small arms such as the Walther PP, which was designed as a civilian police weapon, or the Walther PPK, both of which were favored by officers, whereas the Luger P08 and Walther P38 were used by other ranks. Automatic machine pistols were carried by non-commissioned officers and the Mauser Karabiner 98k rifle was issued but was not widely used. The MG34 and MG42 were used as vehicle-mounted armament for defending road blocks or vehicle checkpoints. As the *Feldgendarmerie* did not have enough manpower to execute all of their tasks, the Wehrmacht established several military police-like troops, some of them with limited authority.[68]

Wehrmacht Prisons

The Wehrmacht had various kinds of military prisons, each kind receiving prisoners of a different category. These prisoners originated from the Replacement Army as well as from the Field Army.

Wehrmacht prisons, which were responsible directly to the Armed Forces High Command, received soldiers who were condemned to terms for more than three months. They were also used for prisoners of war who are sentenced to terms of imprisonment. Wehrmacht Detention Centers accepted prisoners with sentences of up to three months. Wehrmacht Prisons were subordinate to garrison headquarters and took prisoners with sentences of up to six weeks.[69]

Anklam

The Wehrmacht prison at Anklam was one of the eight Wehrmacht military prisons. The building was located west of the Friedlander Straße in the southern part of Anklam. The prison, which was designed for 600 prisoners, was built during 1939–1940 in the yard of the Anklam military academy. There were both group and individual cells. In the basement of the southern wing was the death row, consisting of nineteen cells. The administrative offices were in the adjacent military school in which the court officers were housed.

The prisoners were convicted by military courts of the Military Districts I (Königsberg), II (Stettin), and XX (Danzig), the Kriegsmarine Upper Command (MOK) Baltic Sea Naval forces, and Luftwaffe Field Divisions I and XI. The jurisdiction also extended to Army Group North and the field army in Scandinavia and northern and eastern Europe. Convictions resulted from both military (e.g. desertion, sedition, unlawful removal, cowardice before the enemy, or insubordination) and criminal offenses.

The first prisoners arrived late in 1940 and continued to arrive until 1945. Several thousand convicts passed through the prison. Some of them were used for work details in armament factories such as the Arado aircraft factory in Anklam. At times, the prison, with up to 1,500 prisoners, was overcrowded and the confinement conditions for the prisoners deteriorated. In 1944, several hundred inmates were transferred to the SS *Sturmbrigade Dirlewanger*, which was used for the suppression of the Warsaw Uprising.

Executions of at least 139 condemned prisoners occurred from November 5, 1941 until April 26, 1945. Approximately 100 of the executions occurred during the period from January to April 1945. About 120 clemency requests to death sentences were granted. The evacuation of the Wehrmacht prison took place on April 28, 1945. Guards and the remaining prisoners marched in three groups toward Küstrin, Friedland, Mecklenburg-Vorpommern, and Jarmen in the direction of Bützow. The last group was captured on May 1 by the Red Army.[70]

Fort Zinna

The outwork of Fort Zinna, built in 1810–1813 under the rule of Napoleon, was used as a military prison as early as the nineteenth century. In addition to POWs, military prisoners and so-called work soldiers were held here. During World War I, captured officers were interned at Fort Zinna. After military jurisdiction was abolished under the Weimar constitution, the Prussian judiciary took over the Fort Zinna compound in 1920 as Torgau Prison. In the first few months after the National Socialist takeover in 1933, political opponents were held here in "protective custody." Political prisoners remained in custody in Torgau until late 1935.

In April 1936, the prison was transferred from the Reich judiciary and placed under the authority of the Army High Command. In 1938 and 1939, Fort Zinna was expanded to become the largest Wehrmacht prison in the German Reich. After the Reich Military Court moved from Berlin to Torgau in August 1943, this highest military court held proceedings here as well.

Among those who suffered in the Wehrmacht prison Fort Zinna were not only conscientious objectors, insubordinate personnel, deserters, and military personnel convicted of criminal offences, but also members of the German and European resistance. Prisoners sentenced to death were executed by firing squad in the nearby gravel pit and the moat of Fort Zinna. Fort Zinna was evacuated on April 15, 1945.[71]

Torgau-Brückenkopf

The late nineteenth-century barracks at Torgau-Brückenkopf and the surrounding fortress compound served as a military prison during World War II. On August 27, 1939, immediately before the German invasion of Poland, the commandant of the Torgau Wehrmacht prison had the Brückenkopf compound cleared of its civilian occupants and converted to a prison. At the beginning of World War II, Brückenkopf joined Fort Zinna as Torgau's second military prison. In the first months of the war, it was subordinate to the commandant of Fort Zinna. In autumn of 1939, it was then given the status of an independent Wehrmacht prison. After the former barracks had been remodeled and two huts erected as prisoners' quarters in November 1939, Torgau-Brückenkopf was ready to accommodate approximately 1,000 prisoners. As early as January 8, 1940, the prison was already full to capacity.

As in the Fort Zinna Wehrmacht prison, the inmates here were German military personnel who had been convicted by military courts of resisting conscription, insubordination, desertion, or criminal offences. These prisoners were held under inhuman conditions. The inmates also included foreign POWs and Wehrmacht personnel from the occupied European countries, some of whom had been conscripted into the German armed forces, and members of the German and European resistance.

Life as an inmate in Torgau's two Wehrmacht prisons typically included military drill and degrading treatment. Harassment and abuse, such as drilling for hours, confinement, solitary confinement in the dark, corporal punishment, and reduction of the already meagre rations, characterized prison life.[72]

Germersheim

Opened in 1894, the prison was used for arresting soldiers. From 1936 on, it was used by the German Wehrmacht, and from 1945 until 1954 by the French military. The prison retired in 1956 and was used differently.[73]

Freiberg

Freiberg was a sub-camp of Flossenbürg concentration camp located in Freiberg, Saxony. In Freiberg in December 1943, preparations began for a sub camp of Concentration Camp Flossenbürg to house an outside detail at the Arado aircraft factory. The planning and construction of this housing sub camp is a clear example of the collaboration between the armaments industry, the SS, and the Ministry of Armaments. The SS approved the application for the allocation of a prisoner work-detail that Arado had submitted within the context of the Fighter Staff's measures. In its building application, Arado was represented by a building commissioner of the Reich Ministry for Armaments and War Production based in Dresden. The Reich Industry Group (the lobbying organization for the armaments industry) for the Land of Saxony, Regional Office Dresden, undertook the planning of the sub-camp.[74]

Danzig-Matzkau

Danzig-Matzkau was a rehabilitation camp for Waffen SS, particularly Officers and NCOs charged with disciplinary problems. Usually, rehabilitation period ended with assignment to the SS Sturm Battalion 500, operating near Staraja, Russia. This battalion received a steady flux of replacement from Matzkau and until the end of the war formed two sub-units: DORA I and DORA II. It was in the last weeks of the war, in April 1945, the small detachments, Commando Unit DORA I and DORA II, fought their last and most memorable battle defending Berlin. Both units were destroyed.

Serious offences were insubordination, theft, cowardice, or withdrawal in front of the enemy, and these were punished with fierce discipline. The work was very hard outside work in the camp. A particularly task was to soften boots new from factory destined to front-line troops with forced marches.[75]

SS Parachute Battalions

500th SS Parachute Battalion

The first attempt to form an SS airborne unit was in 1937 when a small group of volunteers from the Germania (Germania was the Roman term for the geographical region in north-central Europe inhabited mainly by Germanic peoples) Regiment of the *SS Verfügungstruppe* (later Waffen SS) gathered at the parachute school at Stendal between May 23 and July 17 for jump training. However, the idea suffered crib-death in its infancy, and the troops were returned to their regular units. When the order came down to form an SS Parachute Battalion, it was decided that there would be an equal percentage of volunteers from both existing Waffen SS units, and more specifically, for opportunities for officially disgraced officers and enlisted men wishing to redeem themselves from minor disciplinary sentences to do so under fire. Most such cases were at the time imprisoned at the prison enforcement camp of the Waffen SS and police in places like SS Penal Camp Dachau, and at Danzig-Matzkau. The former military prisoners were restored their rank and standing, and integrated throughout the new unit, while being overseen by a special probationary staff attached to the Battalion HQ, known as Section III, which included an SS lawyer and a number of clerks to keep track of the records concerning the disciplinary cases in the unit.

Although SS Parachute Battalion 500 is commonly referred to as a penal unit, the SS Parachute Battalion was a 500 series probationary unit in which an enlisted soldier, non-commissioned officer, or officer who had dishonored himself by minor infractions of the military code could be given the chance to prove oneself by service at the front and thereby earn an amnesty. In other words, it was a unit where officers and men convicted by courts-martial of minor infractions and currently in disciplinary straits could redeem their soldierly honor by participation in hazardous duties and operations.[1]

In the case of the Waffen SS men being recruited for the SS Parachute Battalion 500, it would have probably been at one of the harsh SS prison, such as that of the notoriously brutal SS military prison at Danzig-Matzkau, or the punishment section for SS personnel at Dachau. Prisons for Wehrmacht personnel directed by the OKW also existed at the old fortress in Gemersheim, and after 1940 at Ingolstadt and at Fort Alvensleben in Metz, among other places.[2]

The first gathering of recruits for the SS Parachute Battalion 500 was at Chlum in Czechoslovakia in October 1943. The first commander of the mixed battalion was SS Major Herbert Gilhofer, of SS Tank Grenadier Regiment 21. In November 1943, the Battalion began intensive parachute jump training at Madanrushka-Banja, near Sarajevo, at the newly relocated Luftwaffe Parachute School Number 3. The fledgling SS Parachute Battalion 500 later relocated to Papa, Hungary, for their final jump training in early 1944. After training as a unit, the SS Parachute Battalion 500 moved into Yugoslavia in April 1944 for its baptism of fire near Tuzla in Bosnia-Herzegovina.[3]

After spending close to three months moving through the rough terrain of Bosnia-Herzegovina, Serbia, Montenegro, and Macedonia in anti-partisan sweeps, SS Parachute Battalion 500 was returned to barracks at Madarushka-Banja in mid-April 1944 to prepare for a new mission. At this time, SS Major Gilhofer returned to the Frundsberg Division, and SS Captain Kurt Rybka took over command. In what would be the first and only combat parachute drop (and glider-assault) made by the SS Parachute Battalion 500 during the war, the unit was prepared to drop on communist Partisan leader Josef Brosz Tito's headquarters in a heavily armed mountain stronghold above the town of Drvar in western Bosnia. In a concerted effort, along with combined Luftwaffe, Army, and Croatian troops attacking from the ground, elements of the SS Parachute Battalion 500 would boldly land near the top of the citadel and storm Tito's headquarters, situated in a well-defended cave, in an attempt to kill or capture him. This was to be undertaken in an operation known as *Rösselsprung*, or Knights Move, and would be the highlight of a major ground sweep by 2nd Tank Army of Army Group F, of Partisan-held territory in Bosnia-Herzegovina.[4]

SS Captain Rybka planned for a total of 654 Paratroopers to drop in the first assault wave. It was planned that 314 of these men would drop by parachute, while the remainder, organized into six assault groups, would land by DFS230 and GO-242 glider. At the heart of the mission, each glider group was assigned a specific task:

1. Panther group: 110 men to neutralize Tito's bodyguard (350 strong), and capture him in his headquarters.
2. Greifer group: 40 men to destroy the U.K. military mission.
3. Sturmer group: 50 men to destroy the U.S.S.R. military mission.
4. Brecher group: 50 men to destroy the U.S. military mission.
5. Daufnanger group: 50 Paratroopers, and 20 men of a special composite detail of (Defense) Brandenburgers, Air Force signals experts, and interpreters from 7th SS Volunteer Mountain.

6. Division Prinz Eugen, tasked with destroying partisan signals unit and collection of radio code books and signal intelligence references.[5]

The airdrop/air landing mission, which commenced at 7 a.m. on May 25, 1944, was a near debacle. While reaching the citadel in near perfect execution of their plan, and initially stunning the partisan defenders, the assault group quickly came under heavy defensive fire from Tito's bodyguard detachment, which delayed their entrance into the inner-sanctum of Tito's mountain headquarters. In the meantime, Tito, along with Slovenian partisan leader Edvard Kardelj, had escaped through a natural fissure at the top of the cave, heavily escorted by partisan echelons to a nearby mountain-railway, which steamed him west to the coast of the Adriatic, well beyond the immediate grasp of the troops detailed to capture him. The prize had escaped, but the ordeal of the attacking glider-troops of SS Parachute Battalion 500 did not end there. Numerous Partisan brigades, encamped and ranging throughout the hilly fastness around the Drvar citadel, quickly responded to the alarm and began to converge upon their beleaguered comrade's positions. While the assault gliders brought SS Parachute Battalion troops directly on top of the heavily guarded mountainside, other elements of the Battalion were at the same time, parachuting directly into and around the perimeter of the smoldering town of Drvar, which, much to the chagrin of both attacker and defender, was still being area-bombed by the Luftwaffe in a less than elegant synchronization of the operational timetable.[6]

The fighting in Drvar was bitter, and both sides suffered heavy casualties throughout the morning and afternoon of May 25. On the hillside, Rybka and his men had finally subdued the defenders of Tito's cave, only to capture a few scattered maps and documents, and a newly tailored General's uniform, which Tito had not yet worn. Despite an early afternoon glider landing of ammunition and medical supplies, Rybka found his position on the hillside untenable and so ordered his remaining assault force to pull back in an orderly fashion into the valley and still-contested town of Drvar. By nightfall, they ended up in the town cemetery, along with the remnants of the battalion, which had parachuted into the village earlier that morning, surrounded on all sides and taking heavy mortar fire from well-equipped and determined partisan fighters.[7]

Meanwhile, the ground forces of the 373rd Croat Infantry Division and the 7th SS Mountain Volunteer Division Prinz Eugen were relentlessly driving their way from the south-west through heavy partisan defensive fire and rough valley terrain toward Drvar and the SS Parachute Battalion beleaguered positions. At daybreak on May 26, the Reconnaissance Battalion of the Prinz Eugen Division linked up with Rybka and his decimated command, and relieved them of their defensive burden. While SS Captain Kurt Rybka went on to the hospital, the remaining fit members of his Battalion were sent on to Petrovac for a subsequent anti-partisan operation. In early June 1944, the fit elements of the Parachute Battalion were sent to barracks at Ljubljana for rest and a much-needed reorganization.[8]

On June 26, 1944, SS Captain Siegfried Milius took command of SS Parachute Battalion 500. The Battalion's Field Reserve Company had only been able, by this time, to return lightly wounded men and briefly trained replacements to the ready-roster of the battalion. As a result of losses incurred during company operations, the battalion had been greatly reduced in size and effectiveness. Of the 1,000-battle-ready men on May 25, 1944, by June 30, only fifteen officers, eighty-one non-commissioned officers, and 196 enlisted men remained.

With the opening of the Russian summer offensive of late June 1944 and the impending withdrawal of Finland from active hostilities against the Soviet Union, the 292 men of SS Parachute Battalion 500 were ordered to report directly to Naval High Command Baltic at Gotenhafen on the Baltic Coast in East Prussia for a special mission. On June 29, 1944, the battalion entrained from the Balkans for the Eastern Front. A plan had been formulated for their participation in a pre-emptive assault-landing and occupation of the Aaland Islands in the Baltic Sea, to deny them to the Russians; yet by the time of their arrival at Gotenhafen, the plan had been cancelled.[9]

The Battalion was then entrained for Narwa, Estonia, to join the III SS Tank Corps. The unit's stay there was brief, however, and they were further moved by airlift from Rakvere, Estonia, to Kaunas, Lithuania, on the northern flank of the crumbling Army Group Center. Upon its arrival in the area of 3rd Tank Army on July 10, the battalion was immediately dispatched to 39th Tank Corps, and into an *ad hoc* battle group with the 1st Tank Regiment *Grossdeutschland* for the relief of the 11th Army Corps, outflanked in the Lithuanian capital of Vilnius.[10]

The SS Parachute Battalion 500, mounted on the tanks of the *Grossdeutschland*, attacked along the Kaunas-Vilnius highway the very day of their arrival at the front, helping to stem the tide of the Soviet Armored thrust on Vilnius to the south-east, allowing another battlegroup to move in and evacuate the wounded, resupply the units fighting there, and bolster the defense of 11th Army Corps. Despite the hard-fought actions of the 39th Tank Corps and 3rd Tank Army, of which the SS Parachute Battalion 500 was a part, a two-week-long furious see-saw battle eventually pushed the Germans out of the Lithuanian capital for good between the last week of July and the first week of August 1944—the SS Parachute Battalion 500 helped to evacuate the last of Vilnius' defenders near the city's Airport—with the Soviet 51st Army battering its way west toward the Baltic sea and the eventual creation of the Kurland Pocket. On August 19, 1944, fighting alongside Tank Brigade von Werthen, elements of 7th Tank Division, 212th, and 252nd Infantry Division, the much-dwindled and hard-fought SS Parachute Battalion 500 helped secure the front around Raseiniai, well north-west of Kaunus. Ordered to stand down for rest and refit that very day, an emergency on August 20 among the units of

26th Army Corps around Sintauti ordered the last ninety combat-fit men of SS Parachute Battalion 500 to join up with 731st SS Tank Destroyer Battalion to help stem the advance of the Soviet 33rd and 11th Guards Armies. Given a few days rest after this engagement, in September 1944, the unit was again linked with the *Grossdeutschland* and 39th Tank Corps.[11]

The final battle of the SS Parachute Battalion 500 in the east was in early October 1944, north of Memel. There, along with elements of the 7th Tank Division, *Grossdeutschland*, and 58th Infantry Division, they attempted to halt the advance of the Soviet's to the sea: an unsuccessful spoiling operation, which led to the eventual siege of Memel and the entrapment of the formerly named units. At this point, the remnants of the battalion were plucked from disaster and sent to Zichenau in East Prussia. They were recalled to Deutsch-Wagram in Ostmark (Austria) to join their Replacement and Training Company currently involved in the formation of a completely new SS Parachute Battalion, to be numbered 600. The probationary status of the unit was dissolved, and the new battalion was composed totally of volunteers.[12]

600th SS Parachute Battalion

The unit was formally mustered on November 9, 1944, in Neu-Strelitz, their garrison town. As part of the formation of the 600 Battalion, soldiers of the 500th were given back their previous ranks and the right to wear the runic insignia of the SS. The renamed battalion would next see action in the Ardennes Offensive (Battle of the Bulge) when two companies attached as part of Otto Skorzeny's 150th Tank Brigade. After this operation, the remainder of the battalion was rushed to the Oder front to take up positions on the eastern bank of the river to help stem the flow of Soviet forces. The Battalion stayed on the eastern bank until April 1, 1945, when it was forced to withdraw under heavy Russian pressure.

The seriously depleted battalion continued to fight as a fire brigade north-east of Berlin, and at the end of April 1945, it provided the rearguard for German forces pulling back from the Oder front. As the end of the war approached, SS Parachute Battalion 600 found itself fighting many rearguard actions before finally being isolated in one of the many pockets in northern Germany. After being virtually wiped out three times in its eighteen-month existence, the unit surrendered to U.S. forces in early May 1945 near the town of Hagenow, Germany.[13]

36th Waffen SS Grenadier Division

The 36th Waffen SS Grenadier Division was formed on February 20, 1945; this unit is better known as the Dirlewanger Brigade, which was its name before it was upgraded in the last weeks of the war. Most of its members were men taken from concentration camps; a few of its soldiers were Communists or political prisoners, but most were common criminals.[1] Its commander SS Colonel Oscar Dirlewanger, who held a PhD in political science, was a brutal drunkard who had once been expelled from the SS on a morals offense. He was first a member of the Nazi Party but was evicted and imprisoned in 1934 when he raped a fourteen-year-old girl, stole a car, and crashed it while driving drunk. After serving a two-year sentence, he was released and imprisoned soon after for sexual assault. A German police report as late as 1942 concluded him being "...a mentally unstable, violent fanatic and alcoholic, who had the habit of erupting into violence under the influence of drugs."[2]

The brigade was responsible for a number of atrocities, especially against the Poles and Jews during the Warsaw Ghetto uprising during the autumn of 1944. It also fought on the Hungarian sector of the Russian Front in late 1944. As of early October, the brigade had 4,000 men—5 percent poachers, 65 percent Waffen SS, Army, Luftwaffe convicts, and 30 percent political prisoners and civilian convicts. Both the division and its commander were considered notoriously unreliable by the German Army. General Friessner, Commander-in-Chief of Army Group South Ukraine, once gave Dirlewanger orders on how to defend a sector against Russian attack. Returning later to check on how the orders were being carried out, he found that the brigade had departed the area without informing his headquarters or anybody else's and that the Soviets had occupied the positions he had assigned Dirlewanger to defend. Friessner himself narrowly avoided capture by the Russians.

The 36th SS ended the war on the Eastern Front, although Dirlewanger himself fled on May 1, 1945, to escape capture by the Allies. SS major General Fritz Schmedes surrendered the division to the Russians. Dirlewanger ended up in a French prison camp at Altshausen, under an assumed name. Some of the inmates recognized him, however, and beat him to death on June 7, 1945.[3]

The 36th Waffen Grenadier Division of the SS was also known as the *SS Sturmbrigade Dirlewanger* (1944), or simply the Dirlewanger Brigade. It was composed of criminals expected to die fighting in the front-line. Originally formed for anti-partisan duties against the Polish resistance, the unit eventually saw action in Slovakia, Hungary, and against the Soviet Red Army near the end of the war. During its operations, it engaged in the rape, pillaging, and mass murder of civilians.[4]

The unit participated in some of World War II's most notorious campaigns of terror in the East. During the organization's time in Russia, Dirlewanger burned women and children alive and let starved packs of dogs feed on them. He was known to hold large formations with the sole purpose of injecting Jews with strychnine (a highly toxic, colorless, bitter, crystalline alkaloid used as a pesticide, particularly for killing small vertebrates such as birds and rodents). Dirlewanger's unit took part in the occupation of Belarus, where it carved out a reputation within the Waffen SS as an atrocious unit. Numerous Army and SS commanders attempted to remove Dirlewanger from the SS and disband the unit, although he had patrons within the Nazi apparatus who intervened on his behalf. His unit was most notably credited with the destruction of Warsaw, and the massacre of 100,000 of the city's population during the Warsaw Uprising, in addition to participating in the brutal suppression of the Slovak National Uprising in 1944. Dirlewanger's Division of the Waffen SS generated fear throughout Waffen SS Organizations including the SS Command Headquarters and earned the notoriety as the most criminal and heinous SS unit in Hitler's war machine.[5]

The history of the Dirlewanger Brigade is inextricably linked to the life of its commander, Oskar Dirlewanger, a known sadist, often called the most evil man in the SS. After receiving the Iron Cross first and second class while serving in the Imperial German Army during World War I, Dirlewanger joined the *Freikorps* (paramilitary organization) and took part in the crushing of German Revolution of 1918–1919. He joined the Nazi Party in 1923. After graduation from Citizens' University, Dirlewanger worked at a bank and a knit-wear factory. He became a violent alcoholic, and in 1934, he was convicted of the statutory rape of a fourteen-year-old girl and stealing government property. The Nazi Party expelled him and later compelled him to reapply for membership. After serving a two-year jail sentence, Dirlewanger was released. Soon after, he was arrested again for sexual assault. He was interned in a concentration camp. Desperate, Dirlewanger contacted Gottlob Berger, an old *Freikorps* comrade who worked closely with Heinrich Himmler, the *Reichsführer*-SS. Berger secured his friend's release where he travelled to Spain to enlist in the Spanish Foreign Legion and later transferred to the Condor Legion, a German volunteer unit that fought in the Spanish Civil War.[6]

After returning to Germany in 1939, Dirlewanger enlisted with the *Allgemeine SS* (General SS) with the rank of second lieutenant. In mid-1940, following the invasion of Poland, Berger arranged for Dirlewanger to train a partisan-hunting military unit under his own control, composed of men convicted of poaching.

On March 23, 1940, a department in the Ministry of Justice received a telephone call from Himmler's headquarters informing them that Hitler had made a decision to give suspended sentences to so-called honorable poachers and, depending on their behavior at the front, a pardon. A further confirmation of Hitler's order was sent specifying that the poachers should, as far as possible, be Bavarian and Austrian, not be guilty of crimes involving trap setting, and were to be enrolled in marksmen's rifle corps. The men were to combine their knowledge of hunting and woodcraft similar to traditional elite riflemen hunters with the courage and initiative of those who willingly broke the law. In late May 1940, Dirlewanger was sent to Oranienburg to take charge of eighty selected men convicted of poaching crimes who were temporarily released from their sentences. After two months training, fifty-five men were selected with the rest sent back to prison. On June 14, 1940, the Oranienburg Poacher's Unit was formed as part of the Waffen SS. Himmler made Dirlewanger its commander. The unit was sent to Poland where they were joined by four Waffen SS non-commissioned officers selected for their previous disciplinary records and twenty other recruits.[7]

From the beginning, the formation attracted criticism from both the Nazi Party and the SS for the idea that convicted criminals who were forbidden to carry arms, therefore then exempt from conscription in the Wehrmacht could be a part of the elite SS. A solution was found where it was proclaimed that the formation was not part of the SS, but under control of the SS. As the war proceeded with a need for further manpower, Germany recruited other Strafbattalions and penal military units.[8]

Within a couple of years, the unit grew into a band of common criminals. In contrast to those who served in the German penal battalions for committing minor offences, the recruits sent into Dirlewanger's band were convicted of major crimes such as premeditated murder, rape, arson, and burglary. Dirlewanger provided them with an opportunity to commit atrocities on such a scale that even the SS executioners complained. Martin Windrow, the British historian, described them as a terrifying rabble of cut-throats, renegades, sadistic morons, and cashiered rejects from other units. Some Nazi officials romanticized the unit, viewing the men as pure primitive German men who were resisting the law.[9]

By September 1940, the formation numbered over 300 men. Dirlewanger was appointed a first lieutenant by Himmler. With the influx of criminals, the emphasis on poachers was now lost, though many of the former poachers rose to non-commissioned officer ranks to train the unit. Those convicted of other more severe crimes, including the criminally insane, joined the unit. Accordingly, the unit name was changed to Special Unit Dirlewanger. As the unit strength grew, it was placed under the command of the SS *Totenkopfverbände* (Death Head Unit) (the unit responsible for the administration of the concentration camps) and re-designated as the Special Battalion Dirlewanger. In January 1942, to rebuild its strength, the unit was authorized to recruit Russian and Ukrainian volunteers. By February 1943, the number of men in the battalion doubled to 700.[10]

On August 1, 1940, the battalion was assigned to guard duties in the region of Lublin (site of a Nazi-established Jew reservation) in the General Government territory of occupied Poland. According to journalist and author Matthew Cooper: "Wherever the Dirlewanger unit operated, corruption and rape formed an every-day part of life and indiscriminate slaughter, beatings and looting were rife." The General Government's Higher Service and Police Leader Friedrich Wilhelm Krüger was disturbed by the unlawful behavior of the Dirlewanger's battalion. His complaints resulted in its transfer to Belarus in February 1942.[11]

In Belarus, the unit came under the command of local Government's Higher Service and Police Leader Erich von dem Bach. The Dirlewanger battalion resumed anti-partisan activities in this area, working in cooperation with the Kaminski Brigade, a militia of Russians under the command of Bronislav Kaminski. Dirlewanger's preferred method of operation was to gather civilians in a barn, set it on fire, and shoot with machine guns anyone who tried to escape; the victims of his unit numbered about 30,000. According to Timothy Snyder, a Yale historian: "As it inflicted its first fifteen thousand mortal casualties, the Special Command Dirlewanger lost only ninety-two men-many of them, no doubt, to friendly fire and alcoholic accidents. A ratio such as that was possible only when the victims were unarmed civilians."[12]

In September 1942, the unit murdered 8,350 Jews in Baranovichi ghetto and then a further 389 people labelled bandits and 1,274 bandit suspects. According to the British-Canadian historian Martin Kitchen, the unit "committed such shocking atrocities in the Soviet Union, in the pursuit of partisans, that even an SS court was called upon to investigate."[13]

On August 17, 1942, the expansion of the Dirlewanger battalion to regimental size was authorized. Recruits were to come from criminals, eastern volunteers, and military delinquents. The second battalion was established in February 1943 when the regiment's strength reached 700 men, of whom 300 were anti-communists from Soviet territory and the unit was re-designated as the SS Special Regiment Dirlewanger. In May 1943, the eligibility to volunteer for service in the regiment was extended to all criminals, and as a result, 500 men convicted of the most severe crimes were absorbed into the regiment. May and June saw the unit taking part in Operation Cottbus, an anti-partisan operation. In August 1943, the creation of a third battalion was authorized. With its expansion, the Dirlewanger unit were allowed to display rank insignia and a unique collar patch (at first crossed rifles, later crossed stick grenades). During this period, the regiment saw heavy fighting, and Dirlewanger himself led many assaults.[14]

In November 1943, the regiment was committed to front-line action with Army Group Center in an attempt to halt the Soviet advance and suffered extreme casualties due to ineptitude. Dirlewanger received the German Gold Cross on December 5, 1943, in recognition of his earnestness, but by December 30, 1943, the unit consisted of only 259 men. Large numbers of amnestied criminals were sent to rebuild the regiment, and by late February 1944, the regiment was back up to full strength. It was decided that eastern volunteers would no longer be admitted to the unit as the Russians had proven to be particularly unreliable in combat. Anti-partisan operations continued until June 1944, when the Soviets launched Operation Bagration, which was aimed at the destruction of Army Group Centre. The Dirlewanger's troops were caught up in the retreat and began falling back to Poland. The regiment sustained heavy casualties during several rearguard actions but reached Poland.[15]

When the Polish Citizen's Home Army began the Warsaw Uprising on August 1, 1944, Dirlewanger was sent into action as part of the battle group formation led by SS Group Leader Heinz Reinefarth, once again serving alongside Kaminski's. Acting on orders that came directly from Heinrich Himmler, Kaminski's and Dirlewanger's men were given a free hand to rape, loot, torture, and butcher. Over the following days, the troops indiscriminately massacred Polish combatants along with civilian men, women, and children in the Wola District of Warsaw. Mathias Schenk describes some of the crimes he personally witnessed while assigned to the Dirlewanger Brigade:

> After the door of the building was blown off we saw a day care- full of small children, around 500; all with small hands in the air. Even Dirlewanger's own people called him a butcher; he ordered to kill them all. The shots were fired, but he requested his men to save the ammo and finish them off by rifle-butts and bayonets. Blood and brain matter flowed in streams down the stairs. There is also that small child in Dirlewanger's hands. He took it from a woman who was standing in the crowd in the street. He lifted the child high and then threw it into the fire. Then he shot the mother.
>
> Or that Polish woman. Every time, when we stormed the cellars and women were inside the Dirlewanger soldiers raped them. Many times a group raped the same woman, quickly, still holding weapons in their hands. Then after one of the fights, I was standing shaking by the wall and couldn't calm my nerves. Dirlewanger soldiers burst in. One of them took a woman. She was pretty. She wasn't screaming. Then he was raping her, pushing her head strongly against the table, holding a bayonet in the other hand. First he cut open her blouse. Then one cut from stomach to throat. Blood gushed. Do you know, how fast blood congeals in August?[16]

The Dirlewanger Regiment fight against the resistance in Warsaw saw it suffer extremely high losses. Although the regiment arrived in the city numbering only 865 soldiers and sixteen officers, it soon received reinforcements of 2,500 men, including 1,900 German convicts from the SS military camp at Danzig-Matzkau. During the course of the two-month urban warfare, the Dirlewanger Regiment lost 2,733 men. Thus, total casualties numbered 315 percent of the unit's initial strength. While some of the regiment's actions were criticized by von dem Bach and the sector commander, General Major Günter Rohr, Dirlewanger was recommended by Reinefarth for the Knight's Cross of the Iron Cross and promotion to SS Reserve Colonial.[17]

By October 3, 1944, the Poles had surrendered and the depleted regiment spent the next month guarding the line along the Vistula. During this time, the regiment was upgraded to brigade status and named SS Special Brigade. In early October, it was decided to upgrade the Dirlewanger Brigade again, this time to a Waffen SS combat brigade. Accordingly, it was re-designated as the 2nd SS Storm Brigade Dirlewanger in December 1944, and soon reached its complement of 4,000 men.

When the Slovak National Uprising began in late August 1944, the newly formed brigade was committed to action. The conduct of the brigade played a large part in putting down the rebellion, and by October 30, the uprising was put down. With the outcome of the war no longer in doubt, large numbers of communist and socialist political prisoners began applying to join the Storm Brigade Dirlewanger in the hope of defecting to the Soviets. SS Major General Leader Fritz Schmedes, disgraced former commander of the 4th SS Police Division, was assigned to the Dirlewanger Brigade by Himmler as punishment for refusing to carry out orders. With his extensive combat experience, Schmedes became the unofficial advisor to Dirlewanger on front-line combat.[18]

In December, the brigade was sent to the front in Hungary. While several newly formed battalions made up of communist and socialist volunteers fell apart, several other battalions fought well. During a month's fighting, the brigade suffered heavy casualties and was pulled back to Slovakia to refit and reorganize.

In February 1945, orders were given to expand the brigade to a division; however, before this could begin, it was sent north to the Oder-Neisse line in an attempt to halt the Soviet advance. On February 14, 1945, the brigade was re-designated as the 36th SS Waffen Grenadier Division. With its expansion to a division of 4,000 men, the division had regular Army units attached to the formation: a grenadier regiment, a pioneer brigade, and an anti-tank battalion. Individual demolition engineers had already been attached to the force during the fighting in Warsaw.

When the final Soviet offensive began on April 16, 1945, the division was pushed back to the northeast. The next day, Oskar Dirlewanger was seriously wounded in combat for the twelfth time. He was sent to the rear and Major General

Schmedes immediately assumed command; Dirlewanger would not return to the division. Desertion became more and more common: when Schmedes attempted to reorganize his division on April 25, he found it had virtually ceased to exist. The situation was highly fluid, with men of the 73rd Waffen Grenadier Regiment of the SS lynching their commanding officer Ewald Ehlers (a former commandant of Dachau concentration camp who had been convicted of corruption). On May 1, 1945, the Soviets wiped out all that was left of the 36th SS Waffen Grenadier Division in the Halbe Pocket. The small remnant of the division that managed to escape attempted to reach the U.S. Army lines on the Elbe river. Schmedes and his staff managed to reach the Americans and surrendered on May 3. Only about 700 men of the division survived the war.[19]

Order of Battle

> SS-Sturmbrigade 'Dirlewanger' (August 1944)
> > Brigade Staff
> > SS Regiment 1
> > SS Regiment 2
> > > Artillery Battalion
> > > > Fusilier Company
> > > > Pioneer Company
> > > > Signal Company
> 36th Waffen SS Grenadier Division (March 1945)
> > Division Staff
> > 72nd Waffen SS Grenadier Regiment
> > 73rd Waffen SS Grenadier Regiment
> > > Tank Battalion Stansdorf I
> > > 36th Artillery Battalion
> > > > 36th Fusilier Company
> > 1244st Volks Grenadier-Regiment
> 687th Pioneer Brigade
> > 681th Schwere-Anti-tank Battalion[20]

6

Storm and Infantry Units

440th Sturm Division Rhodos

The Sturm Division Rhodos (also called the 440th Sturm Division) was formed on May 19, 1943 on the Order of the Commander of the Army and the formation process was launched during the last days of May 1943. The division's home station was Zittau, in Military District IV. It was formed as an upgrade of the Storm Rhodos Brigade. The division received elements of the 22nd Infantry Division, troops already garrisoned on the island Rhodos, and various small units stationed on the Aegean Islands of the Fortress Crete Division and the 999th Light Africa Division, which were not transferred to North Africa in the spring of 1943.[1]

On September 8, 1943, the Italian garrison on the island of Kastelorizo surrendered to a British detachment, which was reinforced during the following days by ships of the Allied navies. The next day, a British delegation, headed by Lord Jellicoe, was dropped by parachute on Rhodes, in order to persuade the Italian commander, Admiral Inigo Campioni, to join the Allies. This was followed by the immediate reaction of the most important German force in the Dodecanese, the 7,500-strong Sturm-Division Rhodos commanded by Lieutenant General Ulrich Kleemann, and stationed on the administrative center of the Dodecanese Islands, the Island of Rhodes. Without waiting for the Italians to decide, Kleemann attacked the 40,000-strong Italian garrison on September 9, and forced it to surrender on September 11. This successful operation earned him the oak leaves to the Knight's Cross of the Iron Cross.[2]

On October 17, 1944, the division was formally dissolved. A smaller number of divisional units remained on the Island. Larger parts of the division were incorporated to Tank Grenadier Division Brandenburg, when the former Division Brandenburg (commando operations) was restructured to an ordinary combat formation near Belgrade in October 1944.

The Brandenburg Division became the Infantry Division Brandenburg and transferred to the Eastern Front. Approximately 1,800 men were transferred to Otto Skorzeny's 502nd SS Hunter Battalion operating within SS *Jagdverband Mitte* (Hunting Group Centre), but mostly to the SS Hunting Association East until the end of the war. Only the *Kurfürst* Regiment retained its original role as a commando unit. The rest of the Brandenburg members were assigned to Panzer Corps *Grossdeutschland* along with its old training partner from 1940 to 1941, the Grossdeutschland Division. In late 1944, the division was equipped with a Panzer Regiment and re-designated Tank Grenadier Division Brandenburg and returned to the front. The division were involved in heavy fighting near Memel, until their withdrawal, along with the *Grossdeutschland*, via ferry to Pillau. The division was all but annihilated during the heavy fighting near Pillau, and only 800 men escaped to the thin strip of land at Frische Nehrung. While some survivors surrendered to the British in Schleswig-Holstein in May, many soldiers, highly skilled in evading detection, simply disappeared. Others enlisted in the French Foreign Legion and fought in French Indo-China where their skills proved an asset.

The divisional staff was used to reform the staff of 4th Tank Corps. The remaining former Sturm Division elements, together with all army units on the island under command of Tank Grenadier Brigade Rhodos surrendered to British Forces on May 8, 1945. On October 17, 1944, the division was officially dissolved.[3]

Sturm Division Rhodos also had armored reconnaissance assets. When elements of the division were deployed on the Isle of Rhodos in October 1943 to help form Tank Grenadier Division Brandenburg, the remaining assets were reorganized and re-designated a brigade. One of the brigade troops had a unique organization consisting of an armored reconnaissance company with eight armored cars, a wheeled armored scout platoon, a VW-equipped armored reconnaissance company, an antitank company, and a heavy company with a towed anti-tank gun platoon, and a motorized combat engineer platoon.[4]

Order of Battle

Sturm Division Rhodos
    1 Division Staff Section
    1 Motorcycle Platoon (2 80-mm mortars, 3 light anti-tank rifles, 4 heavy machine guns, and 18-light machine guns)
    Rhodos Infantry Regiment
    1 Regimental Staff (former Staff/440th Grenadier Regiment)
    1 Regimental Staff Company
    1 Signals Platoon
    1 Pioneer Platoon (3 light machine guns)
    1 Motorcycle Platoon

1 (motorized) Pioneer Platoon (3 light machine guns and 1 heavy anti-tank rifle)

1st Battalion (former 1/440th Grenadier Regiment)

3 Grenadier Companies (3 heavy machine guns, 12 light machine guns, 3 light anti-tank rifles, and 50-mm mortars)

1 Machine Gun Company (12 heavy machine guns and 6 50-mm mortars)

2nd Battalion (former 2/440th Grenadier Regiment)

3 Grenadier Companies (3 heavy machine guns, 12 light machine guns, 3 light anti-tank rifles, and 3 50-mm mortars) (one on bicycles)

3rd Battalion

3 (tractor drawn) Grenadier Companies (3 heavy machine guns, 12 light machine guns, 2 150-mm heavy infantry guns, and 2 80-mm mortars)

1 (motorized) Machine Gun Company (12 heavy machine guns, 2 150-mm heavy infantry guns, and 3 80-mm mortars)

13th (Infantry Gun) Company (2 150-mm heavy infantry guns and 6 75-mm light artillery gun)

14th (Tank Destroyer) Company (former 14th Co/440th Grenadier Regiment) (12 75-mm anti-tank gun)

Rhodos Tank Troop

1 (tractor drawn) Tank Destroyer Company (former Rhodos Tank Hunter Company) (9 75-mm anti- tank guns and 6 light machine guns)

1 Medium Tank Company (15 III Tanks)

1 Storm Protection Company (15 assault guns)

999th Reconnaissance Battalion

1st Armoured Car Company (24 light machine guns and 18 20-mm guns)

1 Armoured Car Platoon (75-mm guns)

2nd (motorized) Company (2 80-mm mortars, 3 heavy anti-tank rifles, 4 heavy machine guns, and 18 light machine guns)

3rd (motorized) Company

1 Pioneer Platoon (3 light machine guns)

1 (motorized) Tank Destroyer Platoon (3 75-mm anti-tank guns and 3 light machine guns)

1 Signals Platoon

4th (tractor drawn) Tank Destroyer Company (12 75-mm anti-tank guns and 12 light machine guns)

Self-propelled Flak Company (12 20-mm flak guns)

4/999th Artillery Regiment

1 Battalion Staff and (motorized) Staff Battery

1 (tractor drawn) Battery (4 150-mm heavy field howitzers and 2 light machine guns)

1 (tractor drawn) Battery (4 105-mm heavy field howitzers and 2 light machine guns)

1 (tractor drawn) Battery (4 105-mm heavy field howitzers and 2 light machine guns)

999th (tractor drawn) Pioneer Company: (former 3/999th Pioneer Battalion)(9 light machine guns, 3 heavy anti-tank rifles, 3 50-mm anti- tank guns and 6 flamethrowers)

Rhodos Tank Signals Company (former 657th Radio Company) (16 light machine guns)

999th Supply Troops

1/999th (motorized) 90-ton Transportation Company

999th (motorized) Supply Company

The units were later renamed and the division had:

Rhodos Grenadier Regiment
Rhodos Fusilier Battalion
Rhodos Tank Battalion
Rhodos Flak Company
Rhodos Pioneer Company
Rhodos Signals Company

Field returns dated from August 15, 1944 show the division with the following organization and equipment:

1/2/3/Rhodes (tractor drawn) Grenadier Regiment

13th Infantry Gun Company (2 150-mm heavy infantry guns and 6 75-mm light infantry guns)

14th Tank Hunter Company (9 75-mm anti-tank guns)

Rhodos (motorized) Fusilier Battalion

Rhodes Tank Battalion

Staff Company (3 III K tanks)

1st Assault Gun Company (13 75-mm assault guns and 3 105-mm assault guns)

2nd Tank Company (15 IV Tanks)

3rd Tank Destroyer Company (10 75-mm assault guns)

999th Tank Reconnaissance Battalion

1st Light Armoured Car Company

1 Platoon (10 armoured cars with 20-mm guns)

1 Platoon (6 armoured cars with 75-mm guns)

2nd (motorized) Company

3rd (motorized) Company (3 75-mm (tractor drawn) assault guns)

4th (tractor drawn) Company (12 75-mm PAK 40 anti-tank guns)
4/999th (tractor drawn) Artillery Regiment
3rd (tractor drawn) Battery (4 105-mm heavy field howitzers)
4th (tractor drawn) Battery (3 152-mm Russian guns)
5th (tractor drawn) Battery (4 105-mm heavy field howitzers)
6th (tractor drawn) Battery (4 150-mm heavy field howitzers)
Rhodes (motorized) Pioneer Company
999th (motorized) Pioneer Company
999th Supply Troop
1/2/999th (motorized) 90-ton Transportation Companies[5]

502nd SS Light Infantry Battalion

The 502nd SS Light Infantry Battalion was a special forces unit from 1943–1944. Formed in June 1943, the unit was commanded by Otto Skorzeny and was based at Castle Friedenthal just north of Berlin in Sachsenhausen by Oranienburg. The unit originally consisted of the 300 members of the former Provisional Special Unit Friedenthal (this was their official name until April 1944, then it was SS Hunter Battalion 502). After an unsuccessful attempt to train members of an SS penal facility, Skorzeny obtained permission to recruit additional volunteers from the Wehrmacht, and 100 SS personnel, fifty Luftwaffe, and 150 Army personnel were admitted, allowing the formation of a headquarters company and two line companies. An intensive training program was instituted.[6]

In September 1943, fourteen members of this unit took part in the Gran Sasso raid, which resulted in the rescue of deposed Italian dictator Benito Mussolini. They were later placed on standby for several operations that never took place, including a proposed kidnapping of Philippe Pétain.

In February 1944, a third company was formed from mainly Flemish and Dutch personnel with Captain Hoyer as its commanding officer. In the same month, Number 1 and 2 companies of the battalion went to the Kurmark troop training area for four weeks' intensive training, after which they saw combat on the Eastern Front for over a month. On July 20, 1944, Number 1 Company was deployed in Berlin, briefly occupying the Bendlerblock building complex after the attempted assassination of Adolf Hitler. In August 1944, fifty members of the unit carried out Operation Landfried, Romania, destroying road and railway bridges in an attempt to delay the Soviet advance. This mission was commanded by Walter Girg. In September 1944, SS Hunter Battalion 502 was dissolved and its personnel absorbed into a new battalion, the SS Jagdverband Mitte.[7]

Note: The main purpose of the German Hunter (*Jäger*) divisions was to fight in adverse terrain where smaller, coordinated formations were more facilely combat capable than the brute force offered by the standard infantry divisions. The Hunter divisions were more heavily equipped than mountain division, but not as well armed as a larger infantry formation. In the early stages of the war, they were the interface divisions fighting in rough terrain and foothills as well as urban areas, between the mountains and the plains. The hunters relied on a high degree of training and slightly superior communications, as well as their not inconsiderable artillery support. In the middle stages of the war, as the standard infantry divisions were downsized, the Hunter structure of divisions with two infantry regiments became the standard table of organization.[8]

SS Commando Group Centre

On October 1, 1944, SS Parachute Battalion 500 had been officially disbanded, and its survivors became the nucleus of a new unit: SS Parachute Battalion 600. The reason for the change was that the 500 number series was typically used for probationary units, and Himmler had decided that he no longer wished the unit to be tainted with the implication of second-rate character. The percentage of disciplinary cases within the battalion had decreased by now from around 70 percent to 30 percent, and even these were considered the most promising of the potential material. Recruits were by now mostly regular personnel rather than military convicts, including men from the Army and Kriegsmarine as well as the Waffen SS, and by November, unit strength was back up to just under 700 men.[9]

The battalion's association with Skorzeny was made permanent on November 10, when SS Parachute Battalion 600 was formally absorbed into SS *Jagdverband Mitte*. While the title of this unit is open to different interpretations, Skorzeny himself preferred SS Commando Group Centre.

At the end of January 1945, the unit formed part of Otto Skorzeny's force for the defensive bridgehead at Schwedt on the Oder; the Paratroopers were positioned in the Königsberg area, operating with SS Jagdverband Mitte around Grabow. There, on February 4, its third company was completely overrun by the Soviets, suffering heavy casualties; the survivors rook part in efforts to retake the city a few days later, but after some initial progress the battered German formations were once again forced out of Königsberg.[10]

The battalion's defensive positions around Grabow came under repeated attack by Soviet armor, and many tanks fell victim to the bazookas of the SS Paratroopers. It was decided that SS Parachute Battalion 600 and SS *Jagdverband Mitte* were to be temporarily merged to form an SS regiment, which would be held as the reserve for Skorzeny's Schwedt bridgehead. Shortly afterwards, however, Hitler decided that the defenders of the bridgehead could be withdrawn. SS Parachute Battalion 600 was then moved southwards to another east bank bridgehead at Zehenden to the south-west of Königsberg.

On March 6, in its merged form with *Jagdverband Mitte*, the battalion joined a number of other smaller Waffen SS units in a new SS Battle Group Solar, which came under the control of the newly formed Division z.b.V. 610.[11]

On the evening of the same day, a stray Soviet artillery shell hit an explosive charge on the bridge over the Oder, which had been prepared for demolition. The bridge was destroyed, effectively cutting off the SS Parachute Battalion 600 on the east bank as the Red Army approached. The next two weeks passed quietly enough, but on March 25, a new Soviet offensive began. For two days, the SS troops held out against overwhelmingly superior opposition, but on the third day, after sustaining huge losses, they were forced to withdraw. Due to the loss of the bridge, the troops were forced to swim the Oder River, many being lost to drowning or enemy fire.

In the weeks that followed, the battalion was yet again reinforced and brought up to a respectable strength of well over 800 men. In mid-April 1945, the unit was absorbed into a new SS Battle Group Harzer, in which it temporarily became part of SS Police Tank Grenadier Regiment, assigned to the bridgehead around Eberswalde northeast of Berlin. This was intended to threaten the flank of the advancing Soviets, but the Red Army's advance was so fast and powerful that the proposed attack was cancelled.[12]

In late April, the battalion found itself assigned to 36th Tank Corps in the defense of the area around Prenzbu, among German units by now at only around 10 percent of their nominal strength .

The battalion was pushed back to positions west of Flirstenwerder and then to Neubrandenburg, where, on April 28, it was involved in heavy defensive fighting before withdrawing west in an effort to avoid Soviet captivity. The remnants of the unit were under constant attack as they withdrew westwards; in one engagement with Soviet horse cavalry at Neuruppin, the 400 or so SS Parachute Battalion 600 who engaged the enemy suffered more than 50 percent losses. The survivors, numbering fewer than 200 men, surrendered to U.S. forces at Hagenow on May 2, 1945.[13]

The SS *Jagdverband Mitte* was formed November 10, 1944, when SS Parachute Battalion 502 was re-designated. It took part in the Ardennes offensive as a part of Tank Brigade 150 wearing American uniforms and using American equipment. After the failure in the Ardennes, the men received a brief leave before being sent to fight the Red Army on the Oder. In April 1945, it was sent to Austria to fight in the Alpine Redoubt and it ended the war in Linz.[14]

Infantry Units

491st Infantry Battalion
As part of the 471st Division formed on September 28, 1942, in Hannover,

as a staff for the replacement troops and to replace the 171st and 191st Reserve Divisions, which moved to Belgium. In December 1943, the division comprised the following:

551st Grenadier Replacement Regiment (211th, 248th, 588th, 590th Battalions)
561st Grenadier Replacement Regiment (12th, 17th, 191th, 461th, 481th, 491th Battalions)
571st Grenadier Replacement Regiment (82nd, 194th, 396th, 398th Battalions)
13th Artillery Replacement Regiment (13th, 19th, 31st, 49th Battalions)
14th Reconnaissance Replacement Battalion
19th Armoured Pioneer Replacement Battalion
4th Pioneer Replacement Battalion
11th Construction Pioneer Replacement and Training Battalion
11th Transportation Replacement and Training Battalion
11th Driver Replacement and Training Battalion

In January 1945, the division detached units as part of the Gneisenau Force under the former Denecke Division Command to Pommerania to the Vistula Army Group. At the end of March 1945, the entire division was committed with the 551st and 571st Regiments going to the west, the 561st Grenadier Training going to Saxony on the Oder. The division comprised the following:

500th Infantry Battalion.
    3 Infantry Companies (3-50mm mortars and 12 light machine guns)
    1 Infantry Company (6-80mm mortars and 12 heavy machine guns)
540th Infantry Battalion.
    3 Infantry Companies (3-50mm mortars and 12 light machine guns)
    1 Infantry Company (6-80mm mortars and 12 heavy machine guns)
550th Infantry Battalion.
    Infantry Companies (1-heavy machine gun and 9 light machine guns)
    1 Infantry Company (4-80mm mortars and 12 heavy machine guns)[15]

Note: The Gneisenau Force (Denecke Division Command) was an emergency unit that was formed of the Field Replacement Battalion from the Mecklenburg-Vorpommern area. The Prison guards of the Wehrmacht Prison Anklam were send to the unit. The prisoners were sent to the 36th Waffen Grenadier Division SS Dirlewanger. The unit had an overall strength of 3,200 men and was a very well-equipped regiment. The unit had multiple armored fighting vehicles, one with a 20-mm anti-aircraft gun and two with 75-mm long cannon. The unit was in use of the Army Group Weichsel and was used alongside the Wallonien and Nederland SS-Divisions, in the area of Pyritz, in north-west Poland, but was pushed back into west Pomerania. The unit was renamed in 549th Volks Grenadier-Division and took part in the battle of Greifswald but suffered heavy casualties and withdraw into west. On May 2, 1945, the Unit surrendered to U.S. Troops in Mecklenburg in northern Germany.

Army Group Vistula was formed on January 24, 1945. It was put together from elements of Army Group A (shattered in the Soviet Vistula-Oder Offensive), Army Group Centre (similarly largely destroyed in the East Prussian Offensive), and a variety of new or *ad hoc* formations. It was formed to protect Berlin from the Soviet armies advancing from the Vistula River.[16]

86th and 87th Country Regiments

As part of the 408th Division z.b.V. formed on October 24, 1939, in Breslau, it was to oversee the country forces in the Replacement Army. In April 1940, the division contained 86th Country Regiment with the 553th, 554th, 555th, 556th, 557th, 584th, 585th, 586th, and 557th Battalions and the 87th Country Regiment with 398th, 515th, 559th, 560th, 561st, 590th, and 752nd Battalions. With the reorganization of the Replacement Army on October 1, 1942, the 408th Division z.b.V. was re-designated the 408th Division and began operations in Alsace-Lorraine. In December 1943, the division comprised the following:

> 352nd Replacement Grenadier Regiment
> Battalions: 54th, 190th, 354th, 360th, and 375nd
> 518th Replacement Grenadier Regiment
> Battalions: 7th, 49th, 83rd, 318th, 406th, and 472nd
> 8th Replacement Reconnaissance Battalion
> 48th Flak Replacement and Training Battalion
> 273rd Army Flak Replacement and Training Battalion
> 300th Storm Protection Replacement and Training Battalion
> 18th Pioneer Replacement and Training Battalion
> 213th Pioneer Replacement Battalion
> 518th Land Construction Pioneer Battalion
> 28th Construction Pioneer Replacement and Training Battalion
> 8th Transportation Training Battalion
> 8th Transportation Replacement Battalion

In November 1944, the division formed the 408th Division Mission Staff, which became the Liegnitz Division in February 1945. The division was mobilized to the 17th Army, Army Group Centre, in February–March 1945.

On July 31, 1943, a new Country Regiment 86 was set up in Neustadt in

Upper Silesia, in Military District VIII. This regiment was also set up as a staff only. The regiment was set up for deployment in the south-east. The staff was deployed in Salonica under the command of the Salonika-Aegean. On August 20, 1943, the staff was renamed the Security Regiment 86. In 1945, the regiment was deployed with the 117th Destroyer Division in Croatia. The 117th Destroyer Division was in Yugoslavia in May 1941 to conduct anti-partisan and internal security operations. It was then posted to Greece to guard the Peloponnesus until summer 1944, when it took part in the general withdrawal through the Balkans and suffered heavy losses during fighting with the partisans in September. The division ended the war fighting on the Eastern Front and surrendered to the U.S. Army in Austria in May 1945.[17]

609th Infantry Battalion

As part of the 409th Division z.b.V. formed on October 25, 1939, in Cassel, Military District IX, for the oversight of the Country forces. In March 1940, the division contained:

> 93rd Country Regiment

The regiment contained the 602nd, 603rd 604th, 608th, 609th, 612th, 613th, 614th, 615th, 616th, and 9th Country Replacement Battalions. Formed on October 1, 1942, during the reorganization of the Replacement Army, the 409th Division was organized to replace the 159th Reserve Division as it was sent to France. At the end of December 1943, the division comprised the following:

> 519th Replacement Grenadier Regiment
> Battalions: 57th, 88th, 116th, 163rd, 181th, 355th, 451st, and 459th
> 529th Replacement Grenadier Regiment
> Battalions: 36, 81, 106, 205, 367, 388, and 471
> 15th Artillery Replacement and Training Regiment
> Battalions: 9th, 29th, 65th, and 309th
> 15th Replacement Reconnaissance Battalion
> 39th Pioneer Replacement and Training Battalion
> 9th Pioneer Replacement Battalion
> 3rd Railroad Pioneer Replacement and Training Battalion
> Pioneer School Battalion z.b.V. Offenbach
> 9th Construction Pioneer Replacement and Training Battalion
> 9th Transportation Replacement and Training Battalion
> 9th Driver Replacement and Training
> 15th Driver Replacement and Training

In April 1945, the division was reorganized as the Zehler Battle Group near Cassel. On March 25, 1945, the division was built up and contained the following:

519th Grenadier Regimental Staff
529th Grenadier Regimental Staff
36th Grenadier Training Battalion
205th Grenadier Training Battalion
57th Grenadier Training Battalion
116th Grenadier Training Battalion
367th Grenadier Training Battalion
81st Grenadier Training Battalion
88th Heavy Grenadier Training Battalion
451st Heavy Grenadier Training Battalion
459th Heavy Grenadier Training Battalion
163rd Heavy Grenadier Training Battalion
388th Heavy Grenadier Training Battalion
106th Heavy Grenadier Training Battalion
309th (heavy) Artillery Training Battalion
65th (heavy motorized) Artillery Training Battalion
29th (light) Artillery Training Battalion
18th (officer training) Artillery Training Battalion
29th Armoured Pioneer Training Battalion
9th Construction Pioneer Training Battalion
9th Signals Training Battalion
9th Country Training Battalion
VIII School for Infantry in Wetzlar
9th Army Infantry Non-commissioned Officer School Course, Military
  District IX[18]

999th Fortress Infantry Battalion

The 999th Fortress Infantry Battalion as part of the 41st Fortress Division formed on December 11, 1943, the division was formed from the disbanded 39th Infantry Division and various fortress troops. The division served in Greece. The division comprised the following:

938th Fortress Regiment (formerly Fortress Infantry Battalions 3rd/999th
  and 1008th)
965th Fortress Infantry Regiment (formerly Fortress Infantry Battalions
  2nd/4th/7th/999th)

1009th Fortress Infantry Battalion
1012nd Fortress Infantry Battalion
919th Army Coastal Artillery Regiment
819th and 920th Coastal Artillery Battalions
309th Army Flak Battalion
41st Division Service Units

In January 1945, the division withdrew from Greece and was reformed into the 41st Infantry Division:

1230th Grenadier Regiment (from staff/733rd Fortress Grenadier Regiment (from Crete) and 1/746th and 3/733rd Infantry Regiments)
1231st Grenadier Regiment (from staff/938th, 1009th and 3/999th Fortress Battalions)
1232nd Grenadier Regiment (from Staff/965th Fortress Regiment, 7/999th and 2/999th Fortress Regiments)
41st Division Fusilier Battalion (From Rhodes Fusilier Battalion)
141st Artillery Regiment (from 831st, 820th and 819th Army Coastal Defense Battalions and 3/619th Artillery Regiment)
141st Anti-tank Battalion (from Athens Alarm Regiment)
141st Pioneer Regiment (from 2264th Pioneer Battalion and 705th Pioneer School Company)
141st Division Service Units

The 41st Infantry Division, formerly the 41st Fortress Division, took part in German operations in Greece towards the end of the war, and surrendered to the Yugoslav resistance at the end of Germany's part in the war.

Founded as the 41st Fortress Division, this unit was formed in Brück in December 1943, with its command staff being formed from the cadre of the defunct 39th Infantry Division, and was ready for duty at the start of 1944 at a size of twenty-two battalions. In its initial deployment, it was to defend the Peloponnesus area of Greece as a coastal component of LXVIII Army Corps, a corps attached to the Army Group F under General Helmut Felmy.

The 733rd Grenadier Regiment was attached to the division in September 1944, after it was separated from its parent 133rd Fortress Division during the evacuation of Crete. On the 28th, it was located in Greece, though this was only learned by Allied code-breakers the following month. It operated in the Army group's rearguard during the German retreat from Corinth, being attacked by royalist guerrillas and elements of the 2nd British Airborne Division, with minor skirmishes taking place as the division moved through Yugoslavia.

The division was restructured as an Infantry Division in January 1945, and engaged the Soviet Army as such along the Sava and Drava rivers. The 41st was then put under the command of the 117th Hunter Division. The 41st surrendered to the 11th Yugoslavian Shock Division near Zagreb on May 8, 1945.[19]

1st Fortress Infantry Battalion 999

The unit was formed in June 1943 by the re-designation of Africa Protection Regiment 961. It was stationed in Greece with the 41st Fortress Division and later in the Crimea, where it was destroyed in May 1944. The 41st formed the rearguard of Army Group F when the Germans evacuated Greece in the fall of 1944, clashing with royalist guerrillas and the 2nd British Airborne Division during the retreat to Corinth. It was engaged in continuous, small, but bitter rearguard actions as the Nazis retreated through Serbia and Croatia. The replacement for the battalion's personnel came from the Replacement Battalion 999. The battalion came from the Military District VII.[20]

Note: See Appendix E for the Army Group F Order of Battle on August 15, 1944.

2nd Fortress Infantry Battalion 999

The unit was formed in June 1943 by the re-designation of Africa Protection Regiment 962. It was stationed in Greece with 41st Fortress Division, and in January 1945, it was absorbed by the Grenadier Regiment 1232 when the division was reformed into the 41st Infantry Division. In January 1945, the 41st was upgraded to infantry division status and fought the regular Soviet forces between the Drava and the Sava Rivers in early 1945. The division was still serving on the southern sector of the Eastern Front when the war ended. The battalion was set up with 5th to 8th Company as an Army group by the renaming of the 2nd Battalion of the Africa Protection Regiment 962. The battalion was relocated to the Peloponnese. There the battalion was subordinated to the fortress infantry regiment 965 at the 41st fortress division. Later, the battalion was deployed in Bosnia. In January 1945, the battalion was renamed the 2nd Battalion of the Grenadier Regiment 1232 of the 41st Infantry Division. The replacement for the battalion's personnel came from the replacement battalion 999. The battalion came from the Military District VII.[21]

3rd Fortress Infantry Battalion 999

The unit was formed in June 1943 by the re-designation of Africa Protection Regiment 963. It was stationed in Greece with 41st Fortress Division, and in January 1945, it was absorbed by the Grenadier-Regiment 1232 when the division was reformed into the 41st Infantry Division. In January 1945, the 41st was upgraded to infantry division status and fought the regular Soviet forces between the Drava and the Sava Rivers in early 1945. The division was still serving on the southern sector of the Eastern Front when the war ended. The III. Fortress Infantry Battalion 999 was set up on June 10, 1943. The battalion was set up as a group of troops by the renaming of the 1st Battalion of the 963 Protectorate Regiment. The battalion was relocated to the Peloponnese. There the battalion was subordinated to the fortress infantry regiment 965 at the 41st fortress division. Subsequently, the battalion subordinated to the 938 Infantry Regiment and was deployed in Bosnia. In January 1945, the battalion was renamed the Second Battalion of the Grenadier Regiment 1231 of the 41st Infantry Division. The replacement for the battalion's personnel came from the replacement battalion 999. The battalion came from the Military District VII.[22]

4th Fortress Infantry Battalion 999

The unit was formed in June 1943 by the re-designation of Africa Protection Regiment 963. It was stationed in Greece with 41st Fortress Division, and in January 1945, it was absorbed by the Grenadier-Regiment 1232 when the division was reformed into the 41st Infantry Division. In January 1945, the 41st was upgraded to infantry division status and fought the regular Soviet forces between the Drava and the Sava Rivers in early 1945. The division was still serving on the southern sector of the Eastern Front when the war ended. The IV Fortress Infantry Battalion 999 was set up on June 10, 1943. The battalion was set up with the 13th to 16th Company as an army group by the renaming of the 2nd Battalion of the Africa Protection Regiment 963. The battalion was relocated to the Peloponnese. There the battalion was subordinated to the fortress infantry regiment 963. Subsequently, the battalion of the 41st Fortress Division. In January 1945, the battalion was dissolved and integrated into the Grenadier Regiment 1232 of the 41st Infantry Division. The replacement for the battalion's personnel came from the replacement battalion 999. The battalion came from the Military District V.[23]

5th Fortress Infantry Battalion 999

The unit was formed in June 1943 by the re-designation of Africa Protection Regiment 963. It was used as army troops and was stationed in the Balkans. The 5th Fortress Infantry Battalion 999 was set up on June 10, 1943. The battalion was founded as a military group by the 17th to the 20th Company by the renaming of the 3rd Battalion of the Africa Guardian Regiment 963. The battalion was relocated to the island of Skarpanto in the East Aegean. There the battalion was subordinated to the fortress infantry regiment 963. In 1945, the battalion was deployed in Croatia and Bosnia at the fortress brigade 963. The replacement for the battalion's battalion personnel came from the replacement battalion 999. The battalion came from the Military District V.[24]

6th Fortress Infantry Battalion 999

The unit was formed in June 1943 by the assembly staff at Heuberg. It was used as Army troops and later attached to Sturm Division Rhodos. The 6th Fortress Infantry Battalion 999 was set up in the Military District V on June 7. The battalion was set up with the 21st to 24th Company as an Army group by the assembly staff of Heuberg. The battalion was moved to the island of Karpathos, where it was until September 7. There, the battalion was subordinated to the fortress infantry regiment 963 under the Storm Division of Rhodes. The replacements came from the Replacement Battalion 999. The battalion came from the Military District V.[25]

7th Fortress Infantry Battalion 999

The unit was formed in June 1943 by the assembly staff at Heuberg. It was used as Army troops and was stationed in the Balkans. The 7th Infantry Battalion 999 was set up in the Military District V on June 7. The battalion was set up with the 25th to 28th company as an Army group by the assembly staff of Heuberg. The battalion was relocated to the Peloponnese. A larger part of the battalion was transferred to the island of Zakynthos in the Adriatic. There, the battalion was subordinated to the 966 Infantry Regiment. In September 1944, the battalion to Patras was transferred to the 41st Fortress Division, where it was subordinated to the 965 Infantry Regiment. Later, the battalion was deployed in Bosnia. In January 1945, the battalion was renamed the 1st Battalion by the Grenadier Regiment 1232 of the 41st Infantry Division. The replacements came from the Replacement Battalion 999. The battalion came from the Military District VI.[26]

8th Fortress Infantry Battalion 999

The unit was formed in June 1943 by the assembly staff at Heuberg. It was used as Army troops and was stationed in the Balkans. The 8th Fortress Infantry Battalion 999 was set up in the Military District V on June 7. The battalion was set up with the 29th to 32nd Company as an Army group by the assembly staff of Heuberg. The battalion was relocated to the island of Corfu. There, the battalion was subordinated to the 966 Infantry Regiment. From 1944 the battalion on Corfu under the fortress Brigade 1017. From September 1944, the battalion in Albania under the fortress Brigade 1017 was used. Later, the battalion was still deployed in Croatia. The replacements came from the Replacement Battalion 999. The battalion came from the Military District III.[27]

9th Fortress Infantry Battalion 999

The unit was formed in June 1943 by the assembly staff at Heuberg. It was used as Army troops and was stationed in the Balkans. The 9th Fortress Infantry Battalion 999 was set up in the Military District V on June 7. The battalion was set up with the 33rd to the 36th Company as an Army group by the assembly staff of Heuberg. The battalion was relocated to the island of Leros in the East Aegean. There the battalion was subordinated to the fortress infantry regiment 968. An island part of the battalion remained on Leros until the end of the war. The replacements came from the Replacement Battalion 999. The battalion came from the Military District III.[28]

10th Fortress Infantry Battalion 999

The unit was formed in June 1943 by the assembly staff at Heuberg. It was used as Army troops and was stationed in the Balkans until it was disbanded in the end of 1944. The 10th Fortress Infantry Battalion 999 was set up in the Military District V on June 28, 1943. The battalion was set up with the 37th to the 40th Company as an army group by the staff of Heuberg. The battalion was relocated to the island of Sámos in the East Aegean. There the battalion was subordinated to the fortress infantry regiment 967. The battalion was dissolved at the end of 1944. The soldiers came to the 12th Fortress Infantry Battalion 999. The replacement for the battalion's battalion staff came from the Replacement Battalion 999. The battalion came from the Military District VI.[29]

11th Fortress Infantry Battalion 999

The unit was formed in June 1943 by the assembly staff at Heuberg. It was used as Army troops and was stationed in the Balkans. The 11th Fortress Infantry Battalion 999 was put up in the Military District V on June 28, 1943. The battalion was set up with the 41st to the 44th Company as an Army group by the staff of Heuberg. The battalion was relocated to the island of Kos in the East Aegean Sea. There the battalion was subordinated to the Fortress Infantry Regiment 967. An island part of the battalion remained until the end of the war on Kos. The replacement for the battalion's battalion staff came from the Replacement Battalion 999. The battalion came from the Military District VI.[30]

12th Fortress Infantry Battalion 999

The unit was formed in June 1943 by the assembly staff at Heuberg. It was used as Army troops and was stationed in the Balkans. The 12th Fortress Infantry Battalion 999 was put up in the Military District V on June 28, 1943. The battalion was set up with the 45th to 48th Company as an Army group by the staff of Heuberg. The battalion was relocated to the island of Leros in the East Aegean. There the battalion was subordinated to the fortress infantry regiment 968. An island part of the battalion, the 3rd company, remained at Leros until the end of the war. The rest of the battalion was deployed in Bosnia at the turn of the year 1944–45. There the battalion of the fortress brigade underwent 964. The replacement for the battalion's staff came from the Replacement Battalion 999. The came from the Military District VI.[31]

13th Fortress Infantry Battalion 999

The unit was formed in July 1943 by the assembly staff at Heuberg. It was used as Army troops and was stationed in the Balkans. The 13th Fortress Infantry Battalion 999 was put up in the Military District V on July 28, 1943. The battalion was set up with 49th to 52nd Company as an Army group. The battalion was relocated to the island of Samos. At the end of 1944 the battalion was stationed on Leros. There the battalion was subordinated to the fortress brigade 968. The battalion remained on Leros until the end of the war. The replacement for the battalion's battalion staff came from the Replacement Battalion 999. The battalion came from the Military District VI.[32]

14th Fortress Infantry Battalion 999

The unit was formed in July 1943 by the assembly staff at Heuberg. It was used as Army troops on the Eastern Front and was destroyed at Tighina in Romania in August 1944. The 14th fortress infantry battalion 999 was set up in the Military District V on July 28, 1943. The battalion was set up with the 53rd to 56th Company as an Army group by the Heuberg staff. The battalion was relocated to Greece in the autumn of 1943. Already in December 1943, the battalion was loaded into the Eastern Front for transport and subordinated to the 6th Army. On December 27, 1943, the battalion arrived at the 370th Infantry Division and was deployed at the village of Beloserka on the Dnieper. From March 20, 1944, the battalion had to settle down. On the Dniester front, the battalion came into positions near Bendery (Tighina). In August 1944, the battalion at Tighina in Romania was destroyed. The replacements came from the Replacement Battalion 999. The battalion came from the Military District VIII.[33]

15th Fortress Infantry Battalion 999

The unit was formed in July 1943 by the assembly staff at Heuberg. It was used as Army troops on the Eastern Front and was destroyed in at Leontina in Romania in August 1944. The 15th Fortress Infantry Battalion 999 was put up in the Military District V on July 28, 1943. The battalion was set up with the 57th to the 60th Company as an Army group by the staff of Heuberg. The battalion was relocated to Greece in the autumn of 1943. Already in

December 1943, the battalion was loaded into the Eastern Front for transport and subordinated to the 6th Army. First the battalion was unloaded at the end of December 1943 at the Dnieper. The battalion was subordinated to the 101st Panzer Division and moved to the Berislav area, where it arrived on December 31, 1943. From January 15, 1944 to March 1944, the battalion of the 79th Infantry Division. On the Dniester front, the battalion came into positions at Leontina. In August 1944, the battalion at Leontinai in Romania was destroyed. The replacements came from the Replacement Battalion 999. The battalion came from the Military District VIII.[34]

16th Fortress Infantry Battalion 999

The unit was formed in July 1943 by the assembly staff at Heuberg. It was used as Army troops and was stationed in the Balkans. The 16th Fortress Infantry Battalion 999 was put up in the Military District V on June 28, 1943. The battalion was set up with the 61st to the 64th Company as an Army group by the staff of Heuberg. The battalion was relocated to Greece. In October 1944, the battalion was deployed in Serbia. In 1945, the battalion was deployed in Bosnia and Croatia. The replacements came from the Replacement Battalion 999. The battalion came from the Military District VIII.[35]

17th Fortress Infantry Battalion 999

The unit was formed in July 1943. It was used as army troops on the Eastern Front and was destroyed in at Tiraspol in Romania in August 1944. The 17th Fortress Infantry Battalion 999 was put up in the Military District V on June 28, 1943. The battalion was set up with the 65th to the 68th Company as an Army group by the assembly staff of Heuberg. The battalion was relocated to Greece in the autumn of 1943. Already in December 1943, the battalion was loaded into the Eastern Front for transport and subordinated to the 6th Army. First the battalion was deployed in the Kherson area on the west bank of the Dnieper and several islands on the river. On March 20, 1944, the battalion began its retreat in the direction of Odessa. On the Dniester front, the battalion entered Tiraspol. In August 1944, the battalion at Tiraspol in Romania was destroyed. The replacements came from the Replacement Battalion 999. The battalion came from the Military District VIII.[36]

18th Fortress Infantry Battalion 999

The unit was formed in December 1943. It was used as Army troops and was stationed in the Balkans until it was disbanded in the end of 1944. The 18th Fortress Infantry Battalion 999 was set up on December 17, 1943, in

Baumholder, in the XII Army. The battalion was set up with 69th to 72nd Company as an Army group by the replacement brigade 999. The battalion was relocated to the island of Corfu. In September 1944, the battalion of Tirana was deployed in Albania. At the end of 1944, the battalion was dissolved. The replacement for the battalion's personnel came from the Replacement Brigade 999. The battalion came from the Grenadier Replacement Battalion 118.[37]

19th Fortress Infantry Battalion 999

The unit was formed in January 1944. It was used as Army troops and was stationed in the Balkans until it was destroyed in December 1944. The 19th Fortress Infantry Battalion 999 was set up on January 5, 1944, in Baumholder, in the XII Army. The battalion was set up with 73rd to 76th Company as an Army group by the replacement brigade 999. The battalion was deployed in Dalmatia on the Pjeljesar peninsula and Ston. In September 1944, the battalion was destroyed. The replacement for the battalion's personnel came from the Replacement Brigade 999. The battalion came from the Grenadier Replacement Battalion 118.[38]

20th Fortress Infantry Battalion 999

The unit was formed in February 1944. It was used as Army troops and was stationed in the Balkans. In April 1945, it was reformed into Fortress Infantry Battalion 1483. The XX. Fortress Infantry Battalion 999 was set up on February 1, 1944, in Baumholder, in the Military District XII. The battalion was set up at the 77th to the 80th Company as an Army group by the replacement brigade 999. The battalion was deployed in Greece. In the autumn of 1944, the battalion was deployed in Serbia. At the end of 1944–45, the battalion was deployed in Croatia. At the end of April 1945, the battalion was reclassified as a fortress infantry battalion in 1483. The replacement for the battalion's personnel came from the Replacement Brigade 999. The replacements for the battalion came from the Grenadier Replacement Battalion 118.[39]

21st Fortress Infantry Battalion 999

The unit was formed in June 1944. It was used as Army troops and was stationed in the Balkans. The XXI. Fortress Infantry Battalion 999 was set up on June 1, 1944, in Baumholder, in the Armed Forces XII. The battalion was set up with 81th to 84th Company as an Army group by the Replacement Brigade 999. The battalion was deployed in Greece. At the end of 1944–45, the battalion was deployed in Croatia. Lastly, the battalion was deployed at the 963 Fortress Brigade.

The replacement for the battalion's battalion personnel came from the Replacement Brigade 999. The battalion of the battalion came from the Grenadier Replacement Battalion 107.[40]

22nd Fortress Infantry Battalion 999

The unit was formed in July 1944. It was used as Army troops and was stationed in the Balkans. The XXII. Fortress Infantry Battalion 999 was set up on July 1, 1944, in Baumholder, in the XII Army. The battalion was set up with 85th to 88th company as an Army group by the Replacement Brigade 999. The battalion was deployed in Greece. At the end of 1944–45, the battalion was deployed in Croatia. Lastly, the battalion was deployed at the 963 Fortress Brigade. The replacement for the battalion's personnel came from the Replacement Brigade 999. The replacements for the battalion came from the Grenadier Replacement Battalion 107.[41]

23rd Fortress Infantry Battalion 999

The unit was formed in August 1944. It was used as Army troops and was stationed on the Western Front. The XXIII. Fortress Infantry Battalion 999 was set up on August 1, 1944, in Baumholder, in the XII Army District. The battalion was set up with 89th to 92nd Company as an Army group by the Replacement Brigade 999. The battalion was deployed after deployment in the West. Lastly, the battalion was deployed at the 212th People's Grenadier Division in Trier. The replacement for the battalion's personnel came from the Replacement Brigade 999. The replacements for the battalion came from the Grenadier Replacement Battalion 107.[42]

2nd Stellungsbau Pioneer Battalion 999

The unit was formed in December 1943 and was re-designated Second Bau Pioneer Battalion 999 in June 1944.[43]

3rd Bau Pioneer Battalion 999

The unit was formed in July 1944 and was assigned to the 15th Army.[44]

4th Bau Pioneer Battalion 999

The was formed in July 1944 and was assigned to the 1st Army.[45]

999th Light Africa Division

On October 15, 1942, the first 500 recruits were convened for a special formation of the Wehrmacht, which two years later the U.S. magazine *Esquire* designated Hitler's Strangest Division, Hitler's most odd division.[1]

The history of the 999s began in April 1942. At that time, the command of the Wehrmacht feverishly sought replacement for the horrendous losses of the failed fight against the Soviet Union. Those who until then had been regarded as defenseless by virtue of paragraph 13 of the Military Law because of the amount of their criminal records were also targeted. This mainly concerned all those who were punished with brethren and, in the case of political offenses, those who had been condemned only to prison for more than six months. These men could originally be convened only if they had submitted a grace application to the re-entry to the military, and this had been advocated by various state and party services. In order to be able to exploit this potential to a far greater extent, on April 11, 1942, the military district commands were briefly authorized to submit such requests to former penitentiaries.[2]

The military command made ample use of the new authorization. There were, however, great delays, as in each individual case the opinion of the local police and National Socialist agencies as well as the competent judicial authorities had to be collected. In particular, the Gestapo often raised objections.

In September 1942, the OKW decided to call upon criminals and political parties as the need for cannon fodder grew. There were sufficient monitoring possibilities, so that previous hearings of police and other bodies could be dispensed with. From October 1942 to April 1943, about 11,800 unworthy men were assembled in the Africa Division, which was first conceived as a brigade. About one-third of the recruits came directly from prisons and prison camps, while two-thirds were conscripted from civic life after serving prison sentences.[3]

Political criminals made up about a third of the 999 Division. They represented the entire range of anti-fascist resistance-from the anarchist Spanish fighter to the religiously motivated war-fighter. Many of them had also been imprisoned in concentration camps, in addition to imprisonment or penalties. For example, the Düsseldorf Communist Peter Klingen, with two years' imprisonment and a five-and-a-half-year concentration camp in the division, had a particularly long period of detention.[4]

The Africa Division 999 was led from the staff down to the group by a regular Army personnel consisting of nearly 5,500 officers, non-commissioned officers, and civil servant officers. The officers and many non-commissioned, were particularly reliable forces. The command was transferred to Colonel Kurt Thomas, who was soon promoted to General Major, who had previously commanded the Führer Accompanying Battalion.[5]

The first training place of the 999 Division was in Heuberg in the south-west of Germany. Their treatment there followed the principle of "sugar bread and whip." This was made clear at the swearing in. The recruits were introduced to the fact that they were given a great opportunity by the Führer; the unique opportunity to become full-fledged soldiers and citizens by brave and courageous engagement before the enemy. There were no complaints after the soldiers experienced years of imprisonment and suffering from the Gestapo. For those who came directly from the penitentiary, the hope of mitigating or decreasing the remaining punishment was foremost in their minds.

Th order to execute death sentences for hard-to-train soldiers was in place. On December 12 and 19, 1942, the first two members of the 999 Division were executed on the Heuberg. One of these executions was filmed by the commander of the Africa Protection Regiment 962, Lieutenant Burkhard Hering, with his narrow-film camera.[6]

On December 18, 1942, the order to change the brigade was surprising. The decision, however, which had been made under the influence of the crisis in Stalingrad, only lasted for almost two weeks. The withdrawal was probably due to concerns, that the commander Thomas harboured.

In the German African group, the prospect of the criminals, as General Hans-Jürgen von Arnim commented, met with little sympathy. The then commander of the 5th Tank Army in Tunisia worried about the prestige of the armed forces in North Africa. On January 12, 1943, Arnim wrote to General Field Marshal Kesselring about the 999s: "No, it cannot be. These people are much more useful at Stalingrad or Rostov, and they do not hurt the reputation of the 5th Army."[7]

Regardless of the future place of deployment, the transfer of the 999 troops into the Antwerp region took place at the beginning of 1943, where training was to be continued and at the same time the German occupation power was to be reinforced. In Antwerp, the first loss came from enemy action. The leader of the medical company 999 was shot in a streetcar by a Belgian underground fighter. Far more 999ers died from the war court under the direction of Doctor Hans-Werner Giesecke, according to the war district court director in Frankfurt am Main. In January and February 1943, he executed seven death sentences for flagging or unauthorized leave. In addition, there were five trials of the Reich Courts-Martial for the disrespect of the military force. These led at least to four religiously motivated conscientious objectors to death judgments, which were executed in the Zuchthaus Brandenburg-Görden by beheading.[8]

In the middle of February 1943, the Africa Division 999 was moved to the south of France, which was closer to their future operational area. The new accommodation area Nimes/Avignon was a high activity of the Resistance, in whose ranks also German emigrants and former Spaniards were active. Three of them received commendations and special leave, because they contributed to the uncovering of French-Communist organizations by particularly clever behavior, who wanted to seduce them to fly, sabotage, and distribute flyers.[9]

The Africa Division 999 also fell victim to betrayal. Five executions executed in the south of France are known, the actual total number being higher. For March and April 1943, the staff of Heuberg also reported the execution of five death sentences in the presence of recruits. At that time, units were formed and the brigade was increased to the division. In the south of France, the transport to the front began already in mid-March 1943. In the *War Day-Book of the Division*, all the seriousness was noted, "The departing troops are enthusiastic and full of expectation."

By mid-April 1943, some 5,700 members of the Africa Division 999 were to be transferred to the Tunisian war site. Among them were about 1,500 former political prisoners. Their mission lasted only one or two months, depending on the regiment, until the capitulation of the Army Group of Africa on May 13, 1943. First, the reinforced Africa Rifle Regiment 961 was deployed from March 28 on the south-west front at Kairouan. It was to cover the flank of the German *Africakorps*, which retreated from the south to the bridgehead of Tunisia. From April 15, 1943, the battalions of the reinforced Africa Protection Regiment 962 were deployed on the north-west front at Heidous and at Djebel Dardyss.[10]

Africa Division 999 participated in the 2nd Battle of Longstop Hill, which took place in Tunisia during the Tunisia Campaign from April 21–23, 1943. The battle was fought for control over the heights of Djebel el Ahmera and Djebel Rhar, together known as Longstop Hill and vicinity, between the British forces of the First Army and German units of the 5th Panzer Army.[11] The infantry of the 78th Battleaxe Division and Churchill tanks of the North Irish Horse captured Longstop Hill after bitter fighting, in which the tanks created a measure of tactical surprise by driving up the hill, a maneuver that only Churchill tanks could achieve.[12] The attackers broke through the German defenses, which were the last great natural barrier on the road to Tunis.

The Run for Tunis, an Allied effort to capture Tunis in late 1942 following Operation Torch, had failed, and since the end of the year, a stalemate had settled on the theatre as both sides paused to re-build their strength. The 5th Panzer Army defending Tunisia was being strengthened as was the Allied First Army.[13]

In January 1943, the German-Italian Tank Army confronting the Eighth Army had withdrawn westwards and joined the 5th Tank Army. Army Group Africa was formed, with the two Axis armies under command of Rommel. In March, the Army Group was defeated by the Eighth Army at the Battle of Medenine and the Battle of the Mareth Line, which fell after Rommel's return to Germany.[14] In the central west, north of Medjez el Bab, and some 48 kilometers from Tunis, the First Army continued to fight for the dominating, German-held peaks in the Medjerda Valley. This included a massif with the hills known as Djebel Ahmera and Dejebel Rhar.[14]

On the night of December 22–23, 1942, the 2nd Battalion, Coldstream Guards, mounted an attack in heavy rain, capturing what they thought to be the whole massif, before being relieved by the U.S. 18th Regimental Combat Team. The Germans counterattacked, driving the Americans off Djebel el Ahmera, but the next night, the Guards recaptured the hill only to find when daylight came that another summit, Djebel Rhar, remained to be assaulted. During the night, the Guards attacked once again and captured the second hill, but they were later driven off by a German counterattack on Christmas Day.[15] Progress towards Tunis was blocked, so the senior Allied commanders, General Dwight D. Eisenhower, the Supreme Allied Commander in North Africa, and General Sir Harold Alexander, agreed that further advances were to be delayed.[16] Thereafter, the massif was known by the Allies as Longstop Hill and by the Germans as *Der Weihnachten Hügel* (The Christmas Hill). The name Longstop is taken from the lay-back position behind the wicket keeper near the boundary of the cricket field. By mid-April 1943, because of increasing German pressure, the British had withdrawn and had lost possession of Longstop Hill and all of the higher ground to the north-west, culminating in the Djebel et Tanngoucha.[17]

On April 20, British troops of the 1st Battalion East Surrey Regiment supported by the 48th Royal Tank Regiment took a nearby hill known as Djebel Djaffa from the Germans, managing in the process to capture Tiger 131 tank the first to be captured intact by the British. On April 22, the 38th (Irish) Infantry Brigade of the 78th Division captured the fortified town of Heidous and the craggy slopes of Tanngoucha.[18] The capture of these positions made sure that the high ground behind Medjez was taken and the next objective would be Longstop.[19]

The 78th Division commander Vyvyan Evelegh ordered the 36th Infantry Brigade (Brigadier Bernard Howlett) to seize Longstop Hill by an attack from the south-west. The brigade, comprised of the 6th Battalion Royal West Kents, the 5th Buffs (East Kents), the 8th Argyll and Sutherland Highlanders, and the 1st East Surrey Regiment, detailed for the attack on Longstop, supported by the North Irish Horse equipped with Churchill tanks and by most of the 78th Division artillery.[20]

The Royal West Kents and the Buffs were to lead the attack while the Argyles, who were to be held back in reserve at the start, were to pass through the Kents and seize Djebel el Rhar, the right-hand higher end of Longstop.

If successful, the Surreys with the North Irish Horse were to be prepared to exploit north-eastwards along the road to Tebourba. Defending the position was the 999th Light Africa Division, which was composed of the 962nd Africa Protection Regiment and the III/754th Grenadier Regiment. They had adequately prepared the area for defense and were supported by anti-tank guns, mortars, and dug in machine-gun nests.[21]

On May 7, British armor rolled into Tunis, taking the Axis forces there by surprise, some were caught emerging from shops and bars. By May 15, all Axis forces had been cut off and soon surrendered with more than 250,000 taken prisoner.[22]

Many of the members of Africa Division 999 were generally unwilling to throw their lives into the balance for the victory of the Nazi regime. They sought to get into Allied captivity in a healthy condition and, as far as possible, without a fight. However, there were no major joint actions in the company or even battalion scale. In the concrete front-line situation, the parties had hardly any communication possibilities as they were used for closed actions. In the far-flung units, they were usually only a minority against tribesmen and criminals. While from the outset it was clear that the Army personnel consisted largely of fanatical fighters, some of the criminals also showed themselves to be willing to commit themselves. The Berlin Communist Heinz Meyer of the Africa Protection Regiment 961 summarized the situation: "nothing of our old instructions about the decompression of military forces, the only thing left was to look for the opportunity to run."[23]

The first eight defectors-most of them Communists-were reported on April 6, 1943, with the addition of good soldiers. This expressed the tendency of many political figures to appear outwardly as tireless soldiers.[24]

Karl Kuntze, once a member of the resistance group the *Rote Kämpfers* (Red Fighters), wrote in his diary on April 7, 1943:

> Lieutenant Juranek reads an order from General Thomas that some of our unit has been overrun. When this happens again, every tenth man is to be shot. To prevent reprisals against remaining comrades, withdraw campaigns were now carried out in such a way that they could not be recognized as such in the future. This was achieved, in particular, in the early retreats. In other cases, withdraw and sabotage campaigns were still recognized, but they could no longer be reported to higher staff because of the rapid collapse of the African Army Group.[25]

Shortly before the end of the fighting in Tunisia, the OKW had already decided to send the remainders of the Africa Division 999, which had been reassigned shortly afterwards, to Greece for coastal protection. There, the German leadership reckoned with an Allied invasion. The subsequent events, especially in the

Peloponnese, soon led to a disillusionment in the OKW, which affected the 999s. An important role was played by Colonel Erich von Brückner. The commander of Africa Protection Regiment 963, which no longer came to Tunisia, had assured him on April 19, 1943 that he was to be eliminated by a court martial. Three months later, the same man from the Peloponnese reported that the attempt, made by the use of an able officer corps, to form a reliable fighting force from the unusual human material, must be regarded as essentially failed.[26]

The OKW then commissioned Lieutenant Colonel Bernhard Klamroth to get an impression on the ground. Klamroth's report of August 29, 1943, was quite clear: "...thirty to forty percent of all unit members are charged with high treason. The possibility that mutiny is being set up by some activists at the appropriate moment is affirmed."[27]

A fourth battalion of the former Africa Division 999 had been subordinated to the Peloponnese of the 117th Destroyer Division. The commander General le Suire shared the following assessment of the battalion commander: "From a remote base, 6 men were demonstrably overrun with the gangs (i.e. partisans) with full armament within four weeks. These soldiers were previously considered reliable." After Colonel Meichsner had flown back to Berlin on September 28, 1943, the OKW was forced to act. On October 3, 1943, the order was issued for a large-scale cleansing operation. From the 999 units in Greece and in Germany, about 1,500 to 2,000 unreliable elements were segregated. An unknown number, which still had to serve remaining sentences, came back to the penal institutions; 1,250 men with no remaining sentences were placed at the disposal of the Organization Todt, responsible for military construction projects, as unarmed workers.

Almost exactly one year after his command of the Führer to set up the Africa Brigade 999, Hitler had to take note of the fact that the project had largely failed. When General Alfred Jodl, on October 4, 1943, explained the situation on the various battlefields, the events of the 999s were also raised in Greece.[28]

Order of Battle

The division was formed on December 23, 1942, and the division ceased to exist on May 13, 1943.

Africa Brigade 999 Brigade
        Brigade Staff
      961st (motorized) Africa Rifle Regiment
      952nd (motorized) Africa Rifle Regiment
       999th (motorized) Supply Battalion
        999th (motorized) Vehicle Column
          999th (motorized) Vehicle Maintenance Platoon

999th (motorized) Supply Platoon
999th (motorized) Butcher Company
999th (motorized) Bakery Company
999th (motorized) Divisional Administration Company
999th (motorized) Medical Company
999th (motorized) Ambulance Platoon
999th (motorized) Military Police Troop
999th Light Africa Division—March 1, 1943:
Divisional Staff
999th (motorized) Divisional Mapping Detachment
Musical Corps
961st Africa Rifle Regiment
962nd Africa Rifle Regiment
963rd Africa Rifle Regiment
999th (motorized) Anti-tank Battalion
999th (motorized) Artillery Regiment
999th (motorized) Pioneer Battalion
999th (motorized) Reconnaissance Battalion
999th (motorized) Astronomical Calibration Troop
999th (motorized) Maintenance Company
999th (motorized) Decontamination Battery
999th (motorized) Supply Battalion
999th (motorized) Butcher Company
999th (motorized) Bakery Company
999th (motorized) Divisional Administration Company
999th (motorized) Medical Company
999th (motorized) Ambulance Platoon
999th (motorized) Veterinary Company
999th (motorized) Military Police Troop
999th (motorized) Field Post Office

999th Light Africa Division actually serving in Africa:

Divisional Staff
961st Africa Rifle Regiment
962nd Africa Rifle Regiment
963rd Africa Rifle Regiment
999th (motorized) Artillery Regiment
999th (motorized) Pioneer Battalion
999th (motorized) Astronomical Calibration Troop
999th (motorized) Ambulance Platoon
999th (motorized) Military Police Troop[29]

The German Replacement Army

During the course of World War II, the Replacement and Training Divisions of the Third Reich proved to be the lubricant that oiled the formidable German military machine. Formed in the various *Wehrkreis* (military districts), these divisions were tasked, after August 27, 1939, with conscription, training, and replacement of personnel including control of mobilization policies and the actual call-up and induction of men; all types of military training, including the selection and schooling of officers and non-commissioned officers; the dispatch of personnel replacements to field units in response to their requisitions; and the organization of new units.[1] Under control of the Replacement Army, these Replacement and Training Divisions rose in strength from a total of 996,000 men at the start of WWII to a peak of 2,572,000 in December 1944.[2, 3]

After the mobilization order was given by the Armed Forces High Command, each military district of the Replacement Army began forming Replacement and Training Divisions as set down by order of the Chief of Army Equipment and Commander of the Replacement Army.[4] The normal location of the replacement unit was the home station of the affiliated field unit, to which the soldiers expected ultimately to return for their discharge or for reassignment. For example, a soldier who was wounded and went to a reserve hospital in the Zone of the Interior (in Germany) would be sent, upon leaving the hospital, to his affiliated replacement unit before being returned to the field.[5]

In order to understand the intricacies of the replacement system, it is well to trace the successive stages of its development. Originally, each infantry regiment that took to the field at the beginning of the war left behind at its home station a battalion cadre bearing its own number and known as its Ersatz battalion. The primary purpose of this battalion was to receive recruits, train them, and dispatch them as replacements to the field regiments. At any given time, it included reception cadre companies, training companies, convalescent companies, and transfer companies. Typically, the trained inductees combined with the convalescents into transfer companies for movement to a field unit. The regimental staff also controlled from three to five infantry specialist replacement training companies, which provided the personnel for the infantry Howitzer companies, anti-tank companies, signal sub-units, engineer platoons, and mounted platoons or the three infantry field regiments.[6]

The number of replacement division staffs in each military district was regulated by the Army High Command. They were responsible for the uniformity of training in their subordinate replacement training units and were to be kept free from all administrative duties.[7] From September 1, 1939 through to October 1942, the Replacement Army (sometimes, referred to as the Home Army) kept up a steady flow of new divisions and their trained replacement personnel to the far-flung battlefields of Europe, Africa, and almost to the very gates of the Russian capital city of Moscow.

The most far-reaching change in the organization of the Replacement Army took place in October 1942, when all basic replacement training units were broken up into their two elements—one to handle induction and replacement and the other to handle training. The induction and replacement unit retained the designation replacement, but henceforth, it was concerned only with receipt of recruits forwarding of recruits as speedily as possible to the sister training unit; receipt of convalescents and sending them back to a field unit; and the newly created training units bore the same number as and received the men from the replacement unit, gave them their training, and then dispatched them to an affiliated field unit.[8]

Training in replacement companies was abbreviated both for new recruits and for men released from hospitals. Both received from three to eight weeks' basic training, depending on the judgment of the company officers as to when the men were ready. After the men finished basic training, small percentages, usually those destined for the Russian front, were sent to education companies for advanced training.[9] Divisions had a field replacement battalion to provide final training for new replacements. Occasionally, local short-term training was undertaken by the armies, although for major training/schooling, personnel and units were transferred to the Reserve Army. Field Army units, when within greater Germany, were stationed with the military district and attached for administration (rations, accommodation, etc.), but not for command purposes.[10]

In addition to the regular mobile infantry division and the static division, a third class existed in 1943: the reserve division. To make more manpower available for the divisions in Russia, reserve divisions were formed from the training battalions in Germany and assigned to occupation duties in France and Russia. Twelve such reserve divisions were sent to France in 1943 to replace infantry divisions sent to the East.

The creation of the reserve divisions hampered the training of new men to a certain degree. If a new draftee were not selected to go into the air force or the panzer force, he received up to four months of basic individual infantry training in a replacement and training battalion located in a barracks near his home in Germany. He was then sent either to a reserve division in the occupied territories or to a training unit behind the lines in Russia, where he received another four months of training while performing occupation duties or fighting partisans. Finally, he was assigned to a division where he was taught more skills in the replacement battalion.[11]

The Replacement Army constituted a major portion of the armed forces. Its operations played a major role in bolstering the perseverance of the Field Army. Throughout most of the war, for every two or three Field Army soldiers, there was a Replacement Army soldier readying to move to the front. The system functioned surprisingly well. The *Wehrkreis* was also responsible for rebuilding and refitting shattered divisions, a responsibility that also took on more importance as the war continued. It rapidly filled the gaps of Stalingrad and Africa in early 1943. In the summer of 1944, it even managed to plug the gaping holes left by an army group (Army Group Centre) in central Russia and part of another (Army Group Sudukraine) in Romania.[12] There were four special penal battalions of the Replacement Army.

Special Battalions of the Replacement Army

These units received men undergoing their basic training in the Replacement Army, who, by their conduct and character, endangered discipline and were therefore a burden to regular training units. After remaining in the special penal battalions for not longer than nine months, these men were sent to their regular replacement units or, if they were still considered incorrigible, to the Special Field Penal Battalions.[13] There were four special penal battalions of the Replacement Army.

Special Division I

Special Division I of the Reserve Army was located in the Stablack training area near Deutsch-Eylau in Military District I. The department was set up as a criminal department. The department was responsible for the Eastern Military District. On May 31, 1942, the division was dissolved.[14]

Special Division III

Special Division III of the Reserve Army, located in the Wandern training area in Military District, was set up on January 29, 1940 at the military training place near Wander, in the Military District III. The department was set up as a criminal department. The department was responsible for Military Districts II, III, VIII, and X. On May 31, 1942, the division was dissolved.[15]

Special Division IV

Special Division IX of the Reserve Army was located in the Schwarzenborn training area in Military District IX. The department set up in January 1940 as a criminal department. The division was responsible for the Western Military Districts V, VI, IX, and XII. On May 31, 1942, the department was reportedly dissolved. There are indications, however, that the division still existed in March 1945.[16]

Special Division XIII

Special Division XIII of the Replacement Army was in the Grafenwöhr training area located in *Wehrkreis* XIII. The department set up on January 8, 1940 as a criminal department. The division was responsible for the Military Districts VII, X, XI, XIII, XVII, XVIII, and Protectorate. On May 31, 1942, the division was dissolved.[17]

Each of the fifteen Military Districts existing at the outbreak of the war had, in addition to the replacement battalions for combat troops, one to three replacement division staffs, and two to five infantry replacement regimental staffs. Most of the latter controlled three to four infantry specialist replacement companies. Each of these Military Districts (except I and XVIII) also had one to two Panzer Grenadier or motorized replacement regimental staffs, containing two or three specialist replacement companies and one to two artillery replacement regimental staffs. The infantry replacement battalions of both these arms contained reconnaissance battalions. In addition, there are two chemical warfare replacement regimental staffs in Military District X.

Military District XVIII has mostly mountain troops. *Wehrkreis* XX, XXI, and General Government controlled only a very few units.

The strength of battalions fluctuated greatly, depending upon whether they had just received new recruits or convalescents or depleted their organization by sending replacements to the field. Thus, some battalions had a strength of 500 men and others over 1,500.

Affiliated field divisions are given to permit a comparison between the replacement units and their field units. General Headquarters troops and disbanded or destroyed field divisions are not included, and converted field divisions could not be attributed to a specific military district. The present affiliation is the controlling one, even though the division was mobilized in another *Wehrkreis*. At the end of 1943, there were possibly 2 million men in the Replacement Army; at the end of 1944, there were probably considerably less.

Wehrkreis (Military Districts)

I: Königsberg

The territories of the land of East Prussia were assigned to *Wehrkreis* I with its headquarters in Königsberg. The military district was divided into the alternative military districts Königsberg, Allenstein, and Elbing. The division of Poland led to a strong enlargement of the military district around the governmental districts of Bialystok and Zichenau.

II: Stettin

The territories of the state of Mecklenburg and Pomerania with headquarters in Szczecin were assigned to *Wehrkreis* II. The military district was divided into the defense areas of Stettin, Schwerin, and Löslin.

III: Berlin

The territories of the provinces of Berlin and Mark Brandenburg with the headquarters in Berlin-Grunewald were assigned to District III. The military district was divided into the military zones Berlin, Frankfurt (Oder), and Potsdam.

IV: Dresden

The district of the province of Saxony was assigned to District IV, with the headquarters in Dresden. The military district was divided into the military areas Dresden, Leipzig, and Chemnitz.

V: Stuttgart

Wehrkreis Command V were assigned to the territories of the states of Württemberg and Baden, headquartered in Stuttgart. The Commander of the Substitute Troops V surrendered to the commander in the military district V. On October 22, 1939, a second commander of the Substitute troops V came to Ulm, and on October 23, 1939, the Divisional Staff for the special use (z.b.V.) On November 3, 1939, all the replacement troops of the WKV were transferred to the Protectorate of Bohemia and Moravia, in order to liberate the barracks for the West's advance.

VI: Münster

The territories of the provinces of Westphalia, Hanover, and the Rhine province were assigned to *Wehrkreis* VI with the headquarters in Münster–

Westfalen. The military district was divided into the alternate military districts Münster, Dortmund, Düsseldorf, and Cologne.

VII: München

The administrative districts of Swabia, Oberbayern, Niederbayern, and Oberpfalz were assigned to the administrative District VII, with their headquarters in Munich. The military district was divided into the alternate military district Munich.

VIII: Breslau

Wehrkreis Command VIII had its location in Breslau. At the beginning of the war, as deputy commander-in-chief VIII Armada Corps, at the same time, commander in *Wehrkreis* VIII was named. On October 24, 1939, the Divisional Staff (e.g. 408) was responsible for the leadership of the national army in the military district itself, and Division Staff 432 in Kattowitz in the formerly Polish Upper Silesia.

IX: Kassel

Wehrkreis Command IX had its location in Kassel. At the beginning of the war, it was given as deputy general command of the IX. Armed corps and at the same time commander in the military district IX. The commander of the replacement troops IX. On October 25, 1939, the Divisional Staff for Special Use (z.b.V.) 409 came to lead the Landwehr units.

X: Hamburg

The areas of the provinces of Schleswig-Holstein and Hanover with the headquarters in Hamburg were assigned to *Wehrkreis* X. The military district was divided into the German states of Schleswig-Holstein, Hamburg, and Bremen.

XI: Hanover

The areas of the provinces of Hanover and Saxony with headquarters in Hanover were assigned to *Wehrkreis* XI. The military district was divided into the military areas of Hannover and Magdeburg.

XII: Wiesbaden

The territories of the provinces of Rhine province and Hesse-Nassau were assigned to *Wehrkreis* XII with the headquarters in Koblenz. The military district was divided into the defense areas of Koblenz and Mannheim.

XIII: Nürnberg

The administrative districts of Upper and Lower Mittelfranken, Niederbayern, and Oberpfalz as well as Eger with the headquarters in Nuremberg were assigned to *Wehrkreis* XIII. The military district was divided into the alternative military districts Nuremberg, Regensburg, and Eger.

XVII: Wien

Wehrkreis XVII was the 17th German military region which controlled Austria, southern Bohemia, and Moravia for the Wehrmacht.

XVIII: Salzburg

On April 1, 1938, *Wehrkreis* Command XVII and XVIII were created for Austria. In addition, on October 15, 1939, the service of a second commander of the replacement troops 2/XVII in Linz on October 25, 1939 for the leadership of the *Landessschützen* and for special tasks of the Division Stab z.b.V. 417 was created. On November 9, 1939, two commanders of the replacement troops were given the designation 177th and 187th Division. In January 1940, the existing replacement battalions and divisions were doubled so that they could be replaced by two replacement battalions.

XX: Böhmen and Mähren—Prague

The administrative districts of Gdansk, Marienwerder, and Bydgoszcz were assigned to the Armed Forces XX with their headquarters in Gdańsk. The military district was formed after the conquest of Poland on October 23, 1939, and was divided into the military district of Danzig.

XXI: General Government—Cracow

The administrative district of Posen, Hohensalza, and Litzmannstadt, with the headquarters in Posen, were assigned to the administrative district XXI. The *Wehrkreis* was formed after the conquest of Poland on October 23, 1939, and was divided into the military recruitment district Posen.[18]

Kriegsmarine and Luftwaffe Units

Kriegsmarine

The Kriegsmarine (German Navy) established a special section for their disciplinary cases at Hela on the Baltic. The Navy also had specific battalion sized units for its disciplinary cases, the first being the *Sonderabteilung der* Kriegsmarine (Naval Disciplinary Unit), which, after WWII began, was renamed the *Kriegsonderabteilung* (Wartime Naval Disciplinary Unit). Another such unit was formed later in WWII named Wartime Naval Disciplinary Unit East. Also during the war, the 30th Ship Cadre Battalion and 31st Ship Cadre Battalion were formed: the 30th for use in the North Sea area and the 31st in the Baltic Sea area. If further education was not likely, problem men were transferred into a naval company of the Army Field Disciplinary Battalion.[1]

The Navy's education unit was initially attached to the Army Disciplinary Unit I at Stablack (now Stabławki, Poland).[2]

The exact date of the erection is not known, but it most likely was in 1934. In 1934, two barracks were built near a Lake of Warschnesser for a large garrison. In 1935, the construction of the northern storage was started. Simultaneously with its construction began the construction of the garden town Stablack, so called because all houses had garden plants. A large military complex, called *Munasiedlung* (MUNA), was built some distance from the town and the camp north between the towns of Schlauthienen and Jerlauken, partly on the forest grounds of Wackern. This was followed by administrative buildings, canteens, and lounges, where the work houses were located. These were planar and single-story, planted with lawns, shrubs, and trees for camouflage. The finished artillery shells were stacked in a large ammunition bunker, which was situated on the ground. From 1936, Stablack was the second largest military training place beside Arys in East Prussia. The MUNA had its own freight station for loading and unloading. In front of the entrance, there was a passenger station on the route Rositten–Stablack–Eylau, which was opened in December 1937. Two large barracks camps for single female and male employees were erected at Jerlauken. In the vicinity of the MUNA, a residential settlement was built for their officers, sub-officers, and employees with Albrechtstrasse and Bergstrasse.[3]

The camp was about 8 kilometers north-west of Prussian Eylau (now Bagrationovsk, Kaliningrad Oblast, Russia). This was the largest POW camp in East Prussia. Before the war, the settlement of Stablack was built as a garrison town specifically for military personnel. Therefore, it was convenient to set up the main central East Prussian POW camp there. There were over twenty working groups in the camp. The groups were based on the former occupations of the prisoners. The number of the base camp was E1. The first POWs, Polish military personnel, were delivered to the camp in the first days of September 1939. Later, they were joined by Belgians, French, Russians, Italians, and prisoners of other nationalities. In 1940–1941, there were over 100,000 prisoners in the camp. In the first half of 1940, 178 Lithuanian citizens, who had been captured as Polish soldiers in 1939, were released from this camp 18. The camp was evacuated on January 25, 1945, and it is believed that at the time of its evacuation, there were about 50,000 POWs in the camp.[4]

Eventually, the Navy's education unit was designated the Naval Disciplinary Unit and transferred to the island of Hela. The education unit was dissolved in 1942 and replaced by the 30th and 31st Cadre Battalions.

In the 560 Battalion, a whole submarine crew was demobilized and was divided among the various companies. The submarine crew did not follow orders on time. In one case, two or three men were missing in the morning, which the commander did not authorize them to leave. When they came running from their harbor girls, they were sent to the *Strafsache z.b.V.* (Criminal Court). Additionally, this submarine crew went the way of almost all 500 members—to the death. Their hopes for probationary sentences required by law, pardon and reassignment to their submarine was an illusion.[5]

In one case, Doctor Ulrich Abel was 1st Watch Officer of *U-154* under the command of Oskar Kusch. Kusch had given Abel a poor review after their first patrol and rated him unfit for command. This deeply angered Abel, who, along with the boat's other officers, began to conspire against the commander (who was well respected by the crew).[6]

On Christmas Day 1943, just after returning to base after their second patrol, Oskar Kusch gave his 1st Warrant Officer a review stating "that while he was an inflexible, rigid and one-sided officer of average talent. He was, nonetheless, suitable for U-boat commander training." This assessment shocked and further infuriated Abel, who on January 12 filed a formal complaint accusing Kusch of sedition, followed by another on January 25 accusing him of cowardice. Kusch was arrested on January 20 and a court martial convened on January 26. The verdict, a death sentence, was delivered on January 29, 1944.[7]

Having a doctorate in law, Abel would have known that his actions would at the least result in a court martial and heavy punishment, but more likely a death sentence for his commander.

Oskar Kusch was executed by firing squad on May 12, 1944—having just turned twenty-six years of age. The court decided to sentence him to death even though the prosecutor had only asked for ten years' imprisonment. A fellow U-boat commander, Otto Westphalen, had been one of those deciding the sentence. Doctor Abel himself had died three weeks before Oskar Kusch, when his first command, *U-193*, was sunk on its first patrol.[8]

A unusual event occurred on May 13, 1945, five days after the Germans had surrendered to the Allies in World War II, two deserting sailors were shot at Amsterdam. Bruno Dorfer and Rainer Beck were deserters of the Wehrmacht's Kriegsmarine and they were shot by a court-martial conducted by the Wehrmacht itself.[9]

Basically, a pocket of fortified German resistance remained hunkered down in the Netherlands as the war approached its close. That force of 150,000 surrendered to a much smaller number of Canadians on May 5 on terms that maintained German responsibility for administering its armed forces and the civilian areas under its control: a highly anomalous situation in an occupied country as the Third Reich dissolved altogether.[10]

Canadians and Germans, according to Madsen, enjoyed a collegial relationship as the Canadians gradually took German forces into custody or received German forces who helpfully marched themselves into custody. Yet even under guard, these imprisoned Germans still retained significant autonomy and a German command structure that Canadians were unwilling to interfere with an arrangement so expedient that it severely tested the bounds of propriety. So invested were the Canadians in maintaining their opposite numbers' unit cohesion that they handed some deserters back over to the nominal prisoners.

Rainer Beck had been deserted for the best part of a year: the son of a Social Democratic father and a Jewish mother, he had ditched harbor defense the previous September and had been laying low with his sister in Amsterdam. Bruno Dorfer was a more recent deserter. They naturally assumed that with the Canadian takeover, they would be good to go. They turned themselves in to Canadian soldiers with an eye towards improving their status.[11]

Major Oliver Mace, acting commanding officer of the Canadian regiment, ordered Major J. Dennis Pierce, the company commander in charge of the former factory (where the German prisoners were being held), to place the two deserters inside the compound because they were certainly Germans and had no other place to put them.

At 10.05 a.m. on May 13, 1945, Pierce informed 2 Canadian Infantry Brigade of the intended German course of action: "German Marine deserters being tried this morning. German Commander intends [to] shoot them." The

German camp leadership established a court martial within the camp and brought Dorfer and Beck before three officers, a team of military lawyers. [12]

Frigate Captain Alexander Stein regarded the proceedings as a show trial for his authority. At the insistence of the German naval commander, the entire camp population witnessed the event. A report, taken earlier that morning, counted 1,817 German marines inside the camp. The two accused, represented by a German military lawyer, underwent rigorous cross-examination before this large staring crowd; Chief Engineer Frank Trmal, a young German officer present at the fifteen-minute trial, remembered Beck's defense:

> For some reason Beck, who was older, decided to defend himself and told the court that we (the Germans) all knew several weeks ago the war was all over for us and that it was a matter of time before we surrendered. He told the captain and the court that any further fighting by us against the Canadians would be senseless bloodshed. With this the captain jumped to his feet in a rage, screaming at Beck that he was calling all of us, his comrades, and his officers, murderers. It is something that I will never forget.[13]

After the inevitable-yet-incredible conviction, Stein appealed to his Canadian guards for a bit of comradely assistance in carrying out the court-martial's order.

The Canadians delivered up eight captured German rifles with ammunition, plus a heavy truck to help their prisoners execute their deserters. A Canadian military cable testifies to the event: "German marines in Amsterdam have picked up some of their own deserters. They have been tried by military law and sentenced to be shot. May they do this."

The answer was determined not by any senior Canadian officer, but by the German High Commander who had surrendered the week before, Johannes Blaskowitz. It was on his approval that Dorfer and Beck were shot against an air raid shelter wall at 5.40 p.m., not eight hours after their bizarre public trial.[14]

Luftwaffe

The following is an excerpt from an article titled "Military Justice in the German Air Force During World War II" written by Edith Rose Gardner for the *Journal of Criminal Law & Criminology*, Volume 49, Issue 3, 1958. The article is made available as free and open access by Northwestern University School of Law Scholarly Commons. It gives us a good understanding of the legal background behind the establishing of punishment units by the Luftwaffe (German Air Force) during World War II.

Two tenets of German military justice were that comrades-in-arms judged offenses and that discipline was the sole responsibility of the superior officer concerned. The doctrine of trying a soldier by soldiers existed from the time of the earliest German standing armies. Within certain limits, it was the right only of a commanding officer to determine and impose disciplinary action against a subordinate, with no higher authority having a right to intervene or to modify his decision. In criminal offenses, the superior officer concerned submitted a charge sheet or summary of evidence on the offense to the appropriate established court-martial and proceedings were' begun on the basis of his report. Correlatively, any superior officer who knew of an offense had a duty to submit such a charge sheet and was liable for failure to do so. Civil police power and jurisdiction ended at the air station boundary. A court-martial could ask the assistance of the police in investigations, but even if a soldier were apprehended in the act of committing an offense outside the military area, the police were obliged to turn him over to the nearest military authorities.

However, after World War I, this exclusive jurisdiction was abolished by the Social Democratic Government's termination of a 'special military law' for the land forces. Thereafter, members of the military service were tried and sentenced by civil courts, with army lawyers protecting their interests, and with investigations conducted by civil prosecution authorities. Only the units of the Navy afloat were permitted to retain the traditional concept and function of military law. The National Socialist Government re-established military jurisprudence in the Armed Forces by a decree effective January 1, 1934, on the basis of the 1898 Military Penal Code. The German Air Force (GAF) created its own judicial system in October 1935. The 1934 law provided for two superior courts: the court-martial was instituted as a general court of appeal and as the court of first instance for high treason and other serious crimes. During World War I, the Wartime Criminal Proceedings Order abolished the superior courts-martial but retained the Supreme Court of Justice.

The highest supervisory authority of the GAF legal branch was the Director of German Air Force Legal Matters at the High Command of the German Air Force in Berlin. The first Director of the legal department was an individual who had previously dealt with air traffic legislation in the Reich Ministry of Communication. Initially, the Department was a section of the Central Office; in 1942, it was under the Director of Air Administrative Matters and Personnel; in the spring of 1944, it was transferred to the Director of Manpower and National Socialist Indoctrination of the German Air Force. In December 1944, the Department became immediately subordinate to the Reich Minister for Air and Commander-in-Chief.

In 1934, with the foundation of the Reich Air Ministry and the Legal Department, the Director was primarily responsible for advising the entire Air Ministry on all questions relating to matters of contract, civil and public law, air law, air traffic law and Reich legislation. Other departments of the Ministry gradually assumed these problems. The Director was then mainly concerned with air traffic laws, drawing up a new Code of Military Law, and building an independent GAF judicature. These functions became increasingly important with the expansion of the GAF and the outbreak of war. The Director furnished to the Commander-in-Chief legal advice on his rights as Convening Authority after the wartime elimination of the two superior courts-martial; on the confirming or rescinding of sentences for more serious punishments, such as death or degradation of officers; on uniformity in the administration of justice; and on the maintenance of discipline among the troops.

The Director of GAF Legal Matters was the commander of all judges in the GAF. As legal advisor to the Reich Minister for Air and Commander- in-Chief, GAF, he had the right of direct audience with the Commander-in-Chief.

The responsibilities of the Director of GAF Legal Matters were: preparatory work in cases where only the Reichs Marshal could confirm or mitigate a sentence; handling all petitions and requests on sentences submitted to the Reichs Marshal personally; standardizing legal practice in the GAF; organizing and employing personnel in the GAF legal branch; representing the Reich Air Minister in collaboration on Reich legislation; collaborating in the development and application of the penal code; advising the Chief of the General Staff, the Director for Air Matters, and all departments of the Reich Air Ministry on legal matters; superintending and directing all legal disputes concerning the aviation department of the Reich Treasury; and dealing with cases of sabotage in the GAF.

The organization of the Department was frequently revised to handle these manifold obligations. Essentially, there were three Divisions. The first was responsible for the administration and uniformity of military justice; and the third, other affairs not strictly within the scope of military justice. By 1944, the Department numbered sixty people. The approval of the Nazi Party authorities, previously necessary for promotions and appointments, was dispensed with during the war, and the criteria became professional and military aptitude. Wartime responsibilities and increased incidence of serious crimes increased the duties of the Department.

The Director of GAF Legal Matters had, in addition to routine duties, special tasks assigned to him by the Commander-in-Chief. For uniformity in dealing with political cases and crimes of corruption, which were serious enough for a possible death penalty, the German Air Force commissioned a Special Duties Court-Martial to handle them. The Chief of the First Division of the Department was the Convening Authority and an order of the Commander-in-Chief referred cases to it. The 1934 'Malice Law' specified as an offense the making of false, inflammatory or garbled statements in public that might endanger the Reich or damage the prestige of the government, of the National Socialist Party or of leading State or Party personalities.

The Special Duties Court, composed of experienced judges, distinguished itself by its moderate treatment of these cases and inflicted heavy punishment

Above: Soldiers of the 36th Waffen SS fought to suppress the Warsaw Uprising. (*Bundesarchiv*)

Right: Oscar Dirlewanger, leader of the 36th Grenadier Division. (*Der Spiegel*)

Above: 11th SS Panzergrenadier Division infantry soldier with the tank-killing Panzerfaust. (*Bundesarchiv*)

Below: 999th Light Africa Division tanks in North Africa. (*Bundesarchiv*)

Above: SS troops watch as housing blocks burn in Warsaw. (*Bundesarchiv*)

Below: Kriegsmarine-Schiffstammabteilung 30 Naval Infantry. (*Bundesarchiv*)

Above: 11th SS Panzer Grenadier soldiers firing a mortar. (*Bundesarchiv*)

Below: Members of the 36th Grenadier Division. (*Juliusz Bogdan Deczkowski*)

Above: Luftwaffe-Feldbataillone 1 bombs Polish airfield. (*Bundesarchiv*)

Below: Focke-Wulf Fw 190A-3. (*Bundesarchiv*)

Above: 999th Fortress Infantry Battalion advancing. (*Bundesarchiv*)

Below: German 609th Infantry Battalion on the move. (*Bundesarchiv*)

Above: 500th Infantry Battalion troops. (*Bundesarchiv*)

Right: Young Waffen SS soldier. (*Bundesarchiv*)

Above: 500th SS Paratrooper Battalion soldiers. (*Bundesarchiv*)

Below: Men of the 11th SS Panzer-Grenadier Division Nordland during the Battle of Narva on February 11, 1944. (*Bundesarchiv*)

Above: Troops on the move. (*Bundesarchiv*)

Right: Max Rettl. (*Bundesarchiv*)

Left: German infantryman seeking protection from desert dust: Western Desert, 1942. (*Bundesarchiv*)

Below: 6th Army soldiers marching towards Stalingrad in 1941. (*Bundesarchiv*)

Above: Otto Skorzeny in Pomerania visiting the 500th SS Parachute Battalion, February 1945. (*Bundesarchiv*)

Below: Watching housing blocks burn in Warsaw during the uprising. (*Franz Conrad*)

Above: A Jewish rebel leaving a house surrounded by German soldiers during the Warsaw Uprising. (*Holocaust Memorial Day Trust*)

Left: Member of the 172nd Grenadier Battalion after the collapse of Army Group Centre. (*World of Tanks Forum EU*)

Above: Feldgendarmerie soldier. (*Bundesarchiv*)

Below: Members of the Dirlewanger Brigade executing Soviet Partisans. (*Bundesarchiv*)

Left: German MG-34 crew. (*Bundesarchiv*)

Below: Gerhard Lopatka, 90th Light Africa Division. (*Bundesarchiv*)

Opposite above: German and Italian prisoners of war captured after the Axis surrender in Tunisia. (*U.S. National Archives*)

Opposite below: Africa German troops and a field kitchen. (*worldwarphotos.info*)

Above: Heinrich Himmler in conversation with some troops. (*Bundesarchiv*)

Below: German soldiers on the Eastern Front. (*Bundesarchiv*)

only on offenders who, by reviling authorities to subordinates or in public, had endangered discipline to an intolerable extent from a military point of view. The Führer became dissatisfied with the administration of justice by this particular court and with military courts generally for excessive clemency in punishing political offenses. In 1943, he ordered all political cases, breaches of the 'Malice Law,' sedition and high treason committed by service personnel, withdrawn from military jurisdiction and transferred to a special session of the Senate of the Reich Supreme Court. This court proved equally unsatisfactory and "derelict in duty" and the Führer, in 1944, hoping for more severe punishments, ordered that all political offenses occurring in the Armed Forces be referred to the civil courts-People's Courts and Special Courts-and that the Gestapo conduct investigations, even within the Armed Forces. However, these oral instructions were not committed to writing and were never executed, although the Senate was dissolved. As a result, documents were returned without-action to the military courts after months of delay.

In December 1944, the Commander-in-Chief created within the Department a Staff for Special Tasks and Suggestions to replace various special commissions, which investigated abuses in the GAF, including armament, command or operations. Inquiries were instituted after military reverses to assess objectively the sources of error or to determine the cause of failure of a new type of aircraft by investigation in the department directing its development, in the factory constructing it or in testing and experimental stations." Anonymous letters of reports from the Security Service, indicting senior air officers or officials of the aircraft industry were often the basis for such investigations. These were usually proven groundless denunciations and rarely led to court martial proceedings. Although time-consuming and difficult to carry out, objective GAF judges experienced in inquiry procedure conducted these extra-judicial investigations and they proved of value to the authorities by clarifying the situation. For these 'special tasks,' the Chief of the Special Staff had the judicial powers of a Convening Authority with the right to intervene in the sphere of any other Convening Authority and to hold a court-martial of his own, conducting investigations and instituting proceedings on the spot, or, to refer the matter to the GAF Special Duties Court-Martial. He had also the disciplinary powers of a higher commander over all members of the GAF. He could order arrests or investigations, prefer charges, issue instructions to lawyers and military courts, and, within the limits of the powers of the GAF Commander-in-Chief, confirm sentences, except loss of rank by officers, and confer pardons. The Chief of Staff for Special Tasks conferred with the Director of GAF Legal Matters and the Commander-in-Chief, GAF, on verdicts by his courts.

Although the German Air Force had its own legal organization, it was subordinate to the Supreme Command of the Armed Forces, which, without interfering with the organization or courts-martial, issued general orders on legal matters for the whole of the Armed Forces. These orders included treatment of civilians in occupied areas, settlement of jurisdictional disputes between GAF and Army courts and establishment of a combined Armed Forces Court. The Legal Department of the Supreme Command was composed of personnel of all three branches of the military service.

As has been said, the two superior military courts were the court-martial and the high court-martial, with a Supreme Court of Justice for the Armed Forces. The first two of these courts were eliminated but the latter was retained with jurisdiction over cases of general officers of all branches of the service, cases of high treason, treachery and a few other serious crimes against the regime. All political offenses, breaches of the 'Malice Law,' sedition, and high treason, committed by military personnel, were withdrawn from military courts and transferred to civil courts.

The GAF field court-martial, with an independent judiciary, was the *Feidgericht* (Free Tribunal). This is distinguished from the Special Duties Court-Martial Each command had an unspecified number of courts-martial depending on the number of units stationed within an Air Force Command, and each GAF commander with the powers of a Convening Authority regulated his own court martial. By delegated authority, the commander of a unit could supervise courts-martial for lighter offenses. Offenses carrying a sentence of a year or more were referred to trial by the commander of a major air command; as, from a company commander through the regiment and division to the zone. The Convening Authorities or crimes involving heavier penalties were the Commanders-in-Chief of individual Air Forces. The Commander-in-Chief, GAF, reserved to himself the authority in cases for which there could be the most serious sentences, including loss of rank of officers.

Before the war, the powers of a Convening Authority were granted only to officers commanding Air or Flak Division, to officers commanding Air Zones and to Commanders-in-Chief of individual Air Forces. The latter were Higher Convening Authorities, comparable to the United States military General Court-Martial Authority. Gradually powers of a Convening Authority were conferred on officers in charge of corps and independent or isolated units. The participants in a GAF trial were, in addition to the accused, the Judge, court members, Prosecutor, Recorder and Defense Counsel. The number of participants varied with the type of court.

The Judge, a Deputy Judge Advocate was the court president. He was usually the highest legal official attached to the unit but in cases of serious offenses he might be the Chief Judge and Legal Adviser of the appropriate individual Air Force Headquarters. The members of the court were lay persons, one a field grade officer and the other an assessor with a rank at least as high as that of the accused. The 'accessor' was the so-called 'Prisoner's Peer,' an innovation on the 1898 Military Penal Code introduced by the 1934 law. The Prosecutor was a legal official either with the unit, a Deputy Judge Advocate, or a Senior Judge Advocate of field grade rank or he was the Investigating Officer. The latter was the more usual. In a case where the Prosecutor had not conducted the preliminary inquiry, the Investigating Officer was the Recorder, so that both could act as either Recorder or Prosecutor. The Defense Counsels were not required to be legal officials, but it was preferable that they have some legal experience.

The normal court-martial consisted of one Judge, one field grade officer, one Prisoner's Peer and the Counsels. If the offense were one for which 15 years' imprisonment or the death penalty were authorized, there were two Judges, one field grade officer and two Prisoner's Peers. Higher courts-martial were also composed of two Judges, one field grade officer and two Prisoner's Peers, or, in serious cases, an additional one of each. Counsel were always present.

The number of Judges allocated to various courts-martial jurisdictions depended upon the volume of work. Large courts-martial of Air Zones, with territorial powers and many subordinate units, were assigned many judges; for example, the Third Air Command in Berlin had at times more than twenty assigned Judges. The courts of training units were also well-manned, but the courts of the actual fighting forces had few Judges, never less than two: a recorder and prosecutor.

Officers in charge of commands with permanent courts-martial were not trained legal specialists, but in regard to legal matters were known in the judicial capacity of Convening Authorities and were addressed as such. Their duties, before and after trial, included the powers of and responsibilities for: preferring charges after receiving the full report of the Investigating Officer of his preliminary examination; issuing a warrant of arrest or order of confinement to quarters, as necessary; effecting the approved penalty in the shortest possible time; and ordering a stay of execution and reopening the case if he disapproved the decision on the basis of facts known to him, new evidence, or a plea of the accused and counsel that the case was not proven. Further, apparently any Convening Authority was empowered to confirm the imposition of the death penalty in the case of non-commissioned officers and lower grades if the Command Chief Judge and Legal Adviser of the individual Air Force were not readily accessible. He was obliged to have two Deputy Judge Advocates witness and confirm the execution.

The Investigating Officer was a non-legal officer appointed by the Convening Authority to serve within his assigned unit. Transfer to another unit automatically relieved him of his duty and capacity. It was preferable, but not essential, that he have some legal experience. His assignment was undertaken only after an oath was administered by a Deputy Judge Advocate. His duties included conducting investigations, carrying out search and seizure of evidence in the case, arresting an accused if necessary, reporting the arrest to the Convening Authority, working with the competent court-martial, replacing the prosecutor during the trial if the competent legal official were not available and the Convening Authority ordered it, and conducting post-mortem examinations.

As World War II commenced, the GAF had 150 well-trained, active Judges. The number rose to 500 during the war and fell to 350 in 1943 as the younger men were assigned to the fighting forces, after a period of flight training and usually at their own request. The problem of recruitment and training of qualified judicial personnel was more formidable inasmuch as the GAF legal system originated in 1935 and the war ended in 1945.

The original cadre of 150 judge advocates was composed of volunteers who were accepted for service with the GAF by the Reich Ministry of Justice. These were generally judges with experience in civil law; the rest, lawyers. The majority were born about 1900 and were men who no longer felt at home in civil jurisprudence, because of increasing discrimination and political interference, and who feared curtailment of their judicial independence. The young judges who later joined the service did so for some of the same reasons, as well as from the attractions of problems of military justice and of association with contemporaries encountered on reserve tours. The applicants were numerous and the GAF was able to select the best. The qualifications were professional ability, favourable recommendations and, if possible, reserve training. Membership in the Nazi Party was an advantage, but was not essential, as the Armed Forces were traditionally non-political. The wartime additions to the department were deferred service civil judges of provincial, municipal and petty sessions courts. GAF Judges were trained for six months, served six months probation before acceptance with a GAF court-martial, and continued their training in courses and conferences and by attachment to larger courts. There was no political training.

At the inception of German military jurisprudence, lawyers were merely legal advisors to senior officers responsible for exercising judicial powers. They later represented the prosecution and eventually attained the status of Judges, conducting proceedings against military personnel. The Judges, as presidents of courts martial, had less independence than in civil courts, inasmuch as the Convening Authority had to concur in their decisions and acts of opening an inquiry, revoking a charge, ordering arrest and executing a sentence.

The Higher Convening Authorities, Commanders of Air Commands had a senior official as Chief Judge and Legal Advisor and two or three experienced assistant judges to control all courts martial within the command. These Chief Judges managed personnel matters of subordinate judges, drew up reports on verdicts, held conferences and, especially, settled disputed legal points and attempted uniformity in the administration of justice. For these purposes, the courts were grouped into 'inspection districts,' from which a judge came to a quarterly conference with the Chief Judge.

The Air Zone had the largest number of permanent legal officials, with one Senior Judge Advocate, seven Deputy Judge Advocates and eight Recorders. The lowest unit with its own legal department was the Group with two Deputy Judge Advocates and one Recorder, although a company might have a captain to deal with legal matters. All subordinate units performed essentially the same functions as the Air Zone legal office with its wide administrative area and legal problems. The Senior Judge Advocate gave legal advice to his commander, supervised courts-martial within his command and dealt with matters of organization, administration and personnel. The Deputy Judge Advocates rendered legal opinions; appeared in courts; handled verdicts and punishments, including death penalties; gave legal assistance; determined claims for personal injury and property damage; lectured the troops; and assisted the Reich Labour Service and Motor Transportation Corps. By close contact with the troops, they were able not only to discover an offender, but also, often, to prevent wrongdoing.

Criminal action against a member of the GAF was instituted when the Commanding Officer submitted a Charge Sheet on the offense to the appropriate court-martial. On authority of this report, the court began proceedings, conducted its investigation and issued an order for arrest as required. The President or Judge of the court could utilize civil authorities to assist in the investigation, but generally, he used the service personnel, specially trained and appointed by the unit for the purpose. These Investigating Officers had usually already helped draw up the charge sheet and procure the necessary documents.

The Judge referred the results of the investigation to the Convening Authority. If the charges proved groundless, proceedings were suspended. If the offense proved minor or the fault of the guilty party slight, the Convening Authority could dispense with the charges and either impose disciplinary punishment himself or leave this to the discretion of the accused's immediate superior officer. If the charges were sustained, the officer in charge of the inquiry usually acted as Prosecutor before the court-martial.

The Judges had generally had extensive training in civil practice and presumably the courts martial followed the law of evidence and procedure of the criminal courts of German civil jurisdictions.

All unit headquarters commanders were responsible for maintaining a Record of Punishments indicating punishments imposed on personnel of the unit by the commander himself, by a court-martial, or by a civil court. Reports of courts-martial forwarded to the GAF Legal Department aided in checking the quality of judges and directing the administration of justice.

The amount of work of GAF legal officers increased during World War II. During both the First and Second World War, the superior courts were dispensed with and review became only a matter of confirmation of the sentence by the Convening Authority. Prior to confirmation of a sentence, in every case, a report had to be submitted to the Convening Authority concerned by a legal adviser.

The Führer reserved to himself the right to confirm or rescind sentences to death imposed against officers and sentences against general officers. In the absence of such a reservation, these prerogatives were otherwise assigned to the Commanders-in-Chief of the several services. The GAF Commander-in-Chief reserved to himself the right of action on all other death sentences, all sentences involving loss of rank or imprisonment of officers, and all sentences in cases of insubordination and rape. Later the Commanders-in-Chief of Air Commands were granted the power to act on sentences of imprisonment and those not involving loss of rank in officer cases. These commanders had the right to rescind sentences submitted to them for review. The power to confirm other sentences was delegated to the Convening Authorities. If a Convening Authority did not choose to confirm a verdict, he had to submit it to the Air Command Commander-in-Chief, who could confirm or rescind it. If the sentence were disapproved, the case could be referred for retrial either to the same court of different composition or to another court.

In 1944, the responsibility for the execution of all sentences imposed by courts-martial was in the Office for the Execution and Mitigation of Sentences under an Air Marshal as Convening Authority, and directly subordinate to the Commander-in-Chief, GAF. This was to relieve courts-martial of post-sentencing matters, of- execution of sentences, pardons, requests for clemency, automatic revision or remission after a stated period, and supervision of redemption by combat units. In mid-1944, in special cases where the regimental commander was the confirming authority, the death penalty against non-commissioned officers and lower grades could be imposed by his Court on the Spot, without reference to the Convening Authority. In such cases, the Regimental Commander was known as Disciplinary Committee Leader.

In certain special circumstances, Armed Forces Courts-Martial were created, with representatives from all three branches of the service. An example was that organized on Crete in mid-1944 when the island was blockaded and in danger of isolation and invasion. Army, Navy and Air Force personnel were stationed there, but often their competent Convening Authorities were based elsewhere. Ordinarily, an accused might have to be transported to Greece for trial and punitive action would be difficult and delayed. The Führer, Supreme Commander of the Armed Forces, appointed the Commandant of the Fortress of Crete as Convening Authority for all branches of the German forces assigned for duty on the island, with the power of confirming and pardoning sentences. This power extended to prisoners of war and local civilians, always the case in occupied territory. The composition of the Armed Forces Court on Crete was a judge for the civil population, Judge for the Army, Judge for the Navy, Judge for the GAF, Recorders to correspond with the judges assigned, and members chosen from all three branches of the service. The Commander of the Eastern Aegean Theatre operated under the same conditions.

The types of serious punishment, other than mere restriction or reprimand, after court martial action, were death, penal servitude, imprisonment, and dishonour. Capital punishment was apparently inflicted by hanging. Penal servitude was executed by the civil authorities. Imprisonment was for more than six weeks or for less than six weeks arrest. Detention sentences were served in special military prisons, referred to as 'Glasshouses.'

Arrest sentences were executed by the offender's unit. On imposition of imprisonment or servitude, the offender was automatically discharged from the service and the civil authorities carried out the punishment.

Punishment with Dishonour included Dishonourable Discharge Dishonourable Discharge and loss of civil rights could be imposed jointly or singly. Apparently, dishonourable discharge was for life, as no reference to a time element was made in the sentences. Loss of civil rights was for a specified period-five years being the longest reported. Dismissal from the service applied only to officers; loss of rank could be applied in officer cases. Reduction in rank could be imposed on non-commissioned officers. A fine could be imposed only as the result of a court-martial and not as a company punishment. A fine was administered after recording it in the Punishment Book. Apparently fines were rarely imposed and recorded; therefore, it cannot be estimated how often unrecorded fines were imposed.

The power to punish members of the GAF was vested not in the person but in the office; not according to rank but by virtue of the position an officer held in his unit. This was implicit in the power of command and responsibility for the maintenance of discipline within a unit.

Any officer or non-commissioned officer could cause a subordinate to be apprehended temporarily. The apprehension had to be recorded in writing and reported at once to the individual's commanding officer, who was required to order an immediate investigation of the circumstances. The superior officer concerned decided whether the subordinate was to be punished disciplinarily, without any higher authority having the right to intervene or to modify his decision, unless the punishment were contrary to regulations. In criminal cases, the superior officer submitted a charge sheet of the offense to the appropriate court martial and proceedings began. The GAF Commander-in-Chief stressed that each commander had a duty to maintain discipline with all means at his disposal, including heavy court-martial sentences, and, a preeminent duty to have every regard for his subordinates, including consideration for the personal circumstances of the accused, circumstances of the offense, the offender's general conduct and an interpretation of these factors to the maximum advantage of the accused. These matters were often not legally within the scope of a court-martial.

The company commander with the rank of a first lieutenant had the power to impose disciplinary punishments from simple reprimand to fourteen days' confinement in camp or ten days' severe arrest on bread and water. For penalties up to twenty-eight days' confinement to camp or twenty-one days' severe arrest, the division commander was the competent authority. Other types of non-judicial punishment included strong reprimand, punitive guard duty, extra duty, and drill punishment. To prevent injustice by a superior and to preserve rights and privileges, provision was made for individual complaints. Collective complaints were not allowed. Individual complaints could not be made against court decisions or alleged unfairness in pay, clothing or rationing. A complaint had to be submitted, verbally or in writing, depending on the relative ranks of the accuser and accused, to the immediate superior of the one complained against, within seven days of the wrong. In as much as punishment did not commence until twenty-four hours after its imposition, timely complaint could postpone its execution.

The majority of GAF court-martial verdicts were the result of minor offenses that occur everywhere among soldiers. Gradually there was an increase in crimes attributable to the length of the war, service at a great distance from home and, above all, mobilization of almost the entire nation for war. This increase was not striking and, more important militarily, there was no perceptible increase of offenses against discipline.

In a command of almost exclusively technical units, as the GAF, military transportation offenses and negligence in the handling of weapons and equipment, such as damage caused in taxiing aircraft, were frequent charges. Other recurring and typical offenses were minor offenses on guard, particularly in the home defense flak; absence without leave; insubordination; and theft. Thefts, especially from comrades, increased as the war continued and shortages of goods increased. Frauds and embezzlements increased with the employment of less desirable elements.

Among the more serious crimes were those of desertion; sedition; offenses against discipline and military property and comrades; corruption; sabotage; and political crimes. Percentages and numerical comparisons are not available.

All capital punishments had to be approved by the Commander-in-Chief, GAF, resulting in uniformity in the imposition of the maximum penalty. In contrast, commanders of separate Armies had the power to confirm Army death sentences. During the war years from September 1939, to March 1945, some 700-death sentences were imposed on personnel in the GAF. Two-thirds of these were executed and the rest were remitted to prison or detention sentences. The percentage of death sentences was rather low, estimating the GAF strength to have been two million and calculating that some three million men were in the GAF during those years. The percentage was appreciably higher in the German Army. The GAF, composed mainly of volunteers and especially selected recruits, was not obliged, as was the Army, to use the death sentences as a deterrent.

Most of the capital sentences in the GAF were for desertion, but only for aggravated crimes. These included desertion by an airman previously convicted of serious offenses, a common deserter, a deserter abroad, a deserter who committed other serious offenses such as theft and fraud, or by an airman belonging to a penal or 'redemption by combat' unit. Motivation for desertion by members of the GAF was rarely due to fundamental dislike of soldiering, but rather to other causes, such as fear of punishment for a minor offense, homesickness, love of adventure, or association with women, especially outside Germany. As in United States military law, the GAF differentiated between absence without leave and desertion, on the basis of accompanying intention and not on the duration of the absence. Intention permanently to evade service with one's unit amounted to desertion, be absence only one hour; intention to return, even after an extended period, could result in a finding of only absence without leave.

The death sentence was frequently imposed for various types of sedition. In the narrow sense of the offense, capital punishment was imposed only where there was clear incitement to indiscipline, open utterances of a defeatist character, defamation of heads of the State, of authorities or of superior officers. During the first five years of World War II, there were practically no political offenses under the 'Malice Law.' They began to occur after the fall of Stalingrad and increased progressively thereafter. Sedition by sabotage concerned the GAF only for a few months in 1943. Sedition also included serious cases of avoidance of military service by deception and simulation of illness. However, malingering and self-mutilation were relatively rare and were usually pardoned if homesickness or family troubles, rather than cowardice, occasioned them.

Offences against discipline rarely resulted in capital punishment. Cowardice was a grave offense, but a single dereliction by a soldier, of otherwise good conduct and performance was treated with clemency. Culpable negligence or inattention to guard duty frequently resulted in the death sentence. Serious cases of insubordination by soldiers to superiors were rare. Mistreatment of subordinates by superior officers was heavily punished, but clemency was applied in the case of a young and inexperienced superior who erred in his choice of action out of excess of zeal rather than out of chicanery.

Misappropriation of military property or of government funds could result in the death penalty. Exceptional severity was applied in theft of spirits in large quantity; sale of textiles, food, tobacco and goods in short supply drawn from service stocks for financial gain; and exploitation of shortages suffered by local inhabitants.

The few isolated cases of robbery with violence, which were tried in Russia, Italy and France were punished with death sentences. No mercy was granted and orders were given for the execution of the sentence by hanging on the spot.

By special order, all sentences in rape cases had to be submitted to the Commander-in-Chief, GAF, who demanded unrelenting severity in such offenses. Even with a special plea by a superior officer, for an offender, the

Commander-in-Chief seldom exercised clemency. He often rescinded verdicts that he did not consider sufficiently severe and ordered a retrial. Such stringency resulted in an almost complete cessation of rape cases.

Capital punishment was the general rule for the most serious offenses against comrades, that of theft in camp or barracks. Appeals for mercy were always rejected. 'Anti-social crimes,' carried out under cover of blackouts or of air raids-such as, theft, looting, assaults on women in the dark, breaking into air raid shelters and theft when evacuating property after air attacks-were punished by death. Only a few exceptional cases were pardoned.

Offenses committed by officers were mainly those of unauthorized journeys under the influence of alcohol, often resulting in accidents with serious consequences; journeys without "trip tickets" over long distances and carrying unauthorized passengers, especially women; attacks on women while under the influence of alcohol, which were dealt with extreme severity; misappropriation of military property and employment of soldiers for private purposes, thus withdrawing them from their duties, for which loss of rank was imposed in even minor cases. Loss of rank was also imposed when the offense was repeated, when there was serious and obstinate disobedience, or when the offense was accompanied by fraud, as with the forging of a 'trip ticket.' However, maltreatment of soldiers by officers and resistance by soldiers to officers were infrequent.

As the war progressed, GAF authorities concluded that confinement in idleness for minor offenses was an inadequate deterrent to breaches of discipline and an unsound policy when the nation needed all available manpower to conduct the war. Therefore, the GAF organized Confinement Platoons and Penal Platoons such as those established by the Armed Forces on the island of Crete and elsewhere. The theory of the system was punishment designed to arouse in the prisoner a spirit of pride and comradeship and to assure him that at the expiration of punishment he would be returned to his unit to make a fresh start. The work and living conditions were as severe as a member of the GAF could endure without injury to health, with punishment consisting of rigorous conditions rather than work alone.

Specific procedures were followed in the execution of punishment. Prisoners sentenced to hard labour for not over six days were formed into Confinement Platoons within their own units, under control of a senior officer and supervised by a non-commissioned officer. Prisoners sentenced to hard labour for a period between six days and three months for not too serious offenses were attached to a Penal Platoon. *Bewithrungseinsalz* (Redemption by Combat) was substitute for assignment to a Penal Platoon in more serious cases. Sentences in excess of three months were generally for imprisonment or penal servitude. The confinement and penal platoons were organized by a 1944 order and were similar in purpose and operation. The prisoner had to be certified medically fit for confinement, able to work and free from disease. Officers could not be sent to Penal Platoons for punishment. Members of the GAF civilian retinue could be attached to a Penal Platoon, but members of non-German organizations, such as Croatian legionnaires, could not. Non-commissioned officers and other ranks were sent to separate units, with supervisory personnel always superior in rank to those assigned as prisoners. Those serving disciplinary punishment could be attached to such a unit on determination of their unit commander at the time of his imposition of punishment. Prisoners undergoing punishment for court-martial sentence or for disciplinary purposes were not segregated. Penal Platoons did not work in close proximity to other units.

The total number of Penal Platoons authorized is not known. In 1944, six units were established in the Southeast Air Command, including Bulgaria and one in the Belgium-North France area. The major air command Headquarters referred its eligible prisoners to the nearest Penal Platoon in its area. The chain of command was from the Penal Platoon leader to the GAF Station Commandant, who had disciplinary control over and responsibility for the Penal Platoon in his territory, to the Command Headquarters. A maximum of eighty prisoners was assigned to each Platoon. The commander was preferably a captain or a first Lieutenant with experience in handling troops. He had about five non-commissioned officers and twelve other ranks assigned to his staff, all of whom were specifically designated as superior to the prisoners. All were required to understand their difficult and responsible duty, to exhibit exemplary conduct, to train the prisoners to be useful soldiers by strictness and fairness. In turn, they received recognition by promotion. Guards were armed with machine pistols.

Regulations governing the Penal Platoons were detailed, but were considered as guiding principles, with latitude in the Platoon leader. Work was performed seven days a week, with hours dependent on weather, nature of the work, and amount of punishment considered necessary, but not to exceed fifteen hours in the summer and twelve in the winter. Work projects, assigned in consultation with the GAF Station Commandant, included transportation of ammunition or construction of anti-tank ditches, pillboxes and field fortification. Drill, combined with marching to work, was required one hour a week. Inspirational lectures were given after work. Fraternization between prisoners and guards, other prisoners, soldiers or civilians was forbidden. Mail was restricted and pay withheld. Rations were normal, and supplementary rations, tobacco or alcohol, were permitted only as a special privilege granted by the Platoon leader. Quarters were guarded and locked at all times. Straw bedding was used. Prisoners in the Platoon in the Belgium- North France area, close to the front lines, wore authorized gas masks, helmets, weapons and ammunition, but otherwise even knives and matches were forbidden. For an offense committed-while attached to the Platoon, the term of punishment was lengthened. On release, a short expression of opinion by the Platoon leader was sent to the commander who had imposed the disciplinary punishment. An itemized report on the conduct of a prisoner and a final rating was submitted to the president of the court-martial which had sentenced him. The report could recommend that the prisoner be sent to an establishment for incorrigibles.

Another method of punishment designed to utilize all available manpower and give a prisoner a chance to redeem himself and return to his unit, was assignment to a unit for Redemption by Combat. This was a measure of clemency as well as punishment and also a method of preventing evasion of front-line duty. As it was reserved for more serious offenses and confinement up to three months, it was a means of eliminating undesirables.

In early 1942, the Führer ordered that disgraced soldiers who subsequently distinguished themselves in battle were eligible for pardon and reinstatement and that records of punishment of men killed in action would be expunged. In the fall of 1944, the GAF extended this policy to officers and men, directing that persons under court-martial sentence would be assigned to posts of danger and thus have an opportunity to redeem their honour and to evidence worthiness of pardon by combat with the enemy or undergoing other perils of war. Commanding officers were to transfer eligible men to such units with dispatch. Men who had served a full sentence adjudged by a military or civil court could volunteer for assignment to a unit to retrieve their military honour.

Generally, punishment was carried out within the same branch of service, preferably in the same Wing but in a different Squadron. Those prisoners sent to the front lines were given infantry and flak training and were assigned to units engaged in ground combat until they had redeemed themselves, the transfer being controlled by the Convening Authority. Those men not physically fit for combat were used for especially hazardous duty under difficult conditions in the home territory. Flying personnel were sent by the Penal Section to operational aircrews in the front lines. Specialist personnel reported to their basic organization to redeem themselves in their special spheres by outstanding achievements and perfect behaviour under difficult conditions.

Pardons and opportunity to redeem misconduct by service in Redemption by Combat unit were granted increasingly as the war progressed. In almost all cases, men under sentence showed themselves deserving of final pardon by bravery before the enemy. Within six months of assignment to the unit, the prisoner was considered by the Company Commander for pardon and transfer, as well as for promotion and decoration, on the basis of outstanding achievements in battle, unusual courage and exemplary conduct. Exceptional performance in battle accelerated a pardon. Good conduct was not essential to a change in the punishment record of a prisoner killed or seriously wounded in battle. The application by the commander for pardon of a prisoner could include a recommendation for remission of the balance of punishment, reinstatement of' rank and restriction of information of previous punishment only to the courts and the highest authorities of the Reich. The latter was a preliminary step toward expunging the punishment record on the basis that unusual courage and excellent conduct in combat constituted a guarantee of future good conduct. Personnel, with the unit for six months who were considered unworthy of pardon, were rated again after four months. For these and for prisoners who had committed offenses while with the unit or who had not displayed an honest desire for redemption, consideration was given to whether they should remain with the unit or serve the sentence originally imposed.

Special consideration in German military law was given to persons who were neither German nationals nor members of the GAF and who resided outside the Reich, but who were subject to German courts-martial. Regulations for operational areas provided that foreigners and Germans were subject under military law to trial by court martial for all offenses committed in those areas. In April 1944, all territories outside the borders of the Reich were declared operational areas.

The types of offenses were broad. The Convening Authority was permitted to transfer to the general law courts all cases in Holland, Norway and Denmark not affecting the prosecution of the war; such as, contravention of civil police laws or an offense committed prior to the establishment of a court-martial. A 1940 order provided that if a foreigner or a German civilian committed an offense in any occupied territory against German military personnel or against any authority set up by the Führer, and if the offense were punishable by the laws of the German Reich, that person would be punished as though the offense had been committed within the Reich.

After 1942, the order was used against Parasites of the People. A public enemy was defined as a person who, through the wilful commission of crime disturbs the peace of the community to such an extent that he deserves at least the infliction of penal servitude in the opinion of right-minded people. This was a convenient legal method of liquidating persons inconvenient to the Reich. It was legally possible to inflict penalties, including death, more severe than normally imposed, in cases in which the actions of the accused seriously affected the conduct of the war or the security of the Reich and in which customary punishment was not considered sufficient in the opinion of right-minded people. Prisoners of war as well as civilians were subject to GAF courts-martial. Italian soldiers who would not fight for Germany were treated by courts-martial as any other prisoners of war. By order of the High Command of the Armed, applicable to all the Southeast Command, Italian officers captured while fighting as partisans were to be shot on the spot without a trial. In regard to Russian prisoners of war, officers were dealt with as though they were enlisted men; and regimental courts on the spot could conduct a trial and adjudge the death penalty. If the nature of the punishment adjudged made the prisoner of no further value as a worker, he was turned over to the Security Service. No further report on him was required and he was no longer subject to trial by court martial.

The procedure in trials of civilians or prisoners of war was cursory and summary. On complaint against a foreigner and notice of a suspected offense cognizable by a military court, the Convening Authority ordered an inquiry conducted by an Investigating Officer. The method of preferring charges was discretionary with the Convening Authority. By decree of June, 1944, the trial procedure was abbreviated. If the authorized punishment did not exceed one year's imprisonment or a fine, the Convening Authority had the power to issue judgment in writing without a trial, allowing the accused three days' time to protest and object to the punishment If the punishment authorized for the offense did not exceed five years' imprisonment, the Convening Authority could give judgment and impose sentence himself, in consultation with his legal adviser, but without the two other court members, the accessor. Execution of sentences was effected in the speediest way possible. Sentences for more than three years' imprisonment or death required confirmation by the appropriate military commanders, who could order further investigation or pardon. Punishment not involving death was effected by the Security Service. However, sentences, including death, in cases of insurgence, espionage, and sabotage, could be executed immediately without the approval of anyone delegated by the Air Force Supreme Commander if the confirming authority could not be contacted immediately and military necessity did not permit a delay in the execution.

The Reich Minister of Justice designated special prisons to be placed at the disposal of the Armed Forces for foreigners sentenced to imprisonment. Persons were confined in the German prisons specified as appropriate, on the basis of age (over or under 18 years), gender and nationality. Unless the Convening Authority decided otherwise, transfer to a German prison was obligatory for foreigners in France and Belgium sentenced by military courts to imprisonment or penal servitude of nine months or more; those in Yugoslavia, for six months or more; those in Norway and Denmark, for three months or more.

The Luftwaffe had a disciplinary section at testing centre Leipzig-Schünau, and later at Dedelsdorf in Kreis Gifhorn. The Luftwaffe Field Battalions, for example, were probation units of the Luftwaffe. They served soldiers who were a pity for the infantry battalion, for example, because of their air-force-specific training. In the Luftwaffe field huntsman battalions, for example, they should have the opportunity to prove themselves in front of the enemy within the framework of their own defences. The training for these battalions took place until August 6, 1943 in the air force hunt company z.b.V. 14 at the Luftflotte 4 and was then operated in the Luftwaffe Field Battalion 3 in Olomouc. The battalions fought in the field of air force field divisions in earth combat. In contrast to the military units, they had the advantage of preferring air transport. Their frequent relocation makes it difficult to determine their locations. The battalions had enormous losses in their deployment, mainly due to their deployment as "fire brigade" units and the lack of experience of the officers and sub-officers.[15]

1st Air Force Field Battalion

The 1st Luftwaffe Field Division was an infantry division of the Luftwaffe branch of the Wehrmacht. It was formed using surplus ground crew of the Luftwaffe and served on the Eastern Front from late 1942 to early 1944, at which time it was disbanded. The 1st Luftwaffe Field Division, the first of several such divisions, was formed in mid-1942 in Königsberg in Eastern Prussia. Intended to serve as infantry, its personnel were largely drawn from surplus Luftwaffe ground crew. The division included four battalions of infantry, as well as artillery, engineer, and signal units, although it lacked a regimental staff. After training was completed in December 1942, it was sent to Army Group North as part of the 18th Army although still under Luftwaffe command. Stationed near Novgorod, it was transferred to the Army in December 1943. The division saw little fighting until the withdrawal from Leningrad in January 1944, during which it was involved in heavy defensive battles north of Novgorod.

   The division's personnel were inadequately trained for its role as infantry and due to the heavy losses incurred in the Soviet attacks of the 1943–1944 winter, the division itself was disbanded shortly afterwards. Its surviving personnel were absorbed by the 28th Hunter Division.[16]

2nd Air Force Field Battalion

The unit was formed on November 20, 1942 from the Air Force Field Regiment 3 as a probation group of the Luftwaffe as an Army group. The battalion was destined for soldiers who were not trained for the infantry battalion because of their air force-specific training. The soldiers should have the opportunity to prove themselves in front of the enemy as part of their own military power. This battalion was to be used as a construction battalion for the construction, renewal, and restoration of field flights. The battalion was deployed in Staraja Russia and near Ostrov. In 1943, the regiment was renamed Air Force Rifle Battalion Reserve 2 and was transferred to the Army to form the Parole Infantry Battalion 491.[17]

3b Air Force Field Battalion

The unit was formed on March 9, 1943 as Luftwaffe Field Regiment 2 as an Army group. The battalion was set up at Ilmensee. In 1943, the battalion was renamed the Air Force Rifle Battalion Reserve 2. The battalion was dissolved in the autumn of 1944.[18]

6th Air Force Field Battalion

This battalion was formed in September 1942 in Großborn in Flying Regiment 21. In January 1943, it became part of Tank Destroyer Battalion 6, the Artillery Field Division 6, and the Flak Field Division 6. In November 1943, the unit was supported by the Army.[19]

Air Force Field Battalion, z.b.V. 100

Instituted in December 1942 in Döberitz (formerly as parachute hunter battalion Mattheas) with four companies and moved to southern Russia as an Army group. In February 1943, the battalion was assigned to the Parachute Hunter Regiment 6.[20]

Air Force Field Battalion, z.b.V. Finland

Set up in Finland in 1942 with four companies as an Army group. In October 1943, it was renamed to the *Landwehr* Battalion 1 of the Luftwaffe.[21]

Air Force Hunter Battalions

The Luftwaffe Hunter battalions emerged from the Luftwaffe Field Battalions 1–3, and were probation units of the Luftwaffe. They were soldiers who were not suited for the Infantry Battalion 500 because of their air force-specific training. The soldiers had the opportunity to prove themselves in front. The training for these battalions took place until August 6, 1943 in Luftwaffe Hunter Company z.b.V. 14 at Air Fleet 4 and was then operated in the Luftwaffe Field Battalion 3 in Olomouc. The battalions fought in the field of air force field divisions in combat. In contrast to the military units, they had the advantage of using air transport. Their frequent relocation makes it difficult to determine their exact locations. The battalions had enormous losses in their deployments, mainly due to their deployment as "fire brigade" units and the lack of experience of the officers and sub-officers.[22]

Air Force Hunter Battalion 1

Formed on November 3, 1942 from the II/Luftwaffe Field Regiment 4 (probation group of the Luftwaffe) as an Army group. The battalion was a destination for soldiers who did not fit the Infantry Battalion 500 because of their air force-specific training. The soldiers had the opportunity to prove themselves in front. The battalion was deployed at Illmensee and Ostrow. In 1943, the battalion was renamed Luftwaffe Hunter Battalion z.b.V. 1. The battalion was transferred to the Army and was used for the formation of the Infantry Battalion 491.[23]

Air Force Hunter Battalion 2

Created on November 20, 1942 from the II/Luftwaffe Field Regiment 3 (probation group of the Luftwaffe) as an Army group. The battalion was destined for soldiers who did not fit the infantry battalion 500 because of their air force-specific training. The soldiers had the opportunity to prove themselves in front. In this battalion, low-class soldiers were sufficient as it was to be used as a construction battalion for the construction, renewal, and restoration of airfields. The battalion was deployed in Staraja Russia and near Ostrov. In 1943, the battalion was renamed the Luftwaffe Hunter Battalion z.b.V. 2. The battalion was transferred to the Army and was used for the formation of the Infantry Battalion 491.[24]

Air Force Hunter Battalion 3b

Formed on March 9, 1943 from the III/Luftwaffe Field Regiment 2 as an Army group. The battalion was set up at Ilmensee. In 1943, the battalion was probably renamed the Luftwaffe Hunter Battalion z.b.V. 2. The battalion was dissolved in the autumn of 1944. [25]

Guilt by Association

In addition to the punishment of military members for offenses, the Nazi regime utilized the concept of *Sippenhaft* (guilt by association) as a tool to deter criminal behavior. Sippenhaft was threatened against family members for crimes from treason to desertion and cowardice on the battlefield, but was also utilized against various forms on non-compliance.[1] This concept illustrates the Nazi regimes' policy of embracing their medieval principle of collective punishment against the clan and the blood guilt of a family. Varieties of terror were threatened and inflicted against a wider selection of the population by a range of agencies.[2] This created a climate of fear that was increasingly exploited until the end of the war. Despite opportunities, the Nazis refused to codify *Sippenhaft* until the very last months of the war, and even then, the methods used were largely impractical. Instead, the Nazi leadership preferred to leave its use chiefly in the hands of local authorities, who employed it when they saw fit. Threats to families were issued by a variety of agencies ranging from the rank and file of the party, local administrators, labor service, and the military, based on minimal central direction.

After the German defeat at Stalingrad, elements within the regime began a gradual recourse to the implementation of *Sippenhaft* against German civilians on the home front as well as soldiers in the Wehrmacht. After the July 20, 1944 assassination attempt against Hitler, *Sippenhaft* was widely implemented against families of the conspirators involved.[3]

The use of *Sippenhaft* within the Wehrmacht against individual soldiers was usually determined by the discovery of pre-existing racial or political affiliations, such as the prevalence of leftist or communist political views or racial impurity within the targeted family. The assortment of punishment and threats varied greatly from case to case. Over the entire history of the Third Reich, *Sippenhaft* punishment ranged from the murder or imprisonment (temporary or long term) of various family members, frontline postings—most especially to penal or punishments units—for members of the military to less life-threatening, but nonetheless important consequences such as loss of citizenship, employment, pension, or education opportunities. As argued by Peter Phillips, these lesser manifestations of family punishment had real effects:

> Even a man courageous enough to risk that fate [imprisonment] had to weigh his family's circumstances against his own courageous conscience. Even dismissal without the possibility of finding another job meant ruin for his wife and family as well as for himself. Mere demotion could prevent the children obtaining a proper education.[4]

The nature and extent of these actions were determined by the authority of the agency carrying them out. The only consistent feature was an understanding that the relatives of an identified opponent were being punished for his or her crime. What further clouds the identification of cases of *Sippenhaft* is the suggestion that, in many cases, the family of an offender played more than simply a passive part in the original crime.[5] Often, a socialist or communist husband had an equally passionate or involved spouse, siblings, cousin in-laws. Similarly, if a soldier failed to return to his unit after leave, there was always a chance that his family may have aided his deseration.[6]

On August 17, 1938, the German High Command of the Army revised its Special War Law Orders to allow military courts to punish soldiers convicted of treason (where a death sentence or a prison sentence was imposed) with confiscation of their family's property.[7] However, to encourage an awareness of *Sippenhaft*, in the same year, a booklet was published with the acknowledged assistance of the High Command of the Army, called *Spies, Traitors, and Saboteurs: An Information Pamphlet for the German People*. This pamphlet, written for the German people, indicated forms of treason and the consequences that would result. Along with these descriptions, it implied consequences for the relatives a traitor, saying that they will bring misfortune and ruin on their families.[8] It gave an alleged case where an individual was caught committing treason, in their pay of the enemy upon his execution he left nothing for his family except indescribable misfortune.[9] The booklet, which was explicitly designed for public readership, was most likely read and disseminated among the Wehrmacht, the Gestapo, and Nazi Party functionaries, and it points towards how local commanders were also given greater latitude to punish transgressors. Through such publications, the propensity for *Sippenhaft* as a form of punishment within military justice was created. In 1941, Wehrmacht Judge Gerhard Wulle stated in the military justice journal: "even great guilt can be atoned for by blood."[10]

As with other forms of terror in the Nazi regime, Hitler did play a role in setting the tone of this policy. An example of this comes from Hitler's *Table Talk* conversation of July 1, 1942:

Families which exercise considerable political influence have also a family responsibility. If one member abuses the family political influence, it is quite reasonable that the whole should bear the consequences. They are always, after all, at liberty to dissociate themselves from the family black sheep. In Japan the principal of family accountability is so deeply rooted, that every family exercises influence, whether in the Army or in the political field, considers it a duty, as a matter of course, to prevent any member from doing anything contrary to the national interest. If their efforts are not successful and they feel that the national reputation of the family has been smirched by the erring son, then all the male members commit hari-kari, to clear the family honour.[11]

A similar understanding of the consequences for a family of a traitor was apparent within the German Army, as revealed in the taped conversations of the captured Wehrmacht officer, Lieutenant General Willhelm von Thoma, the former commander of the Africa Corps tank forces. On February 14, 1944, following news of the formation of the League of German Officers, a communist sponsored group of German POWs in Soviet captivity, von Thoma commented:

> I have no doubt that there is such a thing, because all the people are known: Seydlitz, Daniels, Steidle and everyone—whoever knows them must admit it too—not the worst people, but people who dare speak their minds. For you must realize that that is a significant decision, for all those people. Daniels and all those are married, and as our Nazi system—the Himmler system—is no different from the Russian system, it can come about [for] the families [it] will become considerably more difficult.[12]

Thoma's comments indicate the understanding of the threat of *Sippenhaft* within the Army prior to the events of July 20, 1944. After July 20, 1944, *Sippenhaft* reached a greater level of importance and a higher profile as its use as a weapon of fear was obvious in the proliferation of *Sippenhaft* orders and directives.

More overtly than in the civil sphere, in military circles, the Nazi leadership began to threaten the Wehrmacht with *Sippenhaft*. It gave local military commanders, Army courts, and elements of the Nazi Party another means of terrorizing troops into following orders, and represents the broadest attempt in the Third Reich to codify the policy.

While Himmler largely retained control of the actual application of punishment, this did not stop military commanders, military courts, and party functionaries on all levels from attempting to exercise forms of *Sippenhaft*.[13]

Epilogue

In the course of the war, the prerequisites for parole were reduced further and further. After all, a soldier had to be physically and mentally fit for infantry. On April 1, 1941, the Infantry Battalion z.b.V. 500 was set up as the first test unit by *Wehrkreis* Command IX in Meiningen. The members of the battalion wore the white-collar mirrors of the infantry. The basic leadership of December 21, 1940 stated that the service in the probationary group was "honorary service like any other military service. The unit has in no way the character of a criminal group." This idea was to change as the war went on. In the case of promotions, a more stringent standard was applied, since the punishment imposed on probation already represented an award. Orders were not awarded, only the wounded badge and the war memorial badge. Vacation were only permitted after service at the front.

As early as 1941, the battalions 540, 550, 560, and 561 were deployed in the east. They consisted of reinforced grenadier battalions with three armored companies, a machine-gun company, a staff company, a huntsman's train, a parachute train, and a pioneer's train. In the battalions of the Confederation, members of all the Wehrmacht and the Armed Forces Auxiliaries served. Up to the end of the war, about 82,000 soldiers had served in the 500 battalions. At least thirteen officers of the permanent staff were awarded the Knight's Cross.

The units with the number 999 had a completely different background. These units contained the so-called dismissed brethren and prisoners. Homosexuals, traitors, gypsies, and Jews were excluded. First, these men were grouped together in Africa Brigade 999 and deployed in Africa. After the loss of Africa, the battalions were deployed on all front sections. The men were employed in the infantry battalions or other units with the number 999, depending on their physical and mental disposition. The estimates range from 25,000 to 40,000 men who served in the 999 units. There were no soldiers who had come directly from the concentration camp to the 999s.

The records of Strafbattalions were mixed. A combination of criminals, political prisoners, and undisciplined soldiers made up the Strafbattalions. They often required harsh measures to be imposed for unit cohesion to be maintained.

Strafbattalions were often ordered to undertake high-risk missions on the front line, with soldiers being coached to regain their lost honor by fighting.

In addition, Wehrmacht military justice carried out death sentences, mostly by firing squad, against deserters and those were found guilty of undermining the military forces. During the course of the war, German military courts also transferred soldiers who had been sentenced to death to execution sites administered by the Reich Judicial Administration, which were usually prisons. Most convicts were beheaded, some were also hanged. Such executions were considered particularly dishonorable. The executioners of the Reich Ministry of Justice killed between 1,500 and 2,000 members of the Wehrmacht, who had been convicted by military courts during the war. It is not possible to determine the number of victims of summary courts held in the final stage of war; this applies to both soldiers and civilians who were shot or hanged without trial in the last months of war.

The Nazi military justice were not only members of the Wehrmacht and its subordinated entourage, but also prisoners of war. The country inhabitants of the occupied areas in contact German interests and rich German civilians under suspicion of espionage, to partisan, military morale, or high treason were wrapped up in the justice system. The military law consisted essentially of regular Wehrmacht courts and state courts, as well as the end of the war convened "flying courts-martial." Overall, the Nazi military justice system led to about 2.5 million procedures toward members of the armed forces and about 1.5 million soldiers were sentenced. Most went to field prisoners' departments, Wehrmacht prisons, detention centers, portable Army prisons, Wehrmacht detention centers, Wehrmacht prisoners' departments, field punishment camp, and Strafbattalion units.

Many of the Strafbattalion soldiers were hopeful and willing to prove their worth. This raised the combat value of the units they were assigned to. In the face of endless physical and mental hazards on the Eastern and Western Fronts, many soldiers showed high commitment and comradeship. Therefore, unmanaged conduct or politically motivated resistance was rare. In fact, the prospect of grace being actually granted was promised, but many soldiers did not experience their rehabilitation. They fell in the field before the lengthy bureaucratic procedures that concerned them had been completed.

Probation was an essential purpose in these units. Missions led to tougher conditions than in regular units. In the case of failure, the probationer was sent back to the detention center or department of the Wehrmacht from which he had come, and then ended up in the concentration camp or was given to the SS or Gestapo. The eradication of such incorruptible elements was expressly encouraged to promote discipline at the front. The death penalty was also used to maintain the group discipline. Many members of the Strafbattalions went beyond the call of duty and provided honorable service, while some could not rise above the reason they were in the German penal system. The story of Max Rettl is an example of Nazi military justice.

The twenty-year-old Max Rettl was a gunner in the Wehrmacht. He became a victim of the military justice. Rettl was in the 1st Company of the Criminal Investigators Division 4 when, in October 1942, he refused an order at the bridgehead of Kirishi, a difficultly contested strategic crossing over the Wolchov River, 150 kilometers south of St. Petersburg. Prior to this, Rettl had repeatedly violated the discipline of the armed forces. On February 9, 1942, he refused an instruction from his instructor during the training at Solbald Hall in Tyrol. For his punishment, he had to write down several times what he did. Rettl refused the order. Rettl was placed in Innsbruck before the Court of Division Number 188 and sentenced to three months' imprisonment for disobedience. During the interrogation, he had written to his friend the following:

> I have never known my father, he is said to be in Switzerland. My mother I've only seen briefly two times in my life as a child. She lived for a long time in Holland and at the moment lived as the wife of a Dutchman in Cologne. I was raised by my grandmother. I wanted to take my life more often since I do not care at all. It was only with regard to my grandmother, whom I did not want to do with this grief, that I omitted.

In an assessment by his service, this presentation is somewhat confirmed. It stated:

> Rett's past, his appearance, and his statements convey the impression of morbid feelings of inferiority, psychological depression, and great weariness. Angry turmoil occasionally caused him to be inscrutable. His mental capacity seems to be questionable. On the basis of this assessment, the punishment of two disciplinary criminal records from the previous year was also relatively small at three months; a release from the military force for reasons of health, however, did not appear to be a question.

It was not long before Max Rettl refused obedience after his release from the prison. In a leadership report in May, his captain wrote: "He tends strongly to the resistance and the lack of command. His naughty, challenging nature, and the shortcomings noted above, are a threat to male husbandry within the troops." On June 11, 1942, a court sentenced him to a two-year prison term.

After the verdict, Max Rettl was sent to the Anklam military center. From there, he came to the Field Prisoners Section 4. In this section, the condemned soldiers were mostly used for mine clearance or the removal of corpses; work, which often had to be carried out under enemy fire. The survival chances were correspondingly low, but Max Rettl did not die by enemy fire. After he had refused an order, now at the front, the sentence of the Wehrmacht justice was death. On October 16, 1942, Max was executed between 5 a.m. and 6 a.m. for disobedience.

Military Organizations of the Third Reich

(First published in English in the Jewish Virtual Library. Republished with permission of the American-Israeli Cooperative Enterprise)

Oberkommando der Wehrmacht

The *Oberkommando der Wehrmacht* or OKW (Wehrmacht High Command, Armed Forces High Command) was part of the command structure of the German armed forces during World War II. In theory, it served as the military general staff for Adolf Hitler's Third Reich, coordinating the efforts of the German Army (*Heer*), Navy (Kriegsmarine), and Air Force (*Luftwaffe*). In theory, the OKW was only Hitler's military office, was charged with translating Hitler's ideas into military orders, and had little real control over the Army, Navy, and the Air Force High Commands. However, as the war progressed, the OKW found itself exercising increasing amounts of direct command authority over military units, particularly in the West. This created a situation such that, by 1942, the OKW was the *de facto* command of Western forces while the OKH (the Army High Command) exercised *de facto* command of the Russian front.

The OKW had been formed in 1938 following the Blomberg-Fritsch Affair, which led to the dismissal of Werner von Blomberg and the dissolution of the Reich's Ministry of War.

There was a rivalry between OKW and the OKH. As most German operations during World War II were Army operations (with air support), the Army High Command demanded the control over the German military forces. Hitler decided against the OKH and in favor of the OKW.

During the war, more and more influence moved from the OKH to the OKW. Norway was the first OKW war theatre. More and more theatres came under complete control of the OKW. Finally, only the Russian front stayed under control of the Army High Command.

The OKW ran military operations on the Western Front, Africa, and in Italy. In the West, operations were further split between the OKW and the Supreme Commander West, who was *Generalfeldmarschall* Gerd von Rundstedt (later it was Field Marshal Günther von Kluge).

There was even more fragmentation as naval and air operations had their own commands (*Oberkommando der Marine* (OKM) and *Oberkommando der Luftwaffe* (OKL, Hermann Göring)), which, while theoretically subordinate, were largely independent from OKW or the OBW.

The OKW was headed for the entire war by Wilhelm Keitel and reported directly to Hitler, from whom most operational orders actually originated as he had made himself Supreme Commander of the Armed Forces and head of the OKH.

Alfred Jodl was Keitel's Chief of Operation Staff, while Walter Warlimont was Deputy Chief. The OKW was indicted, but acquitted of charges during the Nuremberg trials of being a criminal organization. Keitel and Jodl, however, were convicted and sentenced to death by hanging.

Oberkommando des Heeres

The *Oberkommando des Heeres* (OKH) was Germany's Army High Command. In theory, the OKW commanded the OKH. However, the *de facto* situation after 1941 was that the OKW directly commanded operations on the Western Front, while the OKH commanded the Russian front.

The German *Heer* was formed in May 1935. It was formed after the passing of the "Law for the Reconstruction of the National Defense Forces." This law brought back into existence a free standing German Army, Navy, and Air Force, something that had been essentially banned after the end of World War I.

With the end of World War I and the signing of the Treaty of Versailles in 1919, the Weimar Republic—the successor to Imperial Germany—was allowed only a small defensive military force known as the Reichswehr. The Reichswehr's size and composition was strictly controlled by the Allies in the hope that by restricting its constitution, they could prevent future German military aggression. The Reichswehr consisted of 100,000 men divided between a small standing army, the Reichsheer, and a small defensive navy, the Reichsmarine.

In 1933, the National Socialist German Workers Party (NSDAP) came to power and the infamous Third Reich was born. Two years later, in 1935, the Treaty of Versailles was renounced and the Reichswehr became the Wehrmacht. The newly formed Wehrmacht would still consist of an army and a navy—the renamed *Heer* and Kriegsmarine—but a new air force was born as well: the *Luftwaffe*.

The *Heer* initially consisted of twenty-one divisional-sized units and three Army Groups to control them, as well as numerous smaller formations.

Between 1935 and 1945, this force grew to consist of hundreds of divisions, dozens of Army Groups, and thousands of smaller supporting units. Between 1939 and 1945, close to 13 million served in the *Heer*. Over 1.6 million were killed and over 4.1 million were wounded. Of the 7,361 men awarded the initial grade of the highest German combat honor of WWII, the Knights Cross, 4,777 were from the *Heer*, making up 65 percent of the total awarded.

Between 1939 and 1945, the *Heer* bore the majority of six years' worth of fierce combat, some of which was so fierce—as on the Eastern Front—humankind will likely never again see such fighting. Although not immune to the overtones of politics and the occasional brush with questionable actions, the vast majority of German *Heer* units served with great distinction across many thousands of miles of battlefields.

The *Heer* was defeated with the German capitulation on May 8, 1945, although some units continued to fight for a few days longer in fits of sporadic resistance, mainly against the Soviets in the East. The Allied Control Council passed a law formally dissolving the Wehrmacht on August 20, 1946, the official "death" date of the German *Heer*.

There also existed the *Oberkommando der Marine* (OKM) and the *Oberkommando der Luftwaffe* (OKL) for the navy and the air force respectively. These were theoretically subordinate to the OKW, but in actuality, they acted quite independently.

The Army commanders of the Wehrmacht were as follows:

1935 to 1938: Generaloberst Werner von Fritsch.
1938 to December 19, 1941: Generalfeldmarschall Walther von Brauchitsch.
December 19, 1941 to April 30, 1945: Führer and Reichskanzler Adolf Hitler.
April 30, 1945 to May 8, 1945: Generalfeldmarschall Ferdinand Schörner.

Following German tradition, the Commander in Chief of the Army did not plan operations. This task was left to the General Staff, so actually the most important man in the Army (and the Navy, but less so in the Luftwaffe, which was commanded by Hermann Göring) was the chief of the general staff. It should be noted that the *Heer* always had been the leading factor in planning campaigns. Thus, there was no such thing as combined planning of the different services. The position of OKW, which was by definition superior to the OKH, was not intended for that, nor did it have the resources to do so.

Later in the war, the OKH became responsible for fewer and fewer tasks. For example, the invasion of Norway was entirely planned outside the OKH. During World War II, the Chiefs of General Staff were as follows:

September 1, 1938 to September 24, 1942: Generaloberst Franz Halder.
September 24, 1942 to June 10, 1944: Generaloberst Kurt Zeitzler.

June 10, 1944 to July 21, 1944: Generalleutnant Adolf Heusinger.
July 21, 1944 to March 28: 1945, Generaloberst Heinz Guderian.
April 1, 1945 to April 30, 1945: General der Infanterie Hans Krebs.

When Hitler took command of the Army on December 13, 1941, the importance of the General Staff of the Army decreased and Hitler continued to become more and more responsible for operational planning.

Oberkommando der Marine

The *Oberkommando der Marine* (or OKM for short) was Germany's Naval High Command until 1945. The German Kriegsmarine, or navy, was formed in May 1935. It was formed after the passing of the "Law for the Reconstruction of the National Defense Forces." This law brought back into existence a free-standing German Army, Navy, and Air Force, something that had been essentially banned after the end of World War I.

The Kriegsmarine can be said to have consisted of three main components between 1935 and 1945, individual naval vessels, naval formations consisting of specific types of ships, and a wide variety of ground-based units. From these three main components, the Kriegsmarine fielded thousands of ships and hundreds of naval formations and ground units. Between 1939 and 1945, over 1.5 million served in the Kriegsmarine. Over 65,000 were killed, over 105,000 went missing and over 21,000 were wounded. Of the 7361 men awarded the initial grade of the highest German combat honor of WWII, the Knights Cross, 318 were from the Kriegsmarine, making up 4 percent of the total awarded.

Of all the branches of the Wehrmacht, the Kriegsmarine was the most underappreciated. It fought against superior numbers on almost every front with a force greatly limited by a lack of effective coordination and a harsh misunderstanding from within the German High Command (OKW). Although Allied air and naval power largely destroyed the entire German High Seas Fleet and U-boat force, the smaller and auxiliary vessels of the Kriegsmarine continued to serve effectively until the last hours of WWII. These vessels saw service along thousands of miles of coast in every theatre of war and provided an important link in the backbone of the Wehrmacht.

German naval ground units also provided a critical service during WWII, manning massive guns along the Atlantic Wall in the west and naval flak and artillery units all across Western and Eastern Europe. There were also countless naval infantry, engineer, and communications units as well. In the last months of WWII, most all of the naval ground units were involved directly in fighting of some form or another, some naval units even took part in the Battle for Berlin in 1945.

The Kriegsmarine was officially disbanded in August 1946 by the Allied Control Commission, although many smaller Kriegsmarine ships survived on active service, now under Allied control, as a part of the German contingent to clear the oceans and seas of mines sown by Axis and Allies alike.

The commanders of the Kriegsmarine were as follows:

September 24, 1928 to January 30, 1943: Grossadmiral Erich Raeder.
January 30, 1943 to May 1, 1945: Grossadmiral Karl Dönitz.
May 1, 1945 to May 8, 1945: Generaladmiral Hans-Georg von Friedeburg (after Dönitz becomes Head of State when Hitler commits suicide).

The Luftwaffe

The German Luftwaffe, or air force, was formed in May 1935. It was formed after the passing of the "Law for the Reconstruction of the National Defense Forces." This law brought back into existence a free-standing German Army, Navy, and Air Force, something that had been essentially banned after the end of World War I.

Although officially announced in 1935, the Luftwaffe had existed in one form or another practically since the day the treaty banning it had been signed. Initially, there were *Freikorps* (Free Regiments) air units, then later glider and sail plane formations tasked with finding ways around the rigid restrictions of Versailles, a secret training base in the Soviet Union, and various cover organizations for the initial forming of the new German air force.

The Luftwaffe consisted of air units that made up the majority of the German Air Force, as well as parachute units, Luftwaffe field divisions, the elite Herman Göring ground formations, thousands of smaller anti-aircraft, engineer, communications and security units, and a fair number of Luftwaffe naval vessels and formations as well. Between 1939 and 1945, over 3.4 million served in the Luftwaffe. Over 165,000 were killed, over 155,000 went missing, and over 192,000 were wounded. Of the 7361 men awarded the initial grade of the highest German combat honor of WWII, the Knights Cross, 1,785 were from the Luftwaffe, making up 24 percent of the total awarded.

Initially, the Luftwaffe ruled the skies, but thereafter fought an increasingly futile war of attrition, which, when combined with vital mistakes in aircraft production and utilization, was its death knoll. In the face of this, the Luftwaffe produced the most successful air aces of all time. As well, the feats of the parachute in the first airborne operations in history are as heroic as they are tragic. German parachutes suffered appalling losses on Crete and essentially never saw large-scale airborne operations again. Some Luftwaffe ground units fought well during WWII, such as certain Luftwaffe field divisions and the elite Hermann Göring formations, while other units simply served.

Ultimately, the structure of the Luftwaffe was a grand reflection of its commander, Hermann Göring. He strove more so than any other branch to create a personal army with responsibilities as far reaching as possible. It was partly due to this that the Wehrmacht was ultimately defeated. With strain on resources and manpower, such political maneuvering was far reaching.

The Luftwaffe was officially disbanded in August 1946 by the Allied Control Commission.

The SA

The *Sturmabteilung* (SA, German for "Storm Division" and is usually translated as stormtroops or stormtroopers) functioned as a paramilitary organization of the NSDAP—the German Nazi party. It played a key role in Adolf Hitler's rise to power in the 1930s. SA men were often known as brown shirts from the color of their uniform and to distinguish them from the SS who were known as black shirts.

The SA was also the first Nazi paramilitary group to develop pseudo-military titles for bestowal upon its members. The SA ranks would be adopted by several other Nazi Party groups, chief among them the SS.

The SS

The *Schutzstaffel* (Protective Squadron), or SS, was a large paramilitary organization that belonged to the Nazi party. The SS was led by Heinrich Himmler from 1929 until it was disbanded in 1945 with the defeat of Germany in World War II. The Nazis regarded the SS as an elite unit, a Party's "praetorian guard," with all SS personnel selected on racial and ideological grounds. The SS was distinguished from the German military, Nazi Party, and German state officials by their own SS ranks, SS unit insignia, and SS uniforms.

The most recognizable branches of the SS, later charged with war crimes and crimes against humanity, were the departments that comprised the *Reichssicherheitshauptamt* (RSHA, Reich Security Head Office), *Sicherheitsdienst* (SD, Security Service), *Einsatzgruppen* (Special Mission Groups), the concentration camp service known as the SS *Totenkopfverbände* (SS-TV, Death's Head Formations), and the *Gestapo* (Secret State Police).

The SS fighting units, called the Waffen SS, were to evolve into highly skilled and effective soldiers, in many cases superior in these respects to the German Army—the *Heer*.

Of all the German military organizations of WWII, the Waffen SS is one of the most widely studied. This is in part because of the combat record of the Waffen

SS and the elite status of many of its units, and in part because of the brutality attributed to some of its formations and the war crimes some of its members were responsible for. By the end of WWII, over 1 million soldiers in thirty-eight divisions would serve in the Waffen SS, including over 200,000 conscripts.

The Waffen SS was a part of the German *Schutzstaffel* or SS, which saw its rise during the late 1920s and early 1930s. The SS was the single most powerful political organization within the Third Reich and consisted of the *Allgemeine* SS, *Totenkopfverbände*, and the Waffen SS.

The Waffen SS was born in 1933 after Hitler came to power when Political Readiness Detachments were formed under the control of the SS. These units were organized along military lines and were intended to help counter Communist strikes. On October 1, 1934, these units became the SS Special Use Troops. Initially, the *Verfügungstruppen* consisted of small detachments located in larger German cities, but by 1935, they were organized into battalions, and in 1936, into regiments. In 1936, two main SS-V standards existed, *Deutschland* and *Germania*. The *Leibstandarte Adolf Hitler* also existed at this time and although related it was considered somewhat outside the purview of the SS-V.

In 1938, the SS *Verfügungstruppen* took part in the occupation of Austria and Czechoslovakia alongside the Wehrmacht. After the occupation of Austria, a third Standard was formed known as *Der Führer*. In 1939, the SS *Verfügungstruppen* consisted of three standards, the *Leibstandarte Adolf Hitler*, and a number of smaller service and support units. For the campaign in Poland in 1939, all SS-V units were organized into the SS *Verfügungstruppe* Division and placed under the operational command of the Wehrmacht. The SS *Verfügungstruppe* Division also fought in the Western Campaign 1940. After the conclusion of the Western Campaign, the SS *Verfügungstruppen* was renamed and became the Waffen SS.

Waffen SS

Although the Waffen SS is frequently considered an elite organization, not all of its units were actually elite. Some Waffen SS units formed after 1943 had less than ideal combat records. This was in part due to the fact that the number of volunteers eligible for service in the Waffen SS shrank as the war continued, while the need for replacements increased. The number of conscripts taken into the Waffen SS of lesser quality or questionable ability had a direct impact on combat effectiveness.

After WWII ended, the Waffen SS was condemned at the Nuremberg Trials as a criminal organization. This was in part due to a series of high-profile atrocities and because of their connection to the SS and NSDAP. Only those who were conscripted into the Waffen SS were exempt from the Nuremberg declaration. As a result, Waffen SS veterans were generally denied the rights and benefits granted to other WWII German veterans. Waffen SS POWs were often held in strict confinement and were treated harshly by the Soviets. Many foreign volunteers that served in the Waffen SS were also treated severely by their national governments. In the years since WWII, there have been attempts to rehabilitate the image and legality of Waffen SS veterans, both through legislation and in published works by former officers like Paul Hausser (*Soldaten wie andere auch*—Soldiers Like Any Other). To this day, the stigma on veterans from the Waffen SS remains. After the war, the judges of Nuremberg Trials declared the entirety of the SS as a criminal organization, among others because of its implementation of racial policies of genocide.

The *Volkssturm*

The *Volkssturm*, literally translated as People's Storm in the meaning of National Storm, was a German national militia of the last months of the Nazi regime. It was founded on Adolf Hitler's orders on October 18, 1944 and effectively conscripted all males between the ages of sixteen to sixty (who did not already serve in some military unit) as part of the German Home Guard.

National Socialist Motor Corps

The National Socialist Motor Corps (NSKK), also known as the National Socialist Drivers Corps, was a paramilitary organization of the Nazi Party that existed from 1931 to 1945. The group was a successor organization to the older National Socialist Automobile Corps, which had existed since the beginning of 1930.

The National Socialist Motor Corps was the smallest of the Nazi Party organizations and had originally been formed as a motorized corps of the *Sturmabteilung* (SA). In 1934, the group had a membership of approximately 10,000 and was separated from the SA to become an independent organization. This action may have saved the NSKK from extinction, as shortly thereafter, the SA suffered a major purge during the Night of the Long Knives.

The primary aim of the NSKK was to educate its members in motoring skills. They were mainly trained in the operation and maintenance of high-performance motorcycles and automobiles. In the mid-1930s, the NSKK also served as a roadside assistance group, comparable to the modern-day American Automobile Association or the British Automobile Association.

Membership in the NSKK did not require any knowledge of automobiles and the group was known to accept persons for membership without drivers' licenses. It was thought that training in the NSKK would make up for any previous lack of knowledge. The NSKK did, however, adhere to racial doctrine and screened its members for Aryan qualities. The NSKK was also a paramilitary organization with its own system of paramilitary ranks.

With the outbreak of World War II in 1939, the National Socialist Motor Corps became a target of the Wehrmacht for recruitment, since NSKK members possessed knowledge of motorized transport, whereas the bulk of the Wehrmacht relied on horses. Most NSKK members thereafter joined the regular military, serving in the transport corps of the various service branches.

In 1945, the NSKK was disbanded and the group was declared a "condemned organization" at the Nuremberg Trials (although not a criminal one). This was due in part to the NSKK's origins in the SA and its doctrine of racial superiority required from its members.

National Socialist Flyers Corps

The National Socialist Flyers Corps was a paramilitary organization of the Nazi Party that was founded in the early 1930s during the years when a German Air Force was forbidden by the Treaty of Versailles. The organization was based closely on the organization of the *Sturmabteilung* (SA) and maintained a system of paramilitary ranks closely associated with the SA.

During the early years of its existence, the NSFK conducted military aviation training in gliders and private airplanes. When Nazi Germany formed the Luftwaffe, many NSFK members transferred. As all such prior NSFK members were also Nazi Party members, this gave the new Luftwaffe a strong Nazi ideological base in contrast to the other branches of the German military, who were comprised of "Old Guard" officers from the German aristocracy.

The National Socialist Flyers Corps continued to exist after the Luftwaffe was founded, but to a much smaller degree. During World War II, the NSFK mainly performed air defense duties such as reserve anti-aircraft service.

German Army Group North: As of October 13, 1944

(Created by George Nafziger. First published in English online at the U.S. Army Combined Arms Research Library) (The database is open source)

Order of Battle

Army Group Command Reserve
  III SS Corps:
    SS Tank Grenadier Division Northland
      1/2/3/23rd SS Tank Grenadier Regiment Norway
      1/2/3/24th SS Tank Grenadier Regiment Denmark
        11th SS Tank Battalion (4 companies)
        11th SS Reconnaissance Battalion (5 companies)
      1/2/4/11th SS Artillery Regiment
        11th SS Motorcycle Battalion (5 companies)
        11th SS Anti-tank Battalion (3 companies)
        11th SS Storm Protection Battalion (3-batteries)
        11th SS Flak Battalion (4-batteries)
        11th SS Pioneer Battalion (3 companies)
        11th SS Armoured Signal Battalion (2 companies)
          11th SS Division Service Units
    SS Tank Grenadier Division Nederland
      1/2/48th SS Freiwilligen Tank Grenadier Regiment General Seyffardt
      1/2/49th SS Freiwilligen Tank Grenadier Regiment De Ruiter
        54th Reconnaissance Company
        54th Anti-tank Battalion (2 companies)
      1/2/3/54th Artillery Regiment
        54th Pioneer Battalion
          54th Signals Company
        54th Field Replacement Battalion
          Supply Troop
    Field Training Division Norway (no artillery or other support units)
      1/2/3/639th Grenadier (Field Training) Regiment
      1/2/3/640th Grenadier (Field Training) Regiment
18th Army
  I Army Corps:
    11th Infantry Division
      1/2/2nd Grenadier Regiment

1/2/23rd Grenadier Regiment
1/2/44th Grenadier Regiment
1/2/3/11th Artillery Regiment
1/47th Artillery Regiment
    11th Division Fusilier (anti-aircraft) Battalion
    11th Pioneer Battalion
    11th Signals Battalion
        11th Division Service Units
126th Infantry Division
    1/2/422nd Grenadier Regiment
    1/2/424th Grenadier Regiment
    1/2/426th Grenadier Regiment
    126th Fusilier Battalion
    1/2/3/4/126th Artillery Regiment
    125th Pioneer Battalion
    125th Signals Battalion
        125th Division Service Units
X Army Corps
    30th Infantry Division
    1/2/6th Grenadier Regiment
    1/2/26th Fusilier Regiment
    1/2/46th Grenadier Regiment
    1/2/3/30th Artillery Regiment
    1/66th Artillery Regiment
        30th Divisional Fusilier Battalion
        30th Pioneer Battalion
        30th Signals Battalion
            30th Division Service Units
    14th Tank Division
    1/2/103rd Tank Grenadier Regiment
    1/2/108th Tank Grenadier Regiment
        14th Tank Reconnaissance Battalion
    1/2/3/36th Tank Regiment
    1/2/3/4th Artillery Regiment
        4th Anti-tank Battalion
        13th Tank Pioneer Battalion
        4th Tank Signals Battalion
            4th Division Support units
XXXIX Tank Corps
    61st Infantry Division
    1/2/151st Grenadier Regiment
    1/2/162nd Grenadier Regiment
    1/2/176th Grenadier Regiment
        61st Divisional Fusilier Battalion
    1/2/3/4/161st Artillery Regiment
        161st Pioneer Battalion 161st Signals Battalion
            161st Division Service Units
    225th Infantry Division
    1/2/333rd Grenadier Regiment
    1/2/376th Grenadier Regiment
    1/2/377th Grenadier Regiment
    1/2/3/4/225th Artillery Regiment
        225th Fusilier Battalion
        225th Pioneer Battalion
        225th Signals Battalion
            225th Division Support Unit
    4th Tank Division

1/2/12th Tank Grenadier Regiment
1/2/33rd Tank Grenadier Regiment
   4th Tank Reconnaissance Battalion
   49th Anti-tank Battalion
1/35th Tank Regiment
1/2/3/103rd Artillery Regiment
   290th Army Flak Battalion
      79th Division Service Units
   79th Supply Battalion
12th Tank Division
1/2/5th Tank Grenadier Regiment
1/2/25th Tank Grenadier Regiment
1/12th Tank Regiment
   22nd Tank Reconnaissance Battalion (5 companies)
1/2/3/2nd Artillery Regiment
   303rd Army Flak Battalion
   32nd Pioneer Battalion
   2nd Signals Battalion
      2nd Division Support Units
16th Army Reserve
  24th Infantry Division
   1/2/31st Infantry Regiment
   1/2/32nd Infantry Regiment
   1/2/102nd Infantry Regiment
      24th Division Fusilier (anti-aircraft) Battalion
   1/2/3/24th Artillery Regiment
   1/60th Artillery Regiment
      24th Pioneer Battalion
      24th Signals Battalion
      24th Division Service Units
  31st Infantry Division
   1/3/12th Grenadier Regiment
   1/3/17th Grenadier Regiment
   1/2/82nd Grenadier Regiment
      31st Divisional Fusilier (anti-aircraft) Battalion
   1/2/3/31st Artillery Regiment
   1/67th Artillery Regiment
      31st Pioneer Battalion
      31st Signals Battalion
      31st Division Service Units
  87th Infantry Division
   1/2/173rd Grenadier Regiment
   1/2/185th Grenadier Regiment
   1/2/187th Grenadier Regiment
      87th Fusilier Battalion
   1/2/3/4/187th Artillery Regiment
      187th Pioneer Battalion
      187th Signals Battalion
      187th Division Service Units
  132nd Infantry Division
   1/2/436th Grenadier Regiment
   1/2/437th Grenadier Regiment
   1/2/438th Grenadier Regiment
      132nd Divisional Fusilier Battalion
   1/2/3/4/132nd Artillery Regiment
      132nd Pioneer Battalion
      132nd Signals Battalion

132nd Division Service Units
263rd Infantry Division
　1/463rd Grenadier Regiment
　1/2/483rd Grenadier Regiment
　1/485th Grenadier Regiment
　　263rd Division Fusilier Battalion
　1/2/3/4/263rd Artillery Regiment
　　263rd Pioneer Battalion
　　263rd Signals Battalion
　　　263rd Division Support Unit
300th z.b.V. Infantry Division
　　　　Staff/13th Luftwaffe Field Division
　1/2/3/2nd Estonian Border Protection Regiment (Police)
　1/2/3/4th Estonian Border Protection Regiment (Police)
　1/2/3/5th Estonian Border Protection Regiment (Police)
　1/2/3/6th Estonian Border Protection Regiment (Police)
II Army Corps
227th Infantry Division
　1/2/338th Grenadier Regiment
　1/2/366th Grenadier Regiment
　1/2/412th Grenadier Battalion
　　227th Divisional Fusilier (anti-aircraft) Battalion
　1/2/3/4/227th Artillery Regiment
　　227th Pioneer Battalion
　　227th Signals Battalion
　　　227th Division Support Units
563rd Infantry Division
　3 Infantry Regiments (2 battalions)
　　563rd Divisional Fusilier Battalion
　1/2/3/4/563rd Artillery Regiment
　　563rd Pioneer Battalion
　　563rd Signals Battalion
　　　563rd Division Support Units
XXXXIII Army Corps
23rd Infantry Division
　1/2/67th Grenadier Regiment
　1/2/68th Grenadier Regiment
　1/2/3/4/23rd Artillery Regiment
　　23rd Pioneer Battalion
　　23rd Signals Battalion
　　　23rd Division Support Units
83rd Infantry Division
　1/2/251st Grenadier Regiment
　1/2/257th Grenadier Regiment
　　83rd Fusilier Battalion
　1/2/3/4/183rd Artillery Regiment
　　183rd Pioneer Battalion
　　183rd Signals Battalion
　　　183rd Division Service Units
218th Infantry Division
　1/2/323rd Grenadier Regiment
　1/2/386th Grenadier Regiment
　1/2/397th Grenadier Regiment
　　218th Divisional Fusilier Battalion
　1/2/3/4/218th Artillery Regiment
　　218th Pioneer Battalion
　　218th Signals Battalion

218th Division Support Units
12th Luftwaffe Field Division
  1/2/3/23rd Luftwaffe Hunter Regiment
  1/2/3/24th Luftwaffe Hunter Regiment
  1/2/3/4/12th Luftwaffe Artillery Regiment
    Anti-tank Battalion, 12th Luftwaffe Field Division
  12th Luftwaffe Pioneer Battalion
    Bicycle Company
    Signals Company
    Support Troops
207th Security Division
  1/2/3/94th Security Regiment
  2/9th Police Battalion
  207th Eastern Cavalry Battalion
    207th Tank Company
  207th Artillery Battalion
  821st Divisional Signals Battalion
    374th Division Support Units
390th Security Division
L Army Corps
  290th Infantry Division
    1/2/501st Infantry Regiment
    1/2/502nd Infantry Regiment
    290th Divisional Fusilier Battalion
    1/2/4/290th Artillery Regiment
    290th Pioneer Battalion
    290th Signals Battalion
      290th Divisional Support Units
  281st Security Division
    1/2/3/368th Grenadier Regiment
    1/2/3/107th Security Regiment
    3/9th Police Regiment
      281st East Cavalry Battalion (equipped with captured armour)
      822nd Signals Battalion
      368th Division Support Unit
Battle Group Kleffel
  19th SS Grenadier Division
    1/2/42nd Waffen SS Grenadier Regiment
    1/2/43rd Waffen SS Grenadier Regiment
    1/2/44th Waffen SS Grenadier Regiment
    19th SS Fusilier Battalion
    19th SS Flak Battalion (3 batteries)
    19th SS Anti-tank Battalion (initially only 1 company)
    1/2/3/19th SS Volunteer Artillery Regiment
    19th SS Volunteer Pioneer Battalion (3 companies)
    19th SS Signals Battalion (2 companies)
      19th SS Division Support Units
Army Group Grasser
  XXXVIII Army Corps
    32nd Infantry Division
      1/2/4th Grenadier Regiment
      1/2/94th Grenadier Regiment
      1/3/96th Grenadier Regiment
      1/2/3/32nd Artillery Regiment
      1/68th Artillery Regiment
      2nd Pioneer Battalion
      32nd Signals Battalion

32nd Division Service Units
81st Infantry Division
  1/2/161st Grenadier Regiment
  1/2/174th Grenadier Regiment
  1/2/189th Grenadier Regiment
    61st Divisional Fusilier Battalion
  1/2/3/4/181st Artillery Regiment
    181st Pioneer Battalion
    181st Signals Battalion
    181st Division Service Units
121st Infantry Division
  1/2/405th Grenadier Regiment
  1/2/407th Grenadier Regiment
  1/2/408th Grenadier Regiment
  1/2/3/4/121st Artillery Regiment
    121st Division Fusilier Battalion
    121st Pioneer Battalion
    121st Signals Battalion
    121st Division Service Units
122nd Infantry Division
  1/2/409th Infantry Regiment
  1/2/410th Infantry Regiment
  1/2/411th Infantry Regiment
  1/2/3/4/122nd Artillery Regiment
    122nd Division Fusilier Battalion
    122nd Pioneer Battalion
    122nd Signals Battalion
    122nd Divisional Service Units
329th Infantry Division
  1/2/551st Grenadier Regiment
  1/2/552nd Grenadier Regiment
  1/2/42nd Hunter Regiment (Light)
  1/2/4/329th Artillery Regiment
    329th Division Fusilier Battalion
    329th Pioneer Battalion
    329th Signals Battalion
    329th Division Support Units
201st Security Division
21st Luftwaffe Field Division
  1/2/3/31st Luftwaffe Hunter Regiment
  1/2/3/32nd Luftwaffe Hunter Regiment
  1/2/3/4/21st Luftwaffe Artillery Regiment
    Anti-tank Battalion, 21st Luftwaffe Field Division
    21st Luftwaffe Pioneer Battalion
    Reconnaissance Company, 21st Luftwaffe Field Division
      Signals Company, 21st Luftwaffe Field Division
      Supply Troop, 21st Luftwaffe Field Division

German Army Group Centre: As of April 22, 1942

(Created by George Nafziger. First published in English online at the U.S. Army Combined Arms Research Library) (The database is open source)

Order of Battle

6th Tank Division
7th Tank Division
2nd Tank Army
  XXXXVII (motorized) Corps
    10th (motorized) Division (only part present)
      1/2/3/20th (motorized) Infantry Regiment
      1/2/3/41st (motorized) Infantry Regiment
        10th Anti-tank Battalion
        10th Motorcycle Battalion
      1/2/3/4/10th Artillery Regiment
        10th Signals Battalion
        10th Pioneer Battalion
          10th Division Support Units
    17th Tank Division
    1/39th Armoured Regiment
    17th Tank Grenadier Brigade
      1/2/3/40th Tank Grenadier Regiment
      1/2/3/63rd Tank Grenadier Regiment
        27th Anti-tank Battalion
        17th Motorcycle Battalion
      1/2/3/27th Artillery Regiment
        27th Signals Battalion
        27th Pioneer Battalion
          27th Division Support Units
    18th Tank Division
    1/18th Armoured Regiment
    18th Tank Grenadier Brigade
      1/2/3/52nd Tank Grenadier Regiment
      1/2/3/101st Tank Grenadier Regiment
        88th Anti-tank Battalion
        18th Motorcycle Battalion
      1/2/3/88th Artillery Regiment

88th Signals Battalion
98th Pioneer Battalion
  88th Division Support Units
29th (motorized) Division
208th Division (only 2/3rds of division present)
1/2/3/309th Infantry Regiment
1/2/3/337th Infantry Regiment
1/2/3/338th Infantry Regiment
208th Anti-tank Battalion
208th Bicycle Battalion
1/2/3/4/208th Artillery Regiment
208th Pioneer Battalion
208th Signals Battalion
  208th Division Support Units
211th Division (only 2/3rds of division present)
1/2/3/306th Infantry Regiment
1/2/3/317th Infantry Regiment
1/2/3/365th Infantry Regiment
211th Schnell Battalion
1/2/3/211th Artillery Regiment
4/220th Artillery Battalion
211th Pioneer Battalion
211th Signals Battalion
  211th Division Support Units
216th Division (only 1/3rd of division present)
1/2/3/384th Infantry Regiment
1/2/3/396th Infantry Regiment
216th Schnell Battalion
1/2/3/4/216th Artillery Regiment
216th Pioneer Battalion
216th Signals Battalion
  216th Division Support Units
339th Division
1/2/3/691st Infantry Regiment
1/2/3/692nd Infantry Regiment
1/2/3/693rd Infantry Regiment
339th Schnell Battalion
339th Artillery Battalion
339th Pioneer Battalion
339th Signals Battalion
  339th Division Support Units
Eberbach Battle Group
4th Tank Division
1/35th Armoured Regiment
4th Tank Grenadier Brigade
1/2/3/12th Tank Grenadier Regiment
1/2/3/33rd Tank Grenadier Regiment
49th Anti-tank Battalion
34th Motorcycle Battalion
1/2/3/103rd Artillery Regiment
79th Signals Battalion
79th Pioneer Battalion
  79th Division Support Units
10th (motorized) Division (only part present)
LIII Corps
56th Division (small portion detached)
1/2/3/171st Infantry Regiment

1/2/3/192nd Infantry Regiment
1/2/3/234th Infantry Regiment
  156th Schnell Battalion
1/2/3/4/156th Artillery Regiment
  156th Pioneer Battalion
  156th Signals Battalion
    156th Division Support Units
10th (motorized) Division (only part present)
25th (motorized) Division
  1/2/3/35th (motorized) Infantry Regiment
  1/2/3/119th (motorized) Infantry Regiment
    25th Anti-tank Battalion
    25th Motorcycle Battalion
  1/2/3/4/25th Artillery Regiment
    25th Signals Battalion
    25th Pioneer Battalion
112th Division
  1/2/3/110th Infantry Regiment
  1/2/3/256th Infantry Regiment
  1/2/3/258th Infantry Regiment
    120th Schnell Battalion
  1/2/3/4/85th Artillery Regiment
    112nd Pioneer Battalion
    112nd Signals Battalion
      112nd Division Support Units
134th Division
  1/2/3/439th Infantry Regiment
  1/2/3/445th Infantry Regiment
  1/2/3/446th Infantry Regiment
    134th Schnell Battalion
  1/2/3/4/134th Artillery Regiment
    134th Pioneer Battalion
    134th Signals Battalion
      134th Division Support Units
296th Division
  1/2/3/519th Infantry Regiment
  1/2/3/520th Infantry Regiment
  1/2/3/521st Infantry Regiment
    296th Schnell Battalion
  1/2/3/4/296th Artillery Regiment
    296th Pioneer Battalion
    296th Signals Battalion
      296th Division Support Units
XXXV Corps
  29th (motorized) Division (small, unknown portion detached)
  1/2/3/15th (motorized) Infantry Regiment
  1/2/3/71st (motorized) Infantry Regiment
    29th Anti-tank Battalion
    129th Tank Battalion
    29th Motorcycle Battalion
  1/2/3/4/29th Artillery Regiment
    29th Signals Battalion
    29th Pioneer Battalion
      29th Division Support Units
262nd Division
  1/2/3/462nd Infantry Regiment
  1/2/3/482nd Infantry Regiment

1/2/3/486th Infantry Regiment
262nd Schnell Battalion
1/2/3/4/262nd Artillery Regiment
262nd Pioneer Battalion
262nd Signals Battalion
262nd Division Support Units
293rd Division
1/2/510th Infantry Regiment
1/2/511th Infantry Regiment
1/2/512th Infantry Regiment
293rd Schnell Battalion
1/2/3/4/293rd Artillery Regiment
293rd Pioneer Battalion
293rd Signals Battalion
293rd Division Support Units
3rd Tank Division (only small, unknown portion of division present)
4th Army
Staff/and Detachment/5th Tank Division
Staff/15th Infantry Division
442nd Special Task Force (with Gablenz's Group)
Detachment/31st Infantry Division
XXXX (motorized) Corps
19th Tank Division
1/27th Armoured Regiment
19th Tank Grenadier Brigade
1/2/3/73rd Tank Grenadier Regiment
1/2/3/74th Tank Grenadier Regiment
19th Anti-tank Battalion
19th Motorcycle Battalion
1/2/3/19th Artillery Regiment
19th Signals Battalion
19th Pioneer Battalion
19th Division Support Units
216th Division (unknown detachment, organization unknown)
131st Division (unknown detachment, organization unknown)
1/2/557th Infantry Regiment
1/2/3/558th Infantry Regiment
331st Schnell Battalion
1/2/331st Artillery Regiment
331st Pioneer Battalion
331st Signals Battalion
331st Division Support Units
403rd Security Division (some portion, size unknown)
211th Division (some portion, size unknown)
Schlemm Battle Group
XII Corps
1/2/3/282nd Infantry Regiment
1/2/3/289th Infantry Regiment
1/2/3/290th Infantry Regiment
198th Schnell Battalion
198th Pioneer Battalion
198th Signals Battalion
198th Division Support Units
216th Division (some portion, size unknown)
268th Division
1/2/468th Infantry Regiment
2/3/488th Infantry Regiment

        1/2/499th Infantry Regiment
          268th Schnell Battalion
        1/2/3/4/268th Artillery Regiment
          268th Pioneer Battalion
          268th Signals Battalion
            268th Division Support Units
     34th Division
     131st Division (1 unknown regiment and support units)
     268th Division (unknown detachment)
     5th Tank Division
     10th (motorized) Division (unknown detachment)
     17th Division (unknown detachment)
23rd Division (unknown detachment)
  XIII Corps
    52nd Division
      1/2/163rd Infantry Regiment
      1/2/181st Infantry Regiment
      1/2/205th Infantry Regiment
       152nd Anti-tank Battalion
       152nd Bicycle Battalion
      1/2/3/4/152nd Artillery Regiment
       152nd Pioneer Battalion
       152nd Signals Battalion
         152nd Division Support Units
    137th Division
      1/2/447th Infantry Regiment
      2/3/448th Infantry Regiment
      1/2/3/449th Infantry Regiment
       137th Schnell Battalion
      1/2/3/4/137th Artillery Regiment
       137th Pioneer Battalion
       137th Signals Battalion
         137th Division Support Units
      1/2/460th Infantry Regiment
      1/2/470th Infantry Regiment
      1/2/480th Infantry Regiment
       260th Schnell Battalion
      1/2/3/4/260th Artillery Regiment
       653rd Pioneer Battalion
       260th Signals Battalion
         260th Division Support Units
    263rd Division
      2/3/463rd Infantry Regiment
      1/2/483rd Infantry Regiment
      1/2/485th Infantry Regiment
       263rd Schnell Battalion
      1/2/3/4/263rd Artillery Regiment
       263rd Pioneer Battalion
       263rd Signals Battalion
         263rd Division Support Units
  XXXXIII Corps
    31st Division (some minor detachments)
      1/3/12th Infantry Regiment
      1/3/17th Infantry Regiment
      1/2/82nd Infantry Regiment
       31st Anti-tank Battalion
       31st Bicycle Battalion

1/2/3/31st Artillery Regiment
1/67th Artillery Battalion
31st Pioneer Battalion
31st Signals Battalion
  31st Division Support Units
10th (motorized) Division (assigned to 31st) (small detachment, organization unknown)
211th Division (assigned to 31st) (small detachment, organization unknown)
34th Division (1 regiment detached)
1/2/3/80th Infantry Regiment
1/2/3/107th Infantry Regiment
1/2/3/253rd Infantry Regiment
  34th Anti-tank Battalion
  34th Bicycle Battalion
1/2/3/34th Artillery Regiment
1/70th Artillery Battalion
  34th Pioneer Battalion
  34th Signals Battalion
    34th Division Support Units
131st Division (1 regiment detached)
1/2/431st Infantry Regiment
1/2/434th Infantry Regiment
  131st Schnell Battalion
1/2/3/4/131st Artillery Regiment
  131st Pioneer Battalion
  131st Signals Battalion
    131st Division Support Units
266th Security Division (assigned to 131st) (small detachment, organization unknown)
4th Tank Army
267th Division
1/2/3/467th Infantry Regiment
1/2/3/487th Infantry Regiment
1/2/3/267th Fast Battalion
1/2/3/4/267th Artillery Regiment
  267th Pioneer Battalion
  267th Signals Battalion
    267th Division Support Units
213th Security Division (Unknown sized detachment from division)
XX Corps
17th Division (unknown, minor detachments removed)
1/2/3/21st Infantry Regiment
1/2/3/55th Infantry Regiment
1/2/3/95th Infantry Regiment
  17th Anti-tank Battalion
  17th Bicycle Battalion
1/2/3/17th Artillery Regiment
1/53rd Artillery Battalion
  17th Pioneer Battalion
  17th Signals Battalion
    17th Division Support Units
20th Tank Division (unknown, minor detachments removed)
3/21st Armoured Regiment
20th Tank Grenadier Brigade
1/2/3/59th Tank Grenadier Regiment
1/112nd Tank Grenadier Regiment
  92nd Anti-tank Battalion
  20th Motorcycle Battalion
1/2/3/92nd Artillery Regiment

92nd Signals Battalion
92nd Pioneer Battalion
  92nd Division Support Units
183rd Division
  1/2/3/330th Infantry Regiment
  1/2/3/351st Infantry Regiment
  219th Schnell Battalion
  1/2/3/4/219th Artillery Regiment
  219th Pioneer Battalion
  219th Signals Battalion
    219th Division Support Units
255th Division (1 regiment detached)
  1/2/3/465th Infantry Regiment
  1/2/3/475th Infantry Regiment
    1/2/3/255th Schnell Battalion
  1/2/3/4/255th Artillery Regiment
  255th Pioneer Battalion
  255th Signals Battalion
    255th Division Support Units
258th Division
  1/2/3/458th Infantry Regiment
  1/2/3/478th Infantry Regiment
    258th Anti-tank Battalion
    258th Bicycle Battalion
  1/2/3/4/258th Artillery Regiment
    258th Pioneer Battalion
    258th Division Support Units
292nd Division
  1/2/3/507th Infantry Regiment
  1/2/3/508th Infantry Regiment
  292nd Schnell Battalion
  1/2/3/4/292nd Artillery Regiment
  292nd Pioneer Battalion
  292nd Signals Battalion
  292nd Division Support Units
IX Corps
  7th Division (unknown, minor detachments removed)
  1/2/3/19th Infantry Regiment
  1/2/3/61st Infantry Regiment
  1/2/3/62nd Infantry Regiment
    7th Anti-tank Battalion
    7th Bicycle Battalion
  1/2/3/7th Artillery Regiment
    1/43rd Artillery Battalion
    7th Pioneer Battalion
    7th Signals Battalion
    7th Division Support Units
197th Division
  1/2/3/321st Infantry Regiment
  1/2/3/332nd Infantry Regiment
  1/2/347th Infantry Regiment
  229th Schnell Battalion
  1/2/3/4/229th Artillery Regiment
  229th Pioneer Battalion
  229th Signals Battalion
    229th Division Support Units
78th Division

1/2/14th Infantry Regiment
1/2/195th Infantry Regiment
  178th Schnell Battalion
1/2/3/4/178th Artillery Regiment
  178th Pioneer Battalion
  178th Signals Battalion
    178th Division Support Units
252nd Division
255th Division (attached to 252nd Division) (1, unknown regiment and support units)
7th Division (attached to 252nd Division) (minor, unknown detachments)
35th Division
1/2/34th Infantry Regiment
1/2/109th Infantry Regiment
1/3/111th Infantry Regiment
  35th Anti-tank Battalion
1/2/3/35th Artillery Regiment
  1/71st Artillery Battalion
  35th Pioneer Battalion
  35th Signals Battalion
    35th Division Support Units
78th Division (attached to 35th Division) (minor, unknown detachments)
11th Tank Division (Detachment of unknown size)
23rd Division (Detachment of unknown size)
V Corps
23rd Division (minor, unknown detachments)
1/2/3/9th Infantry Regiment
1/2/3/67th Infantry Regiment
1/2/3/68th Infantry Regiment
  23rd Anti-tank Battalion
  23rd Bicycle Battalion
1/2/3/29th Artillery Regiment
  1/59th Artillery Battalion
    23rd Division Support Units
3rd (motorized) Division
1/2/3/8th (motorized) Infantry Regiment
1/2/3/29th (motorized) Infantry Regiment
  103rd Tank Battalion
  53rd Motorcycle Battalion
1/2/3/4/3rd Artillery Regiment
  3rd Signals Battalion
  3rd Pioneer Battalion
    3rd Division Support Units
5th Tank Division (minor, unknown detachments)
1/2/31st Armoured Regiment
  5th Tank Grenadier Brigade
1/2/3/13th Tank Grenadier Regiment
1/2/3/14th Tank Grenadier Regiment
  53rd Anti-tank Battalion
1/2/3/116th Artillery Regiment
  77th Signals Battalion
  89th Pioneer Battalion
    85th Division Support Units
15th Division (minor, unknown detachments)
1/2/3/81st Infantry Regiment
1/2/3/88th Infantry Regiment
1/2/3/106th Infantry Regiment
  15th Anti-tank Battalion

1/2/3/15th Artillery Regiment
1/51st Artillery Battalion
15th Pioneer Battalion
15th Signals Battalion
15th Division Support Units
9th Army (At Army's disposal known as Funck Group)
2nd Tank Division (small, unknown portion of division present)
5th Tank Division (small, unknown portion of division present)
7th Tank Division (bulk of division present)
1/2/25th Armoured Regiment
7th Tank Grenadier Brigade
1/2/3/6th Tank Grenadier Regiment
1/2/3/7th Tank Grenadier Regiment
7th Motorcycle Battalion
1/2/3/7th Artillery Regiment
83rd Signals Battalion
58th Pioneer Battalion
58th Division Support Units
246th Division
1/2/404th Infantry Regiment
1/3/689th Infantry Regiment
246th Anti-tank Company
246th Bicycle Company
1/2/3/246th Artillery Regiment
246th Pioneer Battalion
246th Division Support Units
XXXXI (motorized) Corps
36th (motorized) Division
1/2/3/87th (motorized) Infantry Regiment
1/2/3/118th (motorized) Infantry Regiment
36th Anti-tank Battalion
36th Motorcycle Battalion
1/2/3/4/36th Artillery Regiment
36th Signals Battalion
36th Pioneer Battalion
36th Division Support Units
342nd Division
1/2/3/697th Infantry Regiment
1/2/3/698th Infantry Regiment
1/2/3/699th Infantry Regiment
342nd Fast Battalion
1/2/3/342nd Artillery Regiment
342nd Pioneer Battalion
342nd Signals Battalion
342nd Division Support Units
900th Brigade (only part present)
1/2/900th (motorized) Infantry Regiment
900th Anti-tank Battalion (3 companies)
900th Artillery Battalion (4 batteries)
900th Pioneer Battalion (3 companies)
900th Signals Battalion
900th Administrative Services
2/3rd Armoured Regiment
2nd Tank Grenadier Brigade
1/2/3/2nd Tank Grenadier Regiment
1/2/3/304th Tank Grenadier Regiment
703rd Storm Protection Battery

38th Anti-tank Battalion
2nd Motorcycle Battalion
1/2/3/74th Artillery Regiment
38th Signals Battalion
38th Pioneer Battalion
   38th Division Support Units
6th Tank Division (only an unknown part present)
1/2/11th Armoured Regiment
1/2/3/4th Tank Grenadier Regiment
1/2/3/114th Tank Grenadier Regiment
   41st Anti-tank Battalion
   6th Motorcycle Battalion
1/2/3/76th Artillery Regiment
   82nd Signals Battalion
   57th Pioneer Battalion
   57th Division Support Units
Recke Corps
 129th Division
1/2/3/427th Infantry Regiment
2/3/428th Infantry Regiment
1/2/430th Infantry Regiment
   129th Anti-tank Battalion
   129th Bicycle Battalion
1/2/3/4/129th Artillery Regiment
   129th Pioneer Battalion
   129th Signals Battalion
   129th Division Support Units
 161st Division
1/2/3/336th Infantry Regiment
1/2/3/371st Infantry Regiment
   241st Schnell Battalion
1/2/3/4/241st Artillery Regiment
   241st Pioneer Battalion
   241st Signals Battalion
   241st Division Support Units
 162nd Division (division broken up in May 1943)
1/2/3/303rd Infantry Regiment
1/2/3/314th Infantry Regiment
1/329th Infantry Regiment
1/2/3/4/236th Artillery Regiment
   236th Pioneer Battalion
   236th Signals Battalion
   236th Division Service Units
VI Corps
 6th Division
1/2/18th Infantry Regiment
1/2/37th Infantry Regiment
1/3/58th Infantry Regiment
   6th Anti-tank Battalion
   6th Bicycle Battalion
1/2/3/6th Artillery Regiment
1/42nd Artillery Battalion
   6th Pioneer Battalion
   6th Signals Battalion
   6th Division Support Units
 26th Division
1/2/3/39th Infantry Regiment

1/2/3/77th Infantry Regiment
  26th Anti-tank Battalion
  26th Bicycle Battalion
  26th Signals Battalion
    26th Division Support Units
1/2/3/456th Infantry Regiment
1/2/3/476th Infantry Regiment
1/2/3/481st Infantry Regiment
  256th Schnell Battalion
1/2/3/4/256th Artillery Regiment
  256th Pioneer Battalion
  256th Signals Battalion
    256th Division Support Units
102nd Division (assigned to 256th Division)
339th Division (assigned to 256th Division)
XXXXVI (motorized) Corps
  SS Reich Leader Brigade
  1/2/3/8th SS Infantry Regiment Reich Leader
  1/2/3/10th SS Infantry Regiment Reich Leader
    Radio and Signals Troops
  14th (motorized) Division
  1/2/3/11th (motorized) Infantry Regiment
  1/2/3/53rd (motorized) Infantry Regiment
    14th Anti-tank Battalion
    54th Motorcycle Battalion
    14th Signals Battalion
    14th Pioneer Battalion
      14th Division Support Units
  206th Division
  2/3/301st Infantry Regiment
  1/2/312th Infantry Regiment
  1/2/413th Infantry Regiment
    206th Schnell Battalion
  1/2/3/4/206th Artillery Regiment
    206th Pioneer Battalion
      206th Division Support Units
  129th Division (assigned to 206th Division) (small, unknown detachment)
  251st Division
  1/2/3/451st Infantry Regiment
  1/2/3/459th Infantry Regiment
  1/2/3/471st Infantry Regiment
    251st Schnell Battalion
  1/2/3/4/251st Artillery Regiment
    251st Pioneer Battalion
    251st Signals Battalion
      251st Division Support Units
  216th Division (assigned to 251st Division)
  1 regiment and support units
XXIII Corps
  253rd Division
  1/2/3/453rd Infantry Regiment
  1/2/3/464th Infantry Regiment
  1/2/3/473rd Infantry Regiment
    253rd Schnell Battalion
  1/2/3/4/253rd Artillery Regiment
    253rd Pioneer Battalion
    253rd Signals Battalion

253rd Division Support Units
102nd Division
  1/2/3/84th Infantry Regiment
  1/2/3/232nd Infantry Regiment
  1/2/3/233rd Infantry Regiment
  1/2/3/235th Infantry Regiment
   102nd Bicycle Battalion
  1/2/3/4/102nd Artillery Regiment
   102nd Pioneer Battalion
   102nd Signals Battalion
    102nd Division Support Units
SS Cavalry Brigade
  2nd SS Cavalry Regiment (6 squadrons)
  1/SS Artillery Regiment (3 batteries)
1st Tank Division (most of division present)
  2/1st Armoured Regiment
1st Tank Grenadier Brigade
  1/2/3/1st Tank Grenadier Regiment
  1/2/3/113th Tank Grenadier Regiment
    702nd Storm Protection Battery
   37th Anti-tank Battalion
   1st Motorcycle Battalion
   37th Signals Battalion
   37th Pioneer Battalion
2nd Tank Division (assigned to 1st Tank Division) (detachment of unknown size)
5th Tank Division (assigned to 1st Tank Division) (detachment of unknown size)
208th Division (assigned to 1st Tank Division) (detachment of unknown size)
XXVII Corps
  1/2/3/167th Infantry Regiment
  1/2/184th Infantry Regiment
  1/2/3/216th Infantry Regiment
   186th Schnell Battalion
  1/2/3/4/186th Artillery Regiment
   186th Pioneer Battalion
   186th Signals Battalion
    186th Division Support Units
110th Division (less 1 regiment and support units)
  1/2/3/252nd Infantry Regiment
  1/2/3/254th Infantry Regiment
  1/2/255th Infantry Regiment
   110th Anti-tank Battalion
   110th Bicycle Battalion
  1/2/3/4/110th Artillery Regiment
   110th Pioneer Battalion
   110th Signals Battalion
   110th Division Support Units
7th Tank Division (assigned to 110th Division) (detachment of unknown size)
328th Division (1 regiment and support units)
1st Tank Division
5th Tank Division (detachment of unknown size)
3rd Tank Army
 LIX Corps
  330th Division
   1/2/554th Infantry Regiment
   1/2/555th Infantry Regiment
   1/2/556th Infantry Regiment
    330th Schnell Battalion

1/2/330th Artillery Regiment
  330th Pioneer Battalion
  330th Signals Battalion
   330th Division Support Units
328th Division
(1 regiment and support units)
205th Division
2/3/335th Infantry Regiment
1/2/353rd Infantry Regiment
2/3/358th Infantry Regiment
   205th Anti-tank Company
  205th Bicycle Squadron
1/2/3/4/205th Artillery Regiment
  205th Pioneer Battalion
  205th Signals Battalion
   205th Division Support Units
83rd Division (1 regiment detached)
1/2/3/251st Infantry Regiment
1/2/3/257th Infantry Regiment
1/2/3/277th Infantry Regiment
  183rd Schnell Battalion
1/2/3/4/183rd Artillery Regiment (only 1 regiment and support units present)
  183rd Pioneer Battalion
  183rd Signals Battalion
   183rd Division Support Units
83rd Division
(1 regiment and division staff)
81st Division (only a portion of division was present)
1/2/3/161st Infantry Regiment
1/2/3/174th Infantry Regiment
1/2/3/189th Infantry Regiment
  181st Schnell Battalion
1/3/4/181st Artillery Regiment
  181st Pioneer Battalion
  181st Signals Battalion
   181st Division Support Units
218th Division (1 regiment and support units detached)
1/2/3/323rd Infantry Regiment
1/2/3/386th Infantry Regiment
1/2/3/397th Infantry Regiment
  218th Schnell Battalion
1/2/3/4/218th Artillery Regiment
  218th Pioneer Battalion
  218th Signals Battalion
   218th Division Support Units
  Rear Area Security
11th Tank Division (some detachments removed)
1/2/3/15th Armoured Regiment
11th Tank Grenadier Brigade
1/2/3/110th Tank Grenadier Regiment
1/2/3/111th Tank Grenadier Regiment
  61st Anti-tank Battalion
  61st Motorcycle Battalion
  341st Signals Battalion
  209th Pioneer Battalion
1/8th Police Regiment (mixed mobility companies)
   201st Motorized Signals Company

1/221st Artillery Battalion
  350th Division Support Units
285th Security Division (some minor detachments)
1/2/3/322nd Infantry Regiment
1/2/3/113th Infantry Regiment
1/9th Police Regiment
  823rd Motorized Signals Company
  3/207th Artillery Battalion
  322nd Division Support Units
403rd Security Division (some detachments)
1/2/3/354th Infantry Regiment
1/2/3/177th Infantry Regiment
2/8th Police Regiment
  826th Motorized Signals Company
201st Security Brigade
202nd Security Brigade
707th Division
1/2/3/727nd Infantry Regiment
1/2/3/747th Infantry Regiment
  657th Artillery Battalion
  707th Pioneer Battalion
  707th Signals Battalion
    707th Division Support Units

German Army Group South: As of December 26, 1943

(Created by George Nafziger. First published in English online at the U.S. Army Combined Arms Research Library) (The database is open source)

Order of Battle

1st Tank Army
    A Corps Detachment Command
        161st Divisional Group (Staff/371st Group, 336th and 371st Regimental Groups)
        293rd Divisional Group (Staff/512th Group, 511th and 512th Regimental Groups)
        355th Divisional Group (Staff/866th Group, 510th and 866th Regimental Groups)
      161st Divisional Fusilier Battalion (from 1/364th Group)
      241st Anti-tank Battalion
    241st Artillery Regiment (from 1/355th, 2/241st, 3/293rd and 4/241st Artillery Regiments)
      241st Pioneer Battalion
      241st Signals Battalion
      241st Field Replacement Battalion
      241st Supply Service
  Schörner Group (XXXX Tank Corps)
  XXIX Corps
    9th Division
      1/2/36th Grenadier Regiment
      1/2/57th Grenadier Regiment
      1/2/116th Grenadier Regiment
      9th Anti-tank Battalion
      9th Fusilier Battalion
      1/2/3/4/9th Artillery Regiment
      9th Pioneer Battalion
      9th Signals Battalion
      9th Division Support Units
    97th Hunter Division
      1/2/3/204th Hunter Regiment
      1/2/3/207th Hunter Regiment
      1/2/3/4/97th Artillery Regiment
      97th Bicycle Battalion
      97th Anti-tank Battalion

      97th Pioneer Battalion
      97th Signals Battalion
      97th Field Replacement Battalion
        97th Division Support Units
   335th Division (1 regiment detached)
     1/2/682nd Grenadier Regiment
     2/3/683rd Grenadier Regiment
     1/2/684th Grenadier Regiment
     1/2/3/4/335th Artillery Regiment
      335th Fusilier Battalion
      335th Pioneer Battalion
      335th Signals Battalion
        335th Division Support Units
IV Corps
  17th Division
    1/2/21st Grenadier Regiment
    1/2/55th Grenadier Regiment
    1/2/95th Grenadier Regiment
     17th Anti-tank Battalion
     17th Fusilier Battalion
    1/2/3/17th Artillery Regiment
    1/53rd Artillery Battalion
     17th Pioneer Battalion
     17th Signals Battalion
       17th Division Support Units
  111th Division
    2/3/50th Grenadier Regiment
    2/3/70th Grenadier Regiment
    1/3/117th Grenadier Regiment
     111th Divisional Fusilier Battalion
    1/2/3/4/111th Artillery Regiment
     111th Pioneer Battalion
     111th Signals Battalion
       111th Division Support Units
  258th Division
    1/3/458th Grenadier Regiment
    1/2/3/478th Grenadier Regiment
    1/2/3/479th Grenadier Regiment
     258th Divisional Battalion
     258th Anti-tank Battalion
     258th Bicycle Battalion
    1/2/3/4/258th Artillery Regiment
     258th Pioneer Battalion
     258th Signals Battalion
       258th Division Support Units
  79th Division (subordinated to 258th Division)
    1/2/3/208th Grenadier Regiment
    1/2/3/212th Grenadier Regiment
    1/2/3/226th Grenadier Regiment
     179th Anti-tank Battalion
     179th Fusilier (anti-aircraft) Battalion
    1/2/3/4/179th Artillery Regiment
     179th Pioneer Battalion
     179th Signals Battalion
       179th Division Support Units
  335th Division (subordinated to 258th Division)
    1 unknown regiment

3rd Mountain Division
  1/2/3/138th Mountain Infantry Regiment
  1/2/3/144th Mountain Infantry Regiment
    95th Anti-tank Battalion
    95th Bicycle Battalion
  1/2/112nd Artillery Regiment
    95th Signals Battalion
    95th Pioneer Battalion
      95th Division Support Units
  24th Tank Division (subordinated to 3rd Mountain Division) (unknown detachment)
302nd Division
  1/2/3/570th Grenadier Regiment
  1/2/3/571st Grenadier Regiment
  1/2/3/572nd Grenadier Regiment
    302nd Fusilier Battalion
  1/2/3/302nd Artillery Regiment
    392nd Pioneer Battalion
    392nd Signals Battalion
      392nd Division Support Units
24th Tank Division (some minor detachments)
  1/2/3/24th Armoured Regiment
24th Tank Grenadier Brigade
  1/2/3/21st Tank Grenadier Regiment
  1/2/3/26th Tank Grenadier Regiment
    40th Anti-tank Battalion
    4th Motorcycle Battalion
  1/2/3/4/89th Artillery Regiment
    86th Signals Battalion
    40th Pioneer Battalion
      40th Division Support Units
XVII Corps
  123rd Division
    1/2/415th Grenadier Regiment
    1/3/416th Grenadier Regiment
    1/2/418th Grenadier Regiment
      123rd Schnell Battalion
    1/2/3/4/123rd Artillery Regiment
      123rd Pioneer Battalion
      123rd Signals Battalion
        123rd Division Support Units
  125th Division
    1/3/419th Grenadier Regiment
    1/2/420th Grenadier Regiment
    1/3/421st Grenadier Regiment
      125th Anti-tank Battalion
      125th Fusilier Battalion
    1/2/3/4/125th Artillery Regiment
      125th Pioneer Battalion
      125th Signals Battalion
        125th Division Support Units
  294th Division
    1 unknown regiment
XXX Corps
  46th Division
    1/3/42nd Grenadier Regiment
    2/3/72nd Grenadier Regiment
    1/2/3/97th Grenadier Regiment

42nd Anti-tank Battalion
46th Fusilier Battalion
1/2/3/114th Artillery Regiment
1/115th Artillery Battalion
88th Pioneer Battalion
76th Signals Battalion
    46th Division Support Units
257th Division
1/2/3/457th Grenadier Regiment
1/2/3/466th Grenadier Regiment
1/2/3/477th Grenadier Regiment
257th Fusilier Battalion
1/2/3/4/257th Artillery Regiment
257th Pioneer Battalion
257th Signals Battalion
    257th Division Support Units
304th Division
1/2/3/573rd Grenadier Regiment
1/2/3/574th Grenadier Regiment
1/2/3/575th Grenadier Regiment
304th Schnell Battalion
1/2/3/304th Artillery Regiment
304th Pioneer Battalion
304th Signals Battalion
    304th Division Support Units
387th Division
1/2/3/541st Grenadier Regiment
1/2/3/542nd Grenadier Regiment
1/2/3/543rd Grenadier Regiment
387th Schnell Battalion
1/2/3/4/387th Artillery Regiment
387th Pioneer Battalion
387th Signals Battalion
    387th Division Support Units
Schwerin Group
16th Tank Grenadier Division
1/2/3/60th Tank Grenadier Regiment
1/2/3/156th Tank Grenadier Regiment
    228th Anti-tank Battalion
    116th Tank Battalion
    700th Tank Association
    116th Tank Reconnaissance Battalion
1/2/3/146th Artillery Regiment
    281st Army Flak Battalion
    288th Signals Battalion
    675th Pioneer Battalion
        66th Division Support Units
306th Division
1/2/579th Grenadier Regiment
1/2/580th Grenadier Regiment
1/2/580th Grenadier Regiment
328th Divisional Group
548th Regimental Group
549th Regimental Group
328th Divisional Fusilier Group
306th Schnell Battalion
1/2/3/306th Artillery Regiment

306th Pioneer Battalion
306th Signals Battalion
   306th Division Support Units
LVII Tank Corps
 Great Germany Division
  1/2/3/Grenadier Regiment Great Germany
  1/2/3/Fusilier Regiment Great Germany
   Great Germany Storm Protection Battalion
    Great Germany Tank Troop
   Great Germany Motorcycle Battalion
  1/2/3/4/ Great Germany (motorized) Artillery Regiment
   Great Germany Signals Battalion
   Great Germany Pioneer Battalion
   Great Germany Anti-tank Battalion
 23rd Tank Division
  1/2/3/201st Armoured Regiment
 23rd Tank Grenadier Brigade
  1/2/3/126th Tank Grenadier Regiment
  1/2/3/128th Tank Grenadier Regiment
   128th Anti-tank Battalion
   23rd Motorcycle Battalion
  1/2/3/4/128th Artillery Regiment
   128th Signals Battalion
   51st Pioneer Battalion
    128th Division Support Units
 294th Division (1regiment present and subordinated to 23rd Tank Division)
 SS Death's Head Division (some minor detachments)
  1/2/3/1st Death's Head Motorized Infantry Regiment
  1/2/3/2nd Death's Head Motorized Infantry Regiment
    SS Death's Head Armoured Troop
  SS Death's Head Motorcycle (Volkswagen) Regiment
  1/2/3/4/5/SS Death Head (motorized) Artillery Regiment
   SS Death's Head Reconnaissance Battalion
   SS Death's Head Anti-tank Battalion
   SS Death's Head Signals Battalion
   SS Death's Head Pioneer Battalion
   SS Death's Head Division Support Units
Sperl Group
 9th Tank Division
  1/2/3/33rd Armoured Regiment
 9th Tank Grenadier Brigade
  1/2/3/10th Tank Grenadier Regiment
  1/2/3/11th Tank Grenadier Regiment
    701st Storm Protection Battery
   50th Anti-tank Battalion
   59th Motorcycle Battalion
  1/2/3/4/102nd Artillery Regiment
   85th Signals Battalion
   86th Pioneer Battalion
    60th Division Support Units
 16th Division
  1/2/3/384th Grenadier Regiment
  1/2/3/396th Grenadier Regiment
   216th Schnell Battalion
  1/2/3/4/216th Artillery Regiment
   216th Pioneer Battalion
   216th Signals Battalion

216th Division Support Units
61st Division
  1/2/151st Grenadier Regiment
  1/2/162nd Grenadier Regiment
  1/2/176th Grenadier Regiment
  161st Fusilier Battalion
  1/2/3/4/161st Artillery Regiment
  161st Pioneer Battalion
  161st Signals Battalion
    161st Division Support Units
LII Corps
  76th Division
  2/3/178th Grenadier Regiment
  1/3/203rd Grenadier Regiment
  1/2/230th Fusilier Regiment
  176th Anti-tank Battalion
  176th Divisional Fusilier Battalion
  1/2/3/4/176th Artillery Regiment
  176th Pioneer Battalion
  176th Signals Battalion
    176th Division Support Units
384th Division
  1/2/3/534th Grenadier Regiment
  1/2/3/535th Grenadier Regiment
  1/2/3/536th Grenadier Regiment
  384th Schnell Battalion
  1/2/3/4/384th Artillery Regiment
  384th Pioneer Battalion
  384th Signals Battalion
    384th Division Support Units
17th Tank Division
  1/39th Armoured Regiment
17th Tank Grenadier Brigade
  1/2/3/40th Tank Grenadier Regiment
  1/2/3/63rd Tank Grenadier Regiment
  27th Anti-Tank Battalion
  17th Motorcycle Battalion
  1/2/3/27th Artillery Regiment
  27th Signals Battalion
  27th Pioneer Battalion
    27th Division Support Units
SS Death's Head Division (unknown detachment, rest with LVII Tank Corps)
13th Tank Division
  1/2/3/4th Armoured Regiment
13th Tank Grenadier Brigade
  1/2/3/66th Tank Grenadier Regiment
  1/2/3/93rd Tank Grenadier Regiment
  13th Anti-tank Battalion
  43rd Motorcycle Battalion
  1/2/3/4/13th Artillery Regiment
  13th Signals Battalion
  4th Pioneer Battalion
    13th Division Support Units
2nd Parachute Division
  2/3/2nd Parachute Regiment
  3/4/6th Parachute Regiment
  2/3/7th Parachute Regiment

2nd Parachute Anti-Tank Battalion (6 companies)
1/2nd Parachute Artillery Regiment (4 batteries)
2nd Parachute Pioneer Battalion (4 companies)
2nd Communications and Signal Battalion
Parachute Division (2 companies)
2nd Parachute Division Service Units
2nd Parachute Flak Battalion (5 batteries
2nd Parachute Machine Gun Battalion (3 companies)
8th Army
III Tank Corps
376th Battle Group
672nd Regimental Battle Group
673rd Regimental Battle Group
767th Regimental Battle Group
376th Artillery Regiment
14th Tank Division (some minor detachments)
1/2/3/36th Armoured Regiment
14th Tank Grenadier Brigade
1/2/3/103rd Tank Grenadier Regiment
1/2/3/108th Tank Grenadier Regiment
4th Anti-Tank Battalion
64th Motorcycle Battalion
1/2/3/4/4th Artillery Regiment
4th Signals Battalion
13th Pioneer Battalion
4th Division Support Units
10th Tank Grenadier Division
1/2/3/20th Grenadier Regiment
1/2/3/41st Grenadier Regiment
7th Tank Battalion
110th Tank Reconnaissance Battalion
1/2/3/10th Artillery Regiment
275th Army Flak Battalion
10th Signals Battalion
10th Pioneer Battalion
10th Division Service Units
14th Tank Division (subordinated to 10th Tank Grenadier Division) (small, unknown force)
3rd Tank Division
1/2/3/6th Armoured Regiment
3rd Tank Grenadier Brigade
1/2/3/3rd Tank Grenadier Regiment
1/2/3/394th Tank Grenadier Regiment
543rd Anti-Tank Battalion
3rd Motorcycle Battalion
1/2/3/4/75th Artillery Regiment
39th Signals Battalion
39th Pioneer Battalion
39th Division Support Units
6th Tank Division
1/2/11th Armoured Regiment
6th Tank Grenadier Brigade
1/2/3/4th Tank Grenadier Regiment
1/2/3/114th Tank Grenadier Regiment
41st Anti-Tank Battalion
6th Motorcycle Battalion
1/2/3/76th Artillery Regiment

82nd Signals Battalion
57th Pioneer Battalion
  57th Division Support Units
11th Tank Division
1/2/3/15th Armoured Regiment
11th Tank Grenadier Brigade
1/2/3/110th Tank Grenadier Regiment
1/2/3/111th Tank Grenadier Regiment
  61st Anti-Tank Battalion
  61st Motorcycle Battalion
1/2/3/4/119th Artillery Regiment
  341st Signals Battalion
  209th Pioneer Battalion
   61st Division Support Units
XXXXVII Tank Corps
106th Division
1/2/239th Grenadier Regiment
1/2/240th Grenadier Regiment
39th Division Group (113rd and 114th Regimental Groups)
  106th Anti-Tank Battalion
  106th Bicycle Battalion
1/2/3/4/106th Artillery Regiment
  106th Pioneer Battalion
  106th Signals Battalion
   106th Division Support Units
167th Division (1 regiment detached) (subordinated to 106th Division)
262nd Division
1/2/462nd Grenadier Regiment
1/2/482nd Grenadier Regiment
1/2/486th Grenadier Regiment
  262nd Fusilier Battalion
  262nd Schnell Battalion
1/2/3/4/262nd Artillery Regiment
  262nd Pioneer Battalion
  262nd Signals Battalion
   262nd Division Support Units
282nd Division
1/2/3/848th Grenadier Regiment
1/2/3/849th Grenadier Regiment
1/2/3/850th Grenadier Regiment
1/2/3/282nd Artillery Regiment
  282nd Anti-Tank Battalion
  282nd Bicycle Battalion
  282nd Pioneer Battalion
  282nd Signals Battalion
   282nd Division Support Units
320th Division
1/2/585th Grenadier Regiment
1/2/586th Grenadier Regiment
1/2/587th Grenadier Regiment
  320th Fusilier Battalion
1/2/3/4/320th Artillery Regiment
  320th Pioneer Battalion
  320th Signals Battalion
   320th Division Support Units
329th Division
1/2/511st Grenadier Regiment

1/2/552nd Grenadier Regiment
1/2/553rd Grenadier Regiment
329th Fusilier Battalion
1/2/3/4/329th Artillery Regiment
329th Pioneer Battalion
329th Signals Battalion
329th Division Support Units
SS Cavalry Division Battle Group
XI Corps
57th Division
1/2/3/676th Grenadier Regiment
1/2/3/199th Grenadier Regiment
1/2/3/217th Grenadier Regiment
157th Anti-Tank Battalion
157th Bicycle Battalion
1/2/3/4/157th Artillery Regiment
157th Pioneer Battalion
157th Signals Battalion
157th Division Support Units
72nd Division
1/2/3/105th Grenadier Regiment
1/2/3/124th Grenadier Regiment
1/2/3/266th Grenadier Regiment
72nd Anti-Tank Battalion
172nd Bicycle Battalion
1/2/3/4/172nd Artillery Regiment
72nd Pioneer Battalion
72nd Signals Battalion
172nd Division Support Units
167th Division (1 regiment, subordinated to 72nd Division)
SS Wiking Division
1/2/3/1st SS Wiking Motorized Infantry Regiment
1/2/3/2nd SS Wiking Motorized Infantry Regiment
SS Wiking Armoured Troop
SS Wiking Motorcycle (Volkswagen) Regiment
1/2/3/4/,5/SS Wiking (motorized) Artillery Regiment
SS Wiking Reconnaissance Battalion
SS Wiking Anti-Tank Battalion
SS Wiking Signals Battalion
SS Wiking Pioneer Battalion
SS Wiking Division Support Units
5th SS Volunteer Storm Brigade Wallonien
Staff and Staff Company
373rd Wallon (motorized) Infantry Battalion (3 companies of tank grenadiers)
(motorized) Heavy Anti-tank Company
(motorized) Machinegun Company
(motorized) Infantry Support Gun Company
Storm Protection Battery
(motorized) Light Flak Company
(motorized) Heavy Flak Company
4th Tank Army
20th Tank Grenadier Division (remains of division, organization unknown)
18th Artillery Division
1/2/3/88th Artillery Regiment
1/2/3/288th Artillery Regiment
1/2/3/388th Artillery Regiment
741st Storm Protection Battery (10 Storm Protection)

280th Army Flak Battalions (2 heavy and 2 light batteries)
4th Observation Battery
18th Gun Battery
88th Division Signals Battalion
88th Supply Troop
88th Protect Battalion
XXIV Tank Corps
444th Security Division (staff only)
34th Division
1/2/80th Grenadier Regiment
1/2/107th Grenadier Regiment
1/2/253rd Grenadier Regiment
34th Anti-tank Battalion
34th Bicycle Battalion
1/2/3/34th Artillery Regiment
1/70th Artillery Battalion
34th Pioneer Battalion
34th Signals Battalion
34th Division Support Units
82nd Division
1/2/3/158th Grenadier Regiment
1/2/3/166th Grenadier Regiment
1/2/3/168th Grenadier Regiment
182nd Schnell Battalion
1/2/3/4/182nd Artillery Regiment
182nd Pioneer Battalion
182nd Signals Battalion
182nd Division Support Units
112th Division
1/2/3/110th Grenadier Regiment
1/2/3/256th Grenadier Regiment
1/2/3/258th Grenadier Regiment
120th Fast Battalion
1/2/3/4/85th Artillery Regiment
112th Pioneer Battalion
112th Signals Battalion
112th Division Support Units
VII Corps
75th Division
1/2/172nd Grenadier Regiment
1/2/202nd Fusilier Regiment
1/2/222nd Grenadier Regiment
175th Anti-tank Battalion
175th Fusilier Battalion
1/2/3/4/175th Artillery Regiment
175th Pioneer Battalion
175th Signals Battalion
175th Division Support Units
88th Division
1/2/245th Grenadier Regiment
1/2/246th Grenadier Regiment
1/2/248th Grenadier Regiment
188th Schnell Battalion
188th Fusilier Battalion
1/2/3/188th Artillery Regiment
188th Pioneer Battalion
188th Signals Battalion

88th Division Support Units
198th Division
  1/2/305th Grenadier Regiment
  1/2/306th Grenadier Regiment
  1/2/326th Grenadier Regiment
  1/2/3/235th Artillery Regiment
  298th Fusilier Battalion
  298th Anti-tank Battalion
  298th Pioneer Battalion
  298th Signals Battalion
  298th Division Service Units
XXXXII Corps
 25th Tank Division
  1/214th Armoured Regiment
  1/2/3/,146th Tank Grenadier Regiment
  514th Anti-tank Company
  87th Motorcycle Battalion
  1/91st Artillery Regiment
  87th Signals Battalion
  87th Pioneer Battalion
 168th Division
  1/2/3/417th Grenadier Regiment
  1/2/3/429th Grenadier Regiment
  248th Anti-tank Battalion
  248th Bicycle Battalion
  1/2/3/4/5/248th Artillery Regiment
  248th Pioneer Battalion
  248th Signals Battalion
  248th Division Support Units
XXXXVIII Tank Corps
 1st Tank Division
  2/1st Armoured Regiment
 1st Tank Grenadier Brigade
  1/2/3/1st Tank Grenadier Regiment
  1/2/3/113th Tank Grenadier Regiment
  702nd Storm Protection Battery
  37th Anti-tank Battalion
  1st Motorcycle Battalion
  1/2/3/73rd Artillery Regiment
  37th Signals Battalion
  37th Pioneer Battalion
  37th Division Support Units
 8th Tank Division
  1/10th Armoured Regiment
 8th Tank Grenadier Brigade
  1/2/3/8th Tank Grenadier Regiment
  1/2/3/28th Tank Grenadier Regiment
  43rd Anti-tank Battalion
  8th Motorcycle Battalion
  1/2/3/80th Artillery Regiment
  84th Signals Battalion
  59th Pioneer Battalion
  59th Division Support Units
 19th Tank Division
  1/27th Armoured Regiment
 19th Tank Grenadier Brigade
  1/2/3/73rd Tank Grenadier Regiment

1/2/3/74th Tank Grenadier Regiment
  19th Anti-tank Battalion
  19th Motorcycle Battalion
1/2/3/19th Artillery Regiment
  19th Signals Battalion
  19th Pioneer Battalion
    19th Division Support Units
SS Leibstandarte Adolph Hitler Division
  1/2/3/1st SS LSSAH Motorized Infantry Regiment
  1/2/3/2nd SS LSSAH Motorized Infantry Regiment
    SS Leibstandarte Adolph Hitler Storm Protection Battalion
      SS Leibstandarte Adolph Hitler Armoured Troop
  SS Leibstandarte Adolph Hitler Motorcycle Regiment
  1/2/3/4/SS Leibstandarte Adolph Hitler (motorized) Artillery Regiment
    SS Leibstandarte Adolph Hitler Anti-tank Battalion
    SS Leibstandarte Adolph Hitler Signals Battalion
    SS Leibstandarte Adolph Hitler Pioneer Battalion
SS Das Reich Battle Group
XIII Corps
  213th Security Grenadier Regiment
  68th Division
  1/2/169th Grenadier Regiment
  1/2/196th Grenadier Regiment
    1/2/168th Anti-tank Battalion
    168th Fusilier Battalion
  1/2/3/4/168th Artillery Regiment
    168th Pioneer Battalion
    168th Signals Battalion
      168th Division Support Units
  340th Division
  1/2/695th Grenadier Regiment
  1/2/696th Grenadier Regiment
  327th Divisional Group
  595th and 596th Regimental Groups
    340th Schnell Battalion
  1/2/3/340th Artillery Regiment
  4/327 Artillery Regiment
    340th Pioneer Battalion
    340th Signals Battalion
      340th Division Support Units
  208th Division Battle Group
    Süd Cavalry Regiment
  309th Regimental Battle Group
    337th Regimental Battle Group
    338th Regimental Battle Group
    208th Artillery Regiment
  7th Tank Division Battle Group
LIX Corps
  291st Division
  1/2/504th Grenadier Regiment
  1/2/505th Grenadier Regiment
  1/2/506th Grenadier Regiment
    291st Fusilier Battalion
  1/2/3/4/291st Artillery Regiment
  291st Pioneer Battalion
  291st Signals Battalion
    291st Division Support Units

C Corps Detachment
  454th Security Division
    1/2/3/375th Infantry Regiment
    1/2/602nd Infantry Regiment
     454th Cavalry Battalion
    1/6th Police Regiment (3 companies)
      828th Motorized Signals Company
      445th Armoured Company
     2/221st Artillery Battalion
     360th Division Support Units
VII Hungarian Army Corps
  21st Hungarian Division
  102nd Hungarian Division
LXII Reserve Corps
  143rd Reserve Division
     68th Reserve Grenadier Regiment (169th, 188th and 512th Battalions)
     76th Reserve Grenadier Regiment (230th, 323rd, 386th and 479th Battalions)
     208th Reserve Grenadier Regiment (122nd, 337th, and 397th Battalions)
     257th Reserve Artillery Battalion
     68th Reserve Artillery Battalion
  147th Reserve Division
    212th Reserve Grenadier Regiment (63rd, 316th, 320th, 423rd and 468th Battalions)
     268th Reserve Grenadier Regiment (91st and 488th Battalions)
     27th Reserve Artillery Battalion
     27th Reserve Pioneer Battalion
     947th Division Service Battalion

German Army Group F (South East): As of October 4, 1943

(Created by George Nafziger. First published in English online at the U.S. Army Combined Arms Research Library) (The database is open source)

Order of Battle

1st (Bulgarian) Sofyia Infantry Division
    1/2/3/1st Infantry Regiment
    1/2/3/6th Infantry Regiment
    1/2/3/16th Infantry Regiment
    1/2/3/25th Infantry Regiment
    4th Field Artillery Regiment
    1st Machinegun Battalion
22nd (Reserve Infantry Division
    1/2/3/50th Infantry Regiment
    1/2/3/63rd Infantry Regiment
    1/2/3/66th Infantry Regiment
    22nd Field Artillery Regiment
    22nd Machinegun Battalion
24th (Reserve) Infantry Division
    1/2/3/60th Infantry Regiment
    1/2/3/64th Infantry Regiment
27th (Reserve) Infantry Division
    1/2/3/68th Infantry Regiment
    1/2/3/69th Infantry Regiment
    1/2/3/75th Infantry Regiment
    1/2/3/76th Infantry Regiment
    1/2/3/77th Infantry Regiment
25th Bulgarian Division
2nd Panzer Corps
    1st Brandenburg Regiment
III (Germania) SS Panzer Corps
    1/2/3/14th SS Polizei Regiment
11th SS Freiwilligen Panzer Grenadier Division Nordland
    1/2/3/SS Panzer Grenadier Regiment Norge
    1/2/3/SS Panzer Grenadier Regiment Danmark
      11th SS Panzer Battalion (4 companies)
      11th SS Reconnaissance Battalion (5 companies)

1/2/4/11th SS Artillery Regiment
   1/2/11th SS Reconnaissance Battalion (5 companies)
   11th SS Panzer-Jäger (AT) Battalion (3 companies)
   11th SS Sturmgeschütz Battalion (3 batteries)
   11th SS Flak Battalion (4 batteries)
   11th SS Pioneer Battalion (3 companies)
   11th SS Armored Signal Battalion (2 companies)
     11th SS Division (Einheiten) Service Units
XV Mountain Corps
  1st Jäger Ersatz Regiment
 114th Jäger (former 714th) Division
  1/2/3/721st Jäger Regiment
  1/2/3/741st Jäger Regiment
  1/2/3/66th Artillery Regiment
    Panzerjäger Company
    712th Pioneer Company
   712th Signals Battalion
    712th Division (Einheiten) Support Units
 369th Croatian Division
  1/2/3/369th Croatian Regiment
  1/2/3/370th Croatian Regiment
  1/2/3/4/369th Croatian Artillery Regiment
   369th Panzerjäger Battalion
   369th Bicycle Battalion
   369th Pioneer Battalion
   369th Signals Battalion
    369th Division (Einheiten) Support Units
 373rd Croatian Division
  1/2/3/383rd Croatian Regiment
  1/2/3/384th Croatian Regiment
  1/2/3/4/373rd Croatian Artillery Regiment
   373rd Panzerjäger Battalion
   373rd Bicycle Battalion
   373rd Pioneer Battalion
   373rd Signals Battalion
    373rd Division (Einheiten) Support Units
 SS Prinz Eugen Division
  1/2/3/92nd (mot) Grenadier Regiment
XXI Mountain Corps
 100th Jäger Division
  1/2/3/54th Jäger Regiment
  1/2/3/227th Jäger Regiment
  1/2/3/4/83rd Artillery Regiment
   100th Bicycle Battalion
   100th Panzerjäger Battalion
   100th Pioneer Battalion
   100th Signals Battalion
    100th Division (Einheiten) Support Units
 118th Jäger (former 718th) Division
  1/2/3/738th Jäger Regiment
  1/2/3/750th Jäger Regiment
  1/2/3/668th Artillery Regiment
    Panzerjäger Company
    718th Pioneer Company
    718th Signals Company
    718th Division (Einheiten) Support Units
 181st Division (enroute)

1/2/3/334th Fusilier Regiment
1/2/3/359th Grenadier Regiment
  222nd Panzerjäger Battalion
  222nd Bicycle Battalion
1/2/3/222nd Artillery Regiment
  222nd Pioneer Battalion
  222nd Signals Battalion
    222nd Division (Einheiten) Support Units
  297th Division (forming)
1/2/3/522nd Grenadier Regiment
2/,3/523rd Grenadier Regiment
1/2/3/524th Grenadier Regiment
  297th Panzerjäger Battalion
  297th Bicycle Battalion
1/2/3/4/297th Artillery Regiment
  297th Pioneer Battalion
  297th Signals Battalion
    297th Division (Einheiten) Support Units
LXIX Reserve Corps
  173rd Reserve Division
    17th Reserve Grenadier Regiment (21st, 42nd & 186th Battalions)
    231st Reserve Grenadier Regiment (55th, 95th, & 170th Battalions)
      10th Reserve Artillery Battalion
      46th Reserve Pioneer Battalion
        1073rd Medical Service Formation
        873rd Support Troops
  187th Reserve Division
          Division Staff Agram
    45th Reserve Infantry Regiment (1/130th, 2/135th, 2/462nd Battalions)
    130th Reserve Infantry Regiment (2/130th, 2/133rd Battalions)
    462nd Reserve Infantry Regiment (1/135th, 1/486th, 2/482nd Battalions)
      96th Reserve Artillery Battalion
      86th Reserve Pioneer Battalion
      1087th Reserve Signals Battalion
        1087th Medical Troops
        1087th Administrative Troops
  1st Cossack Division (forming)
  1st Don Cossack Reiter (Cavalry) Brigade
    1/,2/1st Don Cossack Reiter Regiment
    1/,2/2nd (Siberian) Cossack Regiment
    1/,2/3rd Sswodno Cossack Reiter Regiment
    Don Cossack Artillery Battalion
  2/Kaukasus Cossack Reiter Brigade
    4th Kuban Cossack Reiter Regiment
    5th (Don) Cossack Reiter Regiment
    6th Terek Cossack Reiter Regiment
    Kuban Cossack Artillery Battalion
      55th Division Support Troops
E Army
1/2/3/18th SS Polizei Regiment
1/2/3/1st SS Polizei Grenadier Regiment
1/2/3/2nd SS Polizei Grenadier Regiment
  2nd Brandenburg Regiment
  Sturm Division Rhodos
    Rhodos Grenadier Regiment
      Rhodos Fusilier Battalion
      Rhodos Panzer Battalion

Rhodos Flak Company
Rhodos Signals Company
Rhodos Pioneer Company
Rhodos Feldersatz Battalion
11th Luftwaffe Field Division
1/2/3/21st Luftwaffe Jäger Regiment
1/2/3/22nd Luftwaffe Jäger Regiment
1/2/3/4/11th Luftwaffe Artillery Regiment
11th Luftwaffe Field Division Panzerjäger Battalion
Bicycle Company
Pioneer Company
Signals Company
Support Troops
XXII Mountain Corps
1st Mountain Division
1/2/3/98th Mountain Infantry Regiment
1/2/3/99th Mountain Infantry Regiment
44th Panzerjäger Battalion
54th Bicycle Battalion
1/2/3/4/79th Artillery Regiment
54th Feldersatz Battalion
54th Signals Battalion
54th Pioneer Battalion
54th Division (Einheiten) Support Units
104th Jäger Division
1/2/3/724th Jäger Regiment
1/2/3/734th Jäger Regiment
1/2/3/654th Artillery Regiment
704th Pioneer Battalion
704th Signals Battalion
704th Division (Einheiten) Support Units
LXVII Corps
1st Panzer Division
2/1st Armored Regiment
1st Panzer Grenadier Brigade
1/2/3/1st Panzer Grenadier Regiment
1/2/3/113th Panzer Grenadier Regiment
702nd Sturmgeschütz Battery
37th Panzerjäger Battalion
1st Motorcycle Battalion
1/2/3/73rd Artillery Regiment
37th Signals Battalion
37th Pioneer Battalion
37th Division (Einheiten) Support Units
117th Jäger (former 717th) Division
1/2/3/737th Jäger Regiment
1/2/3/749th Jäger Regiment
1/2/3/670th Artillery Regiment
Panzerjäger Company
717th Pioneer Company
717th Signals Company
717th Division (Einheiten) Support Units
Army Field Corps Saloniki
7th Rila Infantry Division
1/2/3/13th Infantry Regiment
1/2/3/14th Infantry Regiment
7th Field Artillery Regiment

7th Machinegun Battalion 5
Crete Command
 Crete Fortress Brigade
  1/2/3/746th Grenadier Regiment
  1/2/619th Artillery Regiment
   721st & 722nd (motorized) Signal Companies

German Army Group B: As of January 1, 1943

(Created by George Nafziger. First published in English online at the U.S. Army Combined Arms Research Library) (The database is open source)

Order of Battle

307th Motorized Mapping Detachment
1/2/3/57th Security Regiment
221st Armored Company (captured equipment)
318th Armored Company (captured equipment)
221st Signals Battalion
382nd Feldausbildungs Division
Fretter-Pico Army Detachment (XXX Corps)
Kreysing Group (part of 3rd Mountain Division)
304th Division
1/2/3/573rd Grenadier Regiment
1/2/3/574th Grenadier Regiment
1/2/3/575th Grenadier Regiment
304th Schnell Battalion
1/2/3/304th Artillery Regiment
304th Pioneer Battalion
304th Signals Battalion
304th Division (Einheiten) Support Units
Nagel Group
Schuldt Brigade (unknown part of brigade present)
3rd Ravenna Division
37th Ravenna Infantry Regiment
38th Ravenna Infantry Regiment
121st Motorized Artillery Regiment
3rd Mortar Battalion
154th Anti-Tank Company
3rd Signal Company
18th Pioneer Company
16th Field Hospital
202nd Field Hospital
32nd Baggage Section
7th CCRR Section
23 March Italian Brigade (subordianted to Ravenna)

8th Italian Army
 Italian Barbo Cavarly Brigade
 Italian II Corps
 Italian XXXV Corps
  901st Lehr Regiment
  Göller Group
  298th Division (bulk of division present)
   1/2/3/525th Grenadier Regiment
   1/2/3/526th Grenadier Regiment
   1/2/3/527th Grenadier Regiment
    298th Panzerjäger Battalion
    298th Bicycle Battalion
   1/2/3/4/298th Artillery Regiment
    298th Pioneer Battalion
    298th Signals Battalion
     298th Division (Einheiten) Support Units
  9th Pasuibo (Semi-Motorized) Division (subordinated to 298th)
   7th Roma Infantry Regiment
   8th Roma Infantry Regiment
   8th Pasubio Artillery Regiment
     13th AA Battery (20mm)
     18th AA Battery (20mm)
     85th AA Battery (20mm)
    9th Mortar Battalion
  52nd Torino (Semi-motorized) Division (subordinated to 298th)
   81st Torino Infantry Regiment
   82nd Torino Infantry Regiment
   52nd Torino Artillery Regiment
    26th Mortar Battalion
    52nd Mortar Battalion
     52nd Anti-Tank Company
     171st Anti-Tank Company
    52nd Engineer Battalion
 19th Panzer Division
  1/27th Armored Regiment
 19th Panzer Grenadier Brigade
  1/2/3/73rd Panzer Grenadier Regiment
  1/2/3/74th Panzer Grenadier Regiment
   19th Panzerjäger Battalion
   19th Motorcycle Battalion
  1/2/3/19th Artillery Regiment
   19th Signals Battalion
   19th Pioneer Battalion
    19th Division (Einheiten) Support Units
 26th Division (enroute)
  1/2/3/39th Fusilier Regiment
  1/2/3/77th Grenadier Regiment
  1/2/3/78th Grenadier Regiment
   26th Panzerjäger Battalion
   26th Bicycle Battalion
  1/2/3/26th Artillery Regiment
   1/62nd Artillery Battalion
   26th Pioneer Battalion
   26th Signals Battalion
    26th Division (Einheinten) Support Units
 Schuldt Brigade (part present)
XIV Panzer Corps

385th Division
   1/2/3/537th Grenadier Regiment
   1/2/3/538th Grenadier Regiment
   1/2/3/539th Grenadier Regiment
    385th Schnell Battalion
   2/3/4/385th Artillery Regiment
    385th Pioneer Battalion
    385th Signals Battalion
    385th Division (Einheiten) Support Units
213th Security Division (subordinated to 385th) (only part present)
   1/2/3/610th Infantry Regiment
   1/2/3/610th Infantry Regiment
     201st Motorized Signals Company
    1/213th Artillery Battalion
    318th Cavalry Battalion (4 squadrons)
     3/9th Police Regiment (3 companies)
    318th Division (Einheiten) Support Units
Fegelein Group
  5th Cosseria Infantry Division (only part of division present)
    89th Salerno Infantry Regiment
    90th Salerno Infantry Regiment
    108th Artillery Regiment
     5th Mortar Battalion
     10th Mortar Battalion
     135th Anti-Tank Battalion (self-propelled)
     355th Anti-Tank Battalion
  3rd Julia Alpini Division (only part of division present)
    8th Alpini Infantry Regiment
    9th Alpini Infantry Regiment
    3rd Alpini Artillery Regiment
     110th Machinegun Battalion
      41st Anti-Tank Company
      83rd Anti-Tank Company
     3rd Engineer Battalion
      113th Signal Company
      123rd Pioneer Company
       103rd Sit. Section
       303rd Medical Section
       309th Medical Section
     629th Field Hospital
     633rd Field Hospital
      207th Motor Transport Detachment
      237th Motor Transport Detachment
       9th Supply Section
      62nd Field Bakery
  387th Division
    1/2/3/541st Grenadier Regiment
    1/2/3/542nd Grenadier Regiment
    1/2/3/543rd Grenadier Regiment
     387th Schnell Battalion
    1/2/3/4/387th Artillery Regiment
     387th Pioneer Battalion
     387th Signals Battalion
      387th Division (Einheiten) Support Units
  27th Panzer Division
    1/2/140th Panzer Grenadier Regiment
     127th Panzer Battalion

1/2/127th Panzer Artillery Regiment
560th Panzerjäger Battalion
127th Pioneer Battalion
127th Signals Battalion
127th Division (Einheiten) Support Troops
Italian Alpine Corps
156th Vicenza Infantry Division
277th Vicenza Infantry Regiment
278th Vicenza Infantry Regiment
156th Artillery Regiment
156th Machinegun Battalion
155th Engineer Battalion
255th Signal Company
155th Pionieer Company
Medical Section
155th Supply Section
255th Field Bakery
125th CCRR Section
135th CCRR Section
2nd Tridentina Alpini Division
5th Alpini Infantry Regiment
6th Alpini Infantry Regiment
2nd Alpini Artillery Regiment
216th Anti-Tank Company
2nd Alpini Engineer Battalion
112th Signal Company
122nd Pionieer Company
102nd Sit. Company
5th Medical Section
302nd Medical Section
263rd Field Hospital
619th Field Hospital
620th Field Hospital
621st Field Hospital
622nd Field Hospital
206th Mixed Motor Transport Section
417th CCRR Section
4th Cuneense Alpini Division
1st Alpini Infantry Regiment
2nd Alpini Infantry Regiment
4th Alpini Artillery Regiment
4th Engineer Battalion
114th Signal Company
104th Pionieer Company
124th Pionieer Company
104th Sit. Section
61st Field Hospital
62nd Field Hospital
613th Field Hospital
201st Motor Transport Section
22nd Transport Detachment
63rd Field Bakery
414th CCRR Section
2nd Hungarian Army
1st Hungarian Armored Division
30th Armored Regiment
1st Motorized Infantry Regiment

1st Reconnaissance Battalion
  51st Anti-Tank Battalion
  1st Engineer Battalion
  1st Artillery Battalion
  5th Artillery Battalion
  51st Artillery Battalion
168th Division (1 unknown regiment detached)
Verband (Task Force) 700
  VII Hungarian Corps
    12th Hungarian Light Division
      18th Infantry Regiment
      48th Infantry Regiment
      12th Artillery Regiment
    19th Hungarian Light Division
      13th Infantry Regiment
      43rd Infantry Regiment
      19th Artillery Regiment
    23rd Hungarian Light Division
      21st Infantry Regiment
      51st Infantry Regiment
      23rd Artillery Regiment
  IV Hungarian Corps
    7th Hungarian Light Division
      4th Infantry Regiment
      35th Infantry Regiment
      7th Artillery Regiment
    10th Hungarian Light Division
      6th Infantry Regiment
      36th Infantry Regiment
      10th Artillery Regiment
    13th Hungarian Light Division
      7th Infantry Regiment
      37th Infantry Regiment
      13th Artillery Regiment
    20th Hungarian Light Division
      14th Infantry Regiment
      23rd Infantry Regiment
      20th Artillery Regiment
    168th Division
  III Hungarian Corps
    6th Hungarian Light Division
      22nd Infantry Regiment
      52nd Infantry Regiment
      6th Artillery Regiment
    9th Hungarian Light Division
      17th Infantry Regiment
      47th Infantry Regiment
      9th Artillery Regiment
2nd Army
  VIII Corp
    88th Division
    57th Division
      1/2/3/199th Grenadier Regiment
      1/2/3/217th Grenadier Regiment
      157th Panzerjäger Battalion
      157th Bicycle Battalion
      1/2/3/4/157th Artillery Regiment

157th Pioneer Battalion
157th Signals Battalion
   157th Division (Einheinten) Support Units
75th Division
1/2/3/172nd Grenadier Regiment
1/2/3/202nd Grenadier Regiment
1/2/3/222nd Grenadier Regiment
  175th Panzerjäger Battalion
  175th Bicycle Battalion
1/2/3/4/175th Artillery Regiment
  175th Pioneer Battalion
  175th Signals Battalion
   175th Division (Einheinten) Support Units
323rd Division
1/2/3/591st Grenadier Regiment
1/2/3/593rd Grenadier Regiment
1/2/3/594th Grenadier Regiment
  323rd Schnell Battalion
1/2/3/4/323rd Artillery Regiment
  323rd Pioneer Battalion
  323rd Signals Battalion
   323rd Division (Einheiten) Support Units
Oberst Roth Group
Don Group (1 unknown regiment of 383rd Division present)
XIII Corps
68th Division
1/2/3/169th Grenadier Regiment
1/2/3/196th Grenadier Regiment
1/2/3/168th Panzerjäger Battalion
  168th Bicycle Battalion
1/2/3/4/168th Artillery Regiment
  168th Pioneer Battalion
  168th Signals Battalion
   168th Division (Einheiten) Support Units
82nd Division
1/2/3/158th Grenadier Regiment
1/2/3/166th Grenadier Regiment
1/2/3/168th Grenadier Regiment
  182nd Schnell Battalion
1/2/3/4/182nd Artillery Regiment
  182nd Pioneer Battalion
  182nd Signals Battalion
   182nd Division (Einheinten) Support Units
340th Division
1/2/3/694th Grenadier Regiment
1/2/3/695th Grenadier Regiment
1/2/3/696th Grenadier Regiment
  340th Schnell Battalion
1/2/3/4/340th Artillery Regiment
  340th Pioneer Battalion
  340th Signals Battalion
   340th Division (Einheiten) Support Units
377th Division
1/2/3/768th Grenadier Regiment
1/2/3/769th Grenadier Regiment
1/2/3/770th Grenadier Regiment
  377th Schnell Battalion

1/2/3/4/377th Artillery Regiment
  377th Pioneer Battalion
  377th Signals Battalion
    377th Division (Einheiten) Support Units
LV Corps
  88th Division (1 unknown regiment of division present)
  45th Division
    1/2/3/130th Grenadier Regiment
    1/2/3/133rd Grenadier Regiment
    1/2/3/135th Grenadier Regiment
     45th Panzerjäger Battalion
     45th Bicycle Battalion
    1/2/3/98th Artillery Regiment
     1/99th Artillery Battalion
     81st Pioneer Battalion
     65th Signals Battalion
      45th Division (Einheinten) Support Units
  299th Division
    1/2/3/528th Grenadier Regiment
    1/2/3/529th Grenadier Regiment
    1/2/3/530th Grenadier Regiment
    1/2/3/4/299th Artillery Regiment
     299th Panzerjäger Battalion
     299th Pioneer Battalion
     299th Signals Battalion
      299th Division (Einheiten) Support Units
  383rd Division (1 regiment detached)
    1/2/3/531st Grenadier Regiment
    1/2/3/532nd Grenadier Regiment
    1/2/3/533rd Grenadier Regiment
     383rd Schnell Battalion
    1/2/3/4/383rd Artillery Regiment
     383rd Signals Battalion
     383rd Pioneer Battalion
     383rd Division (Einheiten) Support Units
Rear Area Security
  213th Security Division (part detached)
    1/2/3/610th Infantry Regiment
    1/2/3/610th Infantry Regiment
     201st Motorized Signals Company
     1/213th Artillery Battalion
     318th Cavalry Battalion (4 squadrons)
     3/9th Police Regiment (3 companies)
      318th Division (Einheiten) Support Units
  105th Hungarian Light Division

Army Group G Troops: As of October 18, 1944

(Created by George Nafziger. First published in English online at the U.S. Army Combined Arms Research Library) (The database is open source)

Order of Battle

Army Group G Troops
    422nd Flak Company
    Security Company
    2/631st (motorized) Mapping Company
    115th Military Police Detachment
    120th (motorized) FA Commando
352nd Artillery Regiment
    717th Secret Field Police
    1025th (motorized) Military Police Detachment
        Staff, 1/6th Pioneer Battalion
3rd (Home) Pioneer Regimental
A (motorized) Signals Brigade
    14th (motorized) Signals Battalion
    606th (motorized) Signals Battalion
19th Army
    Korück Grenadier Brigade
    106th Tank Brigade
    321st (motorized) Artillery Brigade
        2nd Armoured Train Company
            926th Pioneer Staffel Staff
    39th (motorized) Brüko bridge construction unit
    1/403rd (motorized) Brüko bridge construction unit
    1/409th (motorized) Brüko bridge construction unit
    2/416th (motorized) Brüko bridge construction unit
    669th Pioneer Battalion
    Army Pioneer School (Eberle) Battalion
    601st East Bridge Pioneer Battalion
1st Pioneer Bridge Regiment
    3/622nd Landes Pioneer Battalion
    824th (motorized) Brüko bridge construction unit
    2/422nd (motorized) Brüko bridge construction unit
        A Pioneer Brigade Staff

513rd Signals Battalion
  A Signals Brigade
Dehner Corps
  661st Grenadier Regiment
  G2 Special Grenadier Regiment
    Stern Grenadier Battalion
    Söllner Grenadier Battalion
LXXXV Corps
  Böhme Grenadier Regiment
    Lange Grenadier Battalion
    835th Grenadier Battalion
    454th Grenadier Battalion
    403rd Grenadier Battalion
                Witte (OKH)Battalion Regimental Staff
    Belfort Grenadier Battalion
    Külkan Grenadier Battalion
  933rd Artillery Brigade
  72nd (motorized) Artillery Brigade
  485th Signals Brigade
    1/2/23rd Pioneer Battalion
    2/4/698th Pioneer Battalion
  von Oppen Brigade
    Roth Luftwaffe Regiment
    D/V Regiment
  189th Division
    1/2/Young Grenadier Regiment (1007th and 1021st Security Battalions)
    1/2/1000th (motorized) Grenadier Regiment
    1/2/Menke Luftwaffe Regiment
      Rohrmoser Battalion
      Hollermeier Battalion
      1/28th Reserve Artillery Battalion (4-75mm guns)
      242th Signals Battalion
      1089th Engineer Battalion
      1000th Reconnaissance Battalion
  159th Division
    1/2/9th Grenadier Regiment
    1/2/251st Grenadier Regiment
      1181st Artillery Battalion
      1059th Anti-tank Battalion
      1059th Reserve Pioneer Battalion
      1059th Signals Battalion
      1059th Field Replacement Battalion
    933rd Grenadier Regimental Kampfgruppe
    1/2/3/933rd Grenadier Regiment
        105mm Howitzer Battery
Assigned Fortress Troops
    2 unknown Border Protection battalions
    18th Fortress Regiment
    1414th Fortress Regiment
      806th Fortress Machinegun Battalion
      50th Heavy Machinegun Battalion
      3/Volks Grenadier Artillery Battalion
      1314th Fortress Artillery Battalion
IV Luftwaffe Corps
      4th (motorized) Signals Battalion
      746th Pioneer Battalion
  2nd Artillery Brigade

1559th Armoured Battalion
338th Division
  1/2/757th Grenadier Regiment
  2/3/338th Artillery Regiment
    338th Signals Battalion
    338th Pioneer Battalion
    338th Field Replacement Battalion
308th Grenadier Regimental Battle Group
  1/2/308th Grenadier Regiment
  Carro Veloce Regiment (4 battalions)
  1/338th Artillery Regiment
  1198th Artillery Battalion
  200th Security Regiment
    1K/932nd Russian Battalion
    1432nd Fortress Battalion
    1433rd Fortress Battalion
    62nd Fortress Battalion
    40th Fortress Battalion
    807th Heavy Machinegun Battalion
    808th Heavy Machinegun Battalion
LXIV Corps
    Stenger Grenadier Battalion
    360th Cossack Battalion
  Strassen Command Regiment
  Korück Regiment
    607th Self Propelled Flak Battalion
  186th (motorized) Artillery Brigade
    464th (motorized) Signals Battalion
    11th Armoured Infantry Battalion
    671st Security Battalion
    602nd Reconnaissance Battalion
    5th (motorized) Anti-tank Battalion
  198th Division
  1/2/305th Grenadier Regiment
  1/2/308th Grenadier Regiment
  1/2/326th Grenadier Regiment
  235th Artillery Regiment
    235th Signals Battalion
    235th Engineer Battalion
    198th Fusilier Battalion
    198th Field Replacement Battalion
  716th Division
  1/2/726th Grenadier Regiment
  1/2/736th Grenadier Regiment
    716th Fusilier Battalion
  1/2/3/4/1716th Artillery Regiment
    716th Signals Battalion
    716th Engineer Battalion
    716th Field Replacement Battalion
    716th Anti-tank Battalion
    934th East Battalion
      716th Division Service Units
  17th Fortress Regiment
    1417th Fortress Battalion
    39th Fortress Machinegun Battalion
    1523rd Fortress Artillery Battalion
LXXXV Corps

Unknown (motorized) Signals Battalion
685th Flak Battalion
16th Division
1/2/221st Grenadier Regiment
1/2/223rd Grenadier Regiment
1/2/225th Grenadier Regiment
1316th Fusilier Battalion
1/2/3/4/1316th Artillery Regiment
602nd Reconnaissance Battalion
1316th Signals Battalion
1316th Engineer Battalion
1316th Division Support Troops
21st Tank Division
1/2/47th Tank Grenadier Regiment
1/2/104th Tank Grenadier Regiment
1/2/22nd Tank Regiment
1/2/3/155th Artillery Regiment
21st Tank Reconnaissance Battalion
200th Armoured Anti-tank Battalion
200th Tank Flak Battalion
200th Tank Signals Battalion
200th Tank Pioneer Battalion
200th Field Replacement Battalion
200th Division Troops
A/V Fortress Regiment (Supply)
810th Heavy Machinegun Battalion
49th Fortress Machinegun Battalion
269th Infantry Division
1st Army
1st AOK Sturm Battalion (Training)
318th (motorized) Artillery Brigade
Lutz Pioneer Bridge Staffel Staff
846th (motorized) "J" Bridging Column
550th (motorized) "J" Bridging Column
551st (motorized) "J" Bridging Column
243rd Pioneer Battalion
668th (motorized) Pioneer Battalion
2nd Bridge Construction Staff
22nd (motorized) Brüko bridge construction unit
5th (motorized) Brüko bridge construction unit
2nd Pioneer Bridge Construction Regiment
A (motorized) Pioneer Brigade
512th (motorized) Signals Battalion
A (motorized) Signals Brigade
LVIII Tank Corps
16th Luftwaffe Pioneer Battalion
844th (motorized) Brüko "J" Bridging Column
458th (motorized) Signals Battalion
11th Tank Division
1/2/110th Tank Grenadier Regiment
1/2/111th Tank Grenadier Regiment
1/2/15th Tank Regiment
1/2/3/119th Armoured Artillery Regiment
277th Army Flak Battalion
11th Tank Reconnaissance Battalion
61st Armoured Anti-tank Battalion
203rd Tank Pioneer Battalion

89th Tank Signals Battalion
117th Field Replacement Battalion
61st Division Support Units
553rd Division
1/2/1119th Grenadier Regiment
1/2/1120th Grenadier Regiment
1/2/1121st Grenadier Regiment
1/2/3/4/1553rd Artillery Regiment
553rd Divisional Fusilier Company
553rd Signals Battalion
553rd Field Replacement Battalion
553rd Division Service Units
30th Fortress Regiment
1305th Fortress Artillery Battalion
1306th Fortress Artillery Battalion
34th Fortress Artillery Battalion
1/V Fortress Artillery Battalion
XIII SS Corps
17th (motorized) Signals Battalion
113th (motorized) Artillery Brigade
559th Division
1/2/1125th Grenadier Regiment
1/2/1126th Grenadier Regiment
1/2/1127th Grenadier Regiment
1/2/3/4/1559th Artillery Regiment
1559th Tank Signals Battalion
48th Division
1/2/126th Grenadier Regiment
1/2/127th Grenadier Regiment
148th Fusilier Battalion
1/2/3/148th Artillery Regiment
148th Signals Battalion
148th Pioneer Battalion
148th Field Replacement Battalion
148th Division Service Units
17th SS Tank Grenadier Division Götz von Berlichingen
1/2/3/37th SS Tank Grenadier Regiment
1/2/3/38th SS Tank Grenadier Regiment
17th SS Tank Battalion
1/2/3/17th SS Artillery Regiment
17th SS Flak Battalion
17th SS Pioneer Battalion
17th SS Signals Battalion
17th SS Support Troops
Böhme Fortress Brigade (Staff only)
29th Fortress Regiment
1431st Fortress Battalion
1416th Fortress Battalion
56th Machinegun Fortress Battalion
53rd Machinegun Fortress Battalion
51st Machinegun Fortress Battalion
45th Machinegun Fortress Battalion
816th Heavy Machinegun Fortress Battalion
805th Heavy Machinegun Fortress Battalion
1518th Fortress Artillery Battalion
1309th Fortress Artillery Battalion
33rd Fortress Artillery Battalion

LXXXII Corps
    437th (motorized) Signals Battalion
  189th (motorized) Artillery Brigade
  19th Infantry Division
    1/2/59th Infantry Regiment
    1/2/73rd Infantry Regiment
    1/2/74th Infantry Regiment
    1/2/3/4/719th Artillery Regiment
      119th Signals Battalion
      119th Engineer Battalion
      119th Anti-tank Battalion
        19th Division Service Units
  416th Division
    1/2/712th Grenadier Regiment
    1/2/713th Grenadier Regiment
    1/2/3/4/416th Artillery Regiment
  462nd Division
    1/2/Wagner Grenadier Regiment
    13th and 14th Companies, Wagner Grenadier Regiment
    1/2/Stössel Grenadier Regiment
    13th and 14th Companies, Stössel Grenadier Regiment
    1/2/3/4/761st (Palm) Artillery Regiment
      Divisional Fusilier Company
    Pioneer Battalion
      Divisional Service Units
    26th Fortress Regiment
      1415th Fortress Battalion
      1410th Fortress Battalion
      1522nd Fortress Artillery Battalion
      1419th Fortress Artillery Battalion
      1303rd Fortress Artillery Battalion
      7th Fortress Artillery Battalion
  361st Infantry Division

Endnotes

Introduction

1. Bertaud, J.-P., *The Army of the French Revolution: From Citizen-soldier to Instrument of Power (Princeton: Princeton University Press, 1988)*, p. 87.
2. *Ibid.*
3. Lo Presti, F., "French Penal Regiment Organization," www.napoleon-series.org. Retrieved May 5, 2017.
4. Sicard, J., "Les Bataillons d'Infanterie Legere d'Afrique et leurs insignes, 1832-1972," *Militaria Magazine*, September 1994, p. 49.
5. Carles, P., "Les Bataillons d'Afrique," *www.musee-infanterie.com*. Retrieved May 5, 2017.
6. Ricchiardi, E., *The Battalion of Frank Hunters* (The Italian State Archives of Turin, 2014).
7. Suvorov, V., *Inside The Soviet Army* (London: Hamish Hamilton, 1982).
8. Pyl'cyn, A., *Penalty Strike: The Memoirs of a Red Army Penal Company Commander, 1943–45* (Mechanicsburg: Stackpole Books, 2006), p. 45.
9. Brown, D., *The Galvanized Yankees* (Lincoln: University of Nebraska Press), p. 200.
10. Dyer, F. H. A., *Compendium of the War of the Rebellion*, Vol. 2 (Seattle: Morningside Press, 1979), p. 101.
11. Crooks, J. J., *Historical Records of the Royal African Corps 1800–1821* (Dublin: Browne and Nolan Publishers, 1925), p. 356.
12. 1916 Handbook of the Turkish Army (Nashville: Battery Press, 1999), p. 133.
13. "Translation of Wehrkraftzersetzung," *Wörterbuch Englisch-Deutsch dictionary* www. dict.cc/. Retrieved April 16, 2017.
14. Dear, I., and Foot, M., (eds), *The Oxford Companion to World War II* (London: Oxford University Press, 2001), pp. 365-367.
15. Dear and Foot, *op. cit.* p. 366.
16. Walle, H., (ed.), *Uprising of conscience: Military resistance against Hitler and the Nazi regime 1933–1945*, 4th edition (Mittler, Berlin: 1994), pp. 223-248.
17. "Kriegssonderstrafrechtsverordnung (KSSVO)," www.lexexakt.de. Retrieved May 16, 2017.
18. *Ibid.*
19. Päuser, F., *The Rehabilitation of Deserters of the German Wehrmacht under Historical, Juridical and Political Aspects, with Commentary on the Law for the Abolition of National Socialist Judgments* (Munich: University of the German Armed Forces, 2005), p. 76.
20. Paul, G., *Disobedient soldiers: Dissent, Refusal and Resistance of German Soldiers (1939–1945)* (Sankt Ingbert: Rohrig University Publishers, 1994), p. 251.
21. Hoffmann, P., *The History of the German Resistance, 1933–1945* (McGill-Queen's University Press; 3rd edition, 1996), p. 773.
22. Messerschmidt, M., *The Military Justice in the Service of National Socialism: Destruction of a Legend* (Baden-Baden: Nomos Publishing, 1987), p. 222.

23. Faulkner Rossi, L., *Wehrmacht Priests: Catholicism and the Nazi War of Annihilation* (Cambridge: Harvard University Press, 2015), p. 101.
24. Gruchmann, L., *Justice in the 3rd Reich 1933–1940* (Berlin: Oldenbourg Publishing, 2001), p. 284.
25. Stargardt, N., *The German War: A Nation Under Arms, 1939–1945: Citizens and Soldiers* (New York: Basic Books, 2015), p. 659.
26. Wette, W., *The Wehrmacht History, Myth, Reality* (Cambridge: Harvard University Press, 2007), p. 286.
27. Wagner, W., *The People's Court in the National Socialist State* (Munich: 2011), p. 277.
28. Bradley, D., Hildebrand, K.-F., and Roevekamp, M., *The Generals of the Army, 1921–1945: The Military Generations of the Generals, as well as the Doctors, Veterinarians, Directors, Judges and Generals and Admirals* (Osnabrück: Biblio Publishing, 1993), p. 44.
29. *Ibid.*
30. *Law on the Abolition of Military Judicial Jurisdiction of 17 August 1920.* "German Reichsgesetzblatt Part I, 1867–1945," p. 1,579.
31. Gribbohm, G.. *The Reichskriegsgericht. The Institution and its Legal Evaluation* (Berlin: *Wissenschaftliche Publishing,* 2004), p. 6.
32. Haase, N., *The Reichskriegsgericht and the Resistance to National Socialist Rule* (Berlin: Memorial to the German Resistance, 1993), p. 13.
33. Bradley, Hildebrand, and Roevekamp, *op. cit.*, p. 50.
34. Dermot, B., *The Generals of the Army, 1921–1945, volume 6, (Hochbaum-Klutmann)* (Osnabrück: Biblio Publishing, 2002), p. 100.
35. Moll, M., *Fuehrer-Erlasse 1939–1945* (Wiesbaden: Franz Steiner Publishing, 1997), p. 206.
36. Handbook on German Military Forces, 1945, TM-30-451, War Department (Washington D.C.: United States GPO, 1945).

Chapter 1

1. Hoefer, F., "The Nazi Penal System," II, 35 *Journal of Criminal Law & Criminology* 385 (1944-1945), p. 385.
2. *Ibid.*, p. 386.
3. *Ibid.*, p. 387.
4. *Ibid.*, p. 388.
5. *Ibid.*, p. 389.
6. *Ibid.*, p. 390.
7. *Ibid.*, p. 391.
8. *Ibid.*, p. 392.
9. *Ibid.*, p. 393.
10. Hoefer, F., "The Nazi Penal System," I, 35 *Journal of Criminal Law & Criminology* 385 (1944-1945), p. 30.
11. *Ibid.*, p. 31.
12. *Ibid.*, p. 32.
13. *Ibid.*, p. 33.
14. *Ibid.*, p. 34.
15. *Ibid.*, p. 35.
16. *Ibid.*, p. 38.

Chapter 2

1. Schwinge, E., *The German Military Justice in the Time of National Socialism* (Strasbourg: Elwert Publishing, 1978), p. 246.
2. Messerschmidt, M., *The Wehrmacht Justice, 1933–1945* (Schöningh: Paderborn, 2005), p. 69.

3. Messerschmidt, M., and Wüllner, F., *The Wehrmacht judicial in the service of National Socialism* (Baden-Baden: Nomos Publishing, 1987), p. 34.

4. Messerschmidt, *op. cit.*

5. Schwinge, *op. cit.*, p. 280.

6. Block, J., *The Elimination and Restriction of the German Ordinary Military Jurisdiction During the Second World War* (Würzburg: Offsetdruck Gugel, 1967), p. 3.

7. Messerschmidt, *op. cit.*, p. 126.

8. *Ibid.*, p. 127.

9. Wüllner, F., *The Nazi Military Ruling and the Misery of Historiography: A Basic Research Report* (Baden-Baden: Nomos Publishing, 1996), p. 648.

10. Schwinge, *op. cit.*, p. 101.

11. Wüllner, *op. cit.*, p. 636.

12. Klausch, H.-P., *Die Bewährungstruppe 500* (Bremen: Temmen, 1995), pp. 40-41.

13. *Ibid.*, p. 42.

14. Wachsmann, N., *Hitler's Prison: Legal Terror in Nazi Germany* (New Haven: Yale University Press, 2004), p. 66.

15. Mitcham, Jr., S. W., *Hitler's Legions* (London: Martin Secker and Warburg Ltd., 1985), p. 219.

16. *Ibid.*

17. Absolon, R., *The Wehrmacht in the Third Reich—Volume III—August 3, 1934—February 4, 1938* (Boppard am Rhein: Harald Boldt Publisher, 1975), p. 14.

18. Klausch, *op. cit.*, p. 55.

19. Messerschmidt, *op. cit.*, p. 76.

20. Mitcham, *op. cit.*, p. 219.

21. Block, *op. cit.*, p. 55.

22. Angermund, R., *German Judiciary 1919–1945: Crisis Experience, Illusion, Political Jurisprudence* (Frankfurt: Fischer Publishing, 1997), p. 12.

23. Müller, I., *Hitler's Justice: The Courts of the Third Reich* (Cambridge: Harvard University Press, 1992), p. 196.

24. Wachsmann, *op. cit.*, p. 70.

25. *Ibid.*, p. 71.

26. Klausch, *op. cit.*, p. 14.

27. *Ibid.*, p. 15.

28. *Ibid.*

29. Müller, *op. cit.*, p. 200.

30. Messerschmidt and Wüllner, *op. cit.*, p. 50.

31. Mitcham, *op. cit.*, p. 230.

32. Klausch, *op. cit.*, p. 20.

33. *Ibid.*

34. *Ibid.*

35. Seidler, F. W., *Prostitution, Homosexuality, Self-Mutilation* (Berlin: K. Vowinckel, 1977), p. 193.

36. *Ibid.*, p. 201.

37. Westerlund, L., *German Prison Camps in Finland and in the Border Areas from 1941 to 1944* (Helsinki: Tammi, 2008), p. 33.

38. Block, *op. cit.*, p. 10.

39. *Ibid.*

40. *Ibid.*, p. 88.

41. Mitcham, *op. cit.*, p. 205.

42. Brownmiller, S., *Against Out Will* (New York: Ballantine Books, 1993), p. 48.

Chapter 3

1. Messerschmidt, M., *The Wehrmacht Justice, 1933–1945* (Schöningh: Paderborn, 2005), p. 100.

2. *Ibid.*

3. Mitcham, Jr., S. W., *Hitler's Legions* (London: Martin Secker and Warburg Ltd., 1985), p. 299.

4. Absolon, R., *The Wehrmacht in the Third Reich—Volume III—August 3, 1934– February 4, 1938* (Boppard am Rhein: Harald Boldt Publisher, 1975), p. 58.

5. Tessin, G., *Associations and Troops of the German Wehrmacht and Waffen SS in the Second World War 1939–1945*, Volume IV (Osnabrück: Biblio, 1976), pp. 49-55.

6. *Ibid.*, p. 57.

7. *Ibid.*, p. 59.

8. *Ibid.*, p. 61.

9. Tieke, W., *Das Ende zwischen Oder und Elbe* (Stuttgart: Motorbuch Publishing, 1995), p. 137.

10. Ustinow, D. F., *et al.*, *Geschichte des Zweiten Welt Krieges 1939–1945* (Berlin: Militärverlag der DDR, 1982), p. 87.

11. *Nipe, G. M., Decision in the Ukraine: German Tank Operations on the Eastern Front, Summer 1943 (Mechanicsburg: Stackpole Books, 2012).*

12. Tessin, *op. cit.*, p. 80.

13. Klausch, H.-P., *Die Bewährungstruppe 500* (Bremen: Temmen, 1995), p. 22.

14. Lexicon of the Wehrmacht. www.lexikon-der-Wehrmacht.de.

15. *Ibid.*

16. *Ibid.*

17. *Ibid.*

18. *Ibid.*

19. *Ibid.*

20. The German Replacement Army. Military Intelligence Division (Washington D.C: War Department, 1944), p. 41

21. Lexicon of the Wehrmacht. www.lexikon-der-Wehrmacht.de.

22. *Ibid.*

23. *Ibid.*

24. *Ibid.*

25. *Ibid.*

26. *Ibid.*

27. *Ibid.*

28. Bade, C., Skowronski, L., and Viebig, M., *NS-Military Justice in the Second World War* (Göttingen Vandenhoeck and Ruprecht, 2004), p. 284.

29. Lexicon of the Wehrmacht. www.lexikon-der-Wehrmacht.de.

30. *Ibid.*

31. *Ibid.*

32. *Ibid.*

33. *Ibid.*

34. *Ibid.*

35. *Ibid.*

36. *Ibid.*

37. *Ibid.*

38. *Ibid.*

39. *Ibid.*

40. *Ibid.*

41. *Ibid.*

42. *Ibid.*

43. *Ibid.*

44. *Ibid.*

45. *Ibid.*

46. *Ibid.*

47. *Ibid.*

48. *Ibid.*

49. *Ibid.*

50. *Ibid.*

51. Ziemke, E. F., *Stalingrad to Berlin: The German Defeat in the East* (Washington D.C.: Centre of Military History, US Army, 2002), p. 325.

52. Mitcham, Jr., S. W., *The Tank Legions* (Mechanicsburg: Stackpole Books, 2000), p. 104.
53. *"How Panfilov's Twenty-Eight became a symbol of Red Army soldier's heroism,"* www. fort-russ.com. Retrieved October 7, 2016.
54. Braithwaite, R., *Moscow 1941: A City and Its People at War* (Old Saybrook: Tantor Media, 2006), p. 283.
55. *Ibid.*, p. 284.
56. Mitcham, *op. cit.*, 2000, p. 105.
57. *Ibid.*, p. 106.
58. Stoves, R., *The Armoured and Motorised German Divisions and Brigades 1935–45* (Bad Nauheim: Podzun-Pallas Publishing, 1986), p. 300.
59. *"Organizational History of the German Armoured Formation 1939–1945,"* United States Army Command and General Staff College. usacac.army.mil/CAC2/CGSC/CARL/nafziger/939GXPZ.PDF. Retrieved June 20, 2016.
60. Munoz, A. J., *Forgotten Legions: Obscure Combat Formations of the Waffen-SS* (Boulder: Paladin Press, 1991), p. 42
61. *Ibid.*, p. 50.
62. Hamacher, G., *Against Hitler: Germans in the Resistance, in the Armed Forces of the Anti-Hitler Coalition and the Movement "Free Germany": Short Biographies* (Berlin: Karl Dietz Publishing, 2005), p. 76.
63. Brownmiller, S., *Against Our Will* (New York: Ballantine Books, 1993), p. 78.
64. *Ibid.*
65. Kalmbach, P. L., "Polizeiliche Ermittlungsorgane der Wehrmachtjustiz," www.researchgate.net/publication/259929781_Polizeiliche_Ermittlungsorgane_der_Wehrmachtjustiz.
66. *Ibid.*
67. Goeschel, C., *Suicide in Nazi Germany* (Oxford: Oxford University Press, 2009), p. 200.
68. Kalmbach, *op. cit.*
69. Ambrose, S.E., *Handbook of German Military Forces* (Baton Rouge: Louisiana State University Press, 1990), p. 54.
70. *Disobedience as a Virtue: The Anklam Military Arrest and the Military Justice in the Third Reich.* Director: Jörg Hermann, Germany 2009, approx. eighty-minute movie.
71. "The Fort Zinna Prison," Foundation Sachsische Gedenkstatten, en.stsg.de /cms/node/887. Retrieved May 5, 2017.
72. Eberlein, M., Haase, N., and Oleschinski, W.. *Torgau in the Hinterland of the Second World War: Military Justice, Military Prisons, Imperial War Tribunal.* Series of the Sächsische Gedenkstätten to commemorate the victims of political violence, Vol. 6 (Leipzig: 1999).
73. "Military prison—Germersheim, Germany," www.waymarking.com; www.waymarking.com/waymarks/WMFJE9_Military_prison_Germersheim_Germany. Retrieved May 20, 2017.
74. "Flossenburg/Freiberg," The Holocaust Encyclopedia, www.ushmm.org/wlc/en/article.php?ModuleId=10007297. Retrieved May 19, 2017.
75. Seidler, F. W., *The Camp of Gdansk-Matzkau Prison in the Waffen-SS* (Königsberg: Bernard & Graefe, 1992), p. 355.

Chapter 4

1. Munoz, A. J., *Forgotten Legions: Obscure Combat Formations of the Waffen-SS* (Boulder: Paladin Press, 1991), p. 100.
2. *Ibid.*, p. 102.
3. *Ibid.*
4. Bennighof, M., *Air Pollution: The Waffen SS Parachute Battalion* (Avananche Press, 2015); www.avalanchepress.com/AirPollution.php. Retrieved May 22, 2017.
5. Hermes, O., *500th SS Parachute Battalion* (Saarbrücken Bellum Publishing, 2012), p. 88.
6. *Ibid.*
7. *Ibid.*

8. *Ibid.*
9. Munoz, *op. cit.*, p. 141.
10. *Ibid.*, p. 146.
11. Bennighof, *op. cit.*
12. Hermes, *op. cit.*, 90.
13. Munoz, *op. cit.*, p. 160.

Chapter 5

1. Williamson, G., and Andrew, S., *The Waffen-SS: 24. to 38. Divisions, & Volunteer Legions* (Oxford: Osprey Publishing, 2004), p. 16.
2. Stein, G. H., *The Waffen SS* (Ithaca: Cornell University Press, 1984), p. 266.
3. Borodziej, W., *The Warsaw Uprising of 1944* (Madison: University of Wisconsin Press, 2006), p. 101.
4. Snyder, T., *Bloodlands: Europe Between Hitler and Stalin* (New York: Basic Books, 2012), p. 246.
5. Grunberger, R., *The 12-Year Reich: A Social History of Nazi Germany, 1933–1945* (New York: Holt, Rinehart and Winston, 1971), p. 104.
6. Stein, *op. cit.*, p. 268.
7. Senft, W., *From the Holzknecht from the Salzkammergut to the Wilddiebkommando Oranienburg of the Waffen-SS* (Linz: Freya Publishing, 2009), p. 275.
8. MacLean, F. L., *The Cruel Hunters: SS-Sonderkommando Dirlewanger Hitler's Most Notorious Anti-Partisan Unit* (Atglen: Schiffer Publishing, 1998), p. 99.
9. Klausch, H.-P., *Antifascists in SS Uniform. Fate and Resistance of the German Political Concentration Camp Prisoners, Prisoners of Conscience and Wehrmacht Prisoners in the SS-Special Formation Dirlewanger* (Bremen: Edition Temmen, 1993), p. 491.
10. Williamson, *op. cit.*, p. 23.
11. Stein, *op. cit.*, p. 272.
12. Kitchen, M., *The Third Reich: Charisma and Community* (Abingdon: Routledge, 2008), p. 267.
13. Williamson, *op. cit.*, p. 44.
14. Klausch, *op. cit.*, p. 332.
15. *Ibid.*
16. Nowak, W., and Kuźniak, A., *My Warsaw Madness. The Other Side of the Warsaw Uprising* (Warsaw: Gazeta Wyborcza, 2004), p. 29.
17. Weale, A., *The SS: A New History* (London: Abacus Publishing, 2010), p. 400.
18. Michaelis, R., *Das SS-Sonderkommando Dirlewanger. Ein Beispiel deutscher Beatzungspolitik in Weißrussland* (Berlin, Michaelis Verlag, 1999), p. 67.
19. Day, M, "Notorious SS unit traced," *The Daily Telegraph*, April 17, 2009. Retrieved May 23, 2017.
20. Mitcham, Jr., S. W., *German Order of Battle: Panzer, Panzer Grenadier, and Waffen SS Divisions in World War II* (Mechanicsburg: Stackpole Books, 2007), pp. 156-157.

Chapter 6

1. Edwards, R., *Scouts Out: A History of German Armoured Reconnaissance Units in World War II* (Mechanisburg: Stackpole Books, 2014), p. 107
2. *Ibid.*
3. *Ibid.*
4. *Ibid.*
5. *Ibid.*
6. O'Reilly, T.. *Hitler's Irishmen* (Cork: Mercier Press, 2008), p. 301.
7. *Ibid., p. 304.*
8. Tessin, G., *Verbände und Truppen der deutschen Wehrmacht und Waffen-SS im Zweiten Weltkrieg, 1939–1945.* Vol. IV: Die Landstreitkräfte 15-30 (Frankfurt am Main: Mittler, 1970).

9. McNab, C., *Hitler's Elite: The SS 1939–45* (London: Bloomsbury Publishing, 2013), p. 268.

10. *Ibid.*, p. 269.
11. Munoz, A. J., *Forgotten Legions: Obscure Combat Formations of the Waffen-SS* (Boulder: Paladin Press, 1991), p. 198.
12. *Ibid.*, pp. 200–1
13. *Ibid.*
14. *Ibid.*
15. "Organizational History of 371st through 719th German Infantry, Security and Tank Grenadier Divisions 1939-1945," *The Nafziger Orders Of Battle Collection*, Ike Skelton Combined Arms Research Library Digital Library (Ft. Leavenworth U.S. Army Command and General Staff College).
16. *Ibid.*
17. *Ibid.*
18. *Ibid.*
19. Mitcham, Jr., S. W., *German Order of Battle: 1st–290th Infantry Divisions in World War II* (Mechanicsburg: Stackpole Books, 2007), p. 85.
20. Lexicon of the Wehrmacht. www.lexikon-der-Wehrmacht.de.
21. *Ibid.*
22. *Ibid.*
23. *Ibid.*
24. *Ibid.*
25. *Ibid.*
26. *Ibid.*
27. *Ibid.*
28. *Ibid.*
29. *Ibid.*
30. *Ibid.*
31. *Ibid.*
32. *Ibid.*
33. *Ibid.*
34. *Ibid.*
35. *Ibid.*
36. *Ibid.*
37. *Ibid.*
38. *Ibid.*
39. *Ibid.*
40. *Ibid.*
41. *Ibid.*
42. *Ibid.*
43. *Ibid.*
44. *Ibid.*
45. *Ibid.*

Chapter 7

1. Hamacher, G., *Against Hitler: Germans in the Resistance, in the Armed Forces of the Anti-Hitler Coalition and the Movement "Free Germany": Short Biographies* (Berlin: Karl Dietz Publishing, 2005), p. 90.
2. Klausch, H.-P., *The 999: from the Brigade "Z" to the Africa Division 999: Probation Battalions and Their Share of the Anti-Fascist Resistance* (Frankfurt am Main: Röderberg Publishing, 1986), p. 300.
3. *Ibid.*, P. 315
4. Hamacher, *op. cit.*, p. 101.
5. Tessin, G., *Associations and Troops of the German Wehrmacht and the Waffen-SS in the Second World War 1939–1945*, 20 volumes (Osnabrück: Biblio, 1976), p. 200.
6. *Ibid.*

7. *Ibid.*

8. *Ibid.*
9. *Ibid.*
10. *Ibid.*
11. *Blaxland, G., The Buffs (Oxford: Osprey, 2012), p. 35.*
12. *Dougherty, M., Tanks From World War I to the Present Day, Compared & Contrasted (London: Amber Publishing, 2010), p. 94.*
13. *Watson, B. A., Exit Rommel: The Tunisian Campaign, 1942–43 (Mechanicsburg Stackpole Books, 2007), pp. 66-67.*
14. Dear, I. C. B., and Foot, M. R. D., (eds), *The Oxford Companion to World War II* (Oxford: Oxford University Press, 1995), p. 1,138.
15. *Watson, op. cit., p. 69.*
16. *Ibid.*
17. *Perrett, B., At All Companiests: Stories of Impossible Victories (London: Cassell Military Classics, 1998), p. 160.*
18. *Evans, B., With the East Surreys in Tunisia and Italy 1942–1945: Fighting for Every River and Mountain (Philadelphia: Casemate, 2012), p. 125.*
19. *Ford, K., Battle-axe Division: From Africa to Italy with the 78 Division 1942–45 (Stroud: Sutton, 1999) p. 52.*
20. *Perrett, op. cit., p. 163.*
21. *Ford, op. cit., p. 56.*
22. *Ibid.*
23. *Evans, op. cit., p. 126.*
24. *Perrett, op. cit., p. 165.*
25. *Ford, op. cit., p. 77.*
26. *Sulzberger, C. L., World War II (Boston: Houghton Mifflin Harcourt, 1985), p. 114.*
27. *Ibid.*
28. *Ibid.*
29. *Ibid.*

Chapter 8

1. Madej, V. W., *German Army Order of Battle 1939–1945*, Vol. 1 (Allentown: Game Marketing, 1981), p. 50.
2. *Ibid.*
3. *Ibid.*, p. 55.
4. *Ibid.*, p. 57.
5. *Ibid.*, p. 58.
6. *Ibid.*, p. 59.
7. *Ibid.*, p. 60.
8. *Ibid.*, p. 61.
9. Dunn, Jr., W. S., *Second Front Now-1943: An Opportunity Delayed* (Tuscaloosa: University Alabama Press, 2009), p. 148.
10. *Ibid.*, p. 151.
11. *Ibid.*, p. 153.
12. Madej, *op. cit.*, p. 68.
13. Lexicon of the Wehrmacht. www.lexikon-der-Wehrmacht.de.
14. *Ibid.*
15. *Ibid.*
16. *Ibid.*
17. *Ibid.*
18. Handbook on German Military Forces, 1945, TM-30-451, War Department (Washington D.C.: United States GPO, 1945).

Chapter 9

1. Blair, C., *Hitler's U-boat War, Vol. II: The Hunted, 1942-1945* (Random House, 1998), p. 622.
2. Snyder, D. R., and Patchan, S. C., *Sex Crimes Under the Wehrmacht* (Lincoln: University of Nebraska Press, 2007), p. 242.
3. Blaszczyk, M., *Stalag IA Stablack*. The account of a Polish POW at Stalag IA. "The Wartime Memories Project," www.allstalags.com/stalag-ia.html. Retrieved May 10, 2017.
4. *Ibid.*
5. Wüllner, F., *The NS: Military Justice and the Misery of History* (Baden-Baden: Nomos Publishing, 1991), p. 661.
6. Blair, *op. cit.*, p. 648.
7. Busch, R., and Röll, H.-J., *German U-boat Commanders of World War II: A Biographical Dictionary* (United States Naval Institute, 1999), p. 201.
8. *Ibid.*
9. Madsen, C., "Victims of Circumstance: the Execution of German Deserters by Surrendered German Troops Under Canadian Control in Amsterdam, May 1945," *Canadian Military History*, Vol. 2: Issue 1, Article 8, 1993.
10. *Ibid.*
11. "Menschlich bedrückend," *Kriegsgerichte. Der Spiegel*. Issue 38. September 12, 1966.
12. *Ibid.*
13. *Ibid.*
14. *Ibid.*
15. Gardner, E. R., *Military Justice in the German Air Force During World War II*, 49 *Journal of Criminal Law and Criminology*, (1958–1959), p. 195.
16. Ruffner, K., *Luftwaffe Field Divisions, 1941–45* (Oxford: Osprey, 1997), pp. 127-131.
17. *Ibid.*
18. *Ibid.*
19. *Ibid.*
20. *Ibid.*
21. *Ibid.*
22. *Ibid.*
23. *Ibid.*
24. *Ibid.*
25. *Ibid.*

Chapter 10

1. O'Kand, R., *Terror, Force and States: The Path from Modernity* (London: Cheltham Publishing, 1996), p. 19.
2. Thurston, R., "The Family during the Great Terror 1935-1941." *Soviet Studies*. 43, 3 (1991), p. 553.
3. *Ibid.*, p. 574.
4. Phillips, P., *The Tragedy of Nazi Germany* (London: Routledge & Kegan Paul PLC, 1969), p. 156.
5. Hoffman, P., *The History of the German Resistance, 1933–1945* (Montreal: McGill-Queen's University Press, 2001), p. 519.
6. Phillips, *op. cit.*, p. 160.
7. Bundesarchiv Millitärarchiv, Freiburg. *Reichsgesetzblatt Teil 1*, 1939 (2 Halbahr), p. 1,455.
8. *Ibid.*, p. 1,457.
9. Phillips, *op. cit.*, p. 165.
10. *Oberkommando der Heers, Spione, Verräter und Saboteure* (OKH 1938), p. 12.
11. Hitler, A., and Hugh-Roper, T., (ed.), *Hitler's Table Talk* (Oxford: Enigma Books, 2001) p. 544.
12. Horbach, M., *Out of the Night* (London: Vallentine Mitchell, 1967), p. 38.
13. Kershaw, I., *Hitler 1936–1945: Hubris* (New York: W. W. Norton & Company, 1999), p. 374.

Bibliography

"Flossenburg/Freiberg," *The Holocaust Encyclopedia*, www.ushmm.org/wlc/en/article. php?ModuleId=10007297

"How Panfilov's Twenty-Eight became a symbol of Red Army soldier's heroism" www. fort-*russ.com*

"Kriegssonderstrafrechtsverordnung (KSSVO)," www.lexexakt.de

"Law on the Abolition of Military Judicial Jurisdiction of 17 August 1920," *German Reichsgesetzblatt Part I, 1867–1945*

"Menschlich bedrückend," *Kriegsgerichte. Der Spiegel.* Issue 38. September 12, 1966.

"Military prison—Germersheim, Germany," www.waymarking.com; www.waymarking.com/ waymarks/WMFJE9_Military_prison_Germersheim_Germany

"Organizational History of 371st through 719th German Infantry, Security and Tank Grenadier Divisions 1939-1945." *The Nafziger Orders Of Battle Collection.* Ike Skelton Combined Arms Research Library Digital Library. (Ft. Leavenworth U.S. Army Command and General Staff College)

"Organizational History of the German Armoured Formation 1939–1945" United States Army Command and General Staff College, usacac.army.mil/ CAC2/CGSC/CARL/ nafziger/939GXPZ.PDF

"The Fort Zinna Prison," Foundation Sachsische Gedenkstatten, en.stsg.de/cms/node/887

"The German Replacement Army," *Military Intelligence Division* (Washington D.C: War Department, 1944)

"Translation of Wehrkraftzersetzung," *Wörterbuch Englisch-Deutsch dictionary*; www.dict.cc/

1916 Handbook of the Turkish Army. (Nashville: Battery Press, 1999)

Absolon, R., *The Wehrmacht in the Third Reich—Volume III—August 3, 1934–February 4, 1938* (Boppard am Rhein: Harald Boldt Publisher, 1975)

Ambrose, S. E., *Handbook of German Military Forces* (Baton Rouge: Louisiana State University Press, 1990)

Angermund, R., *German Judiciary 1919–1945: Crisis Experience, Illusion, Political Jurisprudence* (Frankfurt: Fischer Publishing, 1997)

Bade, C., Skowronski, L., and Viebig, M., *NS-Military Justice in the Second World War* (Göttingen Vandenhoeck and Ruprecht, 2004)

Bennighof, M., *Air Pollution: The Waffen SS Parachute Battalion* (Avananche Press, 2015); www.avalanchepress.com/AirPollution.php

Bertaud, J.-P., The Army of the French Revolution: From Citizen-soldier to Instrument of Power (Princeton: Princeton University Press, 1988)

Blair, C., *Hitler's U-boat War, Vol. II: The Hunted, 1942–1945* (Random House, 1998)

Blaszczyk, M., *Stalag IA Stablack.* The account of a Polish POW at Stalag IA. "The Wartime Memories Project," www.allstalags.com/stalag-ia.html

Blaxland, G., The Buffs (Oxford: Osprey, 2012)

Block, J., *The Elimination and Restriction of the German Ordinary Military Jurisdiction During the Second World War* (Würzburg: Offsetdruck Gugel, 1967)

Borodziej, W., *The Warsaw Uprising of 1944* (Madison: University of Wisconsin Press, 2006)

Bradley, D., Hildebrand, K.-F., and Roevekamp, M., *The Generals of the Army, 1921–1945: The Military Generations of the Generals, as well as the Doctors, Veterinarians, Directors, Judges and Generals and Admirals* (Osnabrück: Biblio Publishing, 1993)

Braithwaite, R., *Moscow 1941: A City and Its People at War* (Old Saybrook: Tantor Media, 2006)

Brown, D., *The Galvanized Yankees* (Lincoln: University of Nebraska Press)

Brownmiller, S., *Against Our Will* (New York: Ballantine Books, 1993)

Bundesarchiv Millitärarchiv, Freiburg. *Reichsgesetzblatt Teil 1*, 1939 (2 Halbahr)

Busch, R., and Röll, H.-J., *German U-boat Commanders of World War II: A Biographical Dictionary* (United States Naval Institute, 1999)

Carles, P., "Les Bataillons d'Afrique," *www.musee-infanterie.com*

Crooks, J. J., *Historical Records of the Royal African Corps 1800–1821* (Dublin: Browne and Nolan Publishers, 1925)

Day, M., "Notorious SS unit traced," *The Daily Telegraph*, April 17, 2009

Dear, I. C. B., and Foot, M. R. D., (eds), *The Oxford Companion to World War II* (Oxford: Oxford University Press, 1995); *The Oxford Companion to World War II* (London: Oxford University Press, 2001)

Dermot, B., *The Generals of the Army, 1921–1945, volume 6, (Hochbaum-Klutmann)* (Osnabrück: Biblio Publishing, 2002)

Disobedience as a Virtue: The Anklam Military Arrest and the Military Justice in the Third Reich Director: Jörg Hermann, Germany 2009, approx. eighty-minute movie.

Dougherty, M., Tanks From World War I to the Present Day, Compared & Contrasted (London: Amber Publishing, *2010)*

Dunn, Jr., W. S. *Second Front Now-1943: An Opportunity Delayed* (Tuscaloosa: University Alabama Press, 2009)

Dyer, F. H. A., *Compendium of the War of the Rebellion*, Vol. 2 (Seattle: Morningside Press, 1979)

Eberlein, M., Haase, N., and Oleschinski, W., *Torgau in the Hinterland of the Second World War: Military Justice, Military Prisons, Imperial War Tribunal.* Series of the Sächsische Gedenkstätten to commemorate the victims of political violence, Vol. 6 (Leipzig, 1999)

Edwards, R., *Scouts Out: A History of German Armoured Reconnaissance Units in World War II* (Mechanisburg: Stackpole Books, 2014)

*Evans, B., With the East Surreys in Tunisia and Italy 1942–1945: Fighting for Every River and Mountain (*Philadelphia: Casemate, *2012)*

Faulkner Rossi, L., *Wehrmacht Priests: Catholicism and the Nazi War of Annihilation* (Cambridge: Harvard University Press, 2015)

Ford, K., *Battle-axe Division: From Africa to Italy with the 78 Division 1942–45. (Stroud: Sutton, 1999)*

Gardner, E. R., *Military Justice in the German Air Force During World War II*, 49 *Journal of Criminal Law & Criminology*, 195 (1958–1959)

Goeschel, C.. *Suicide in Nazi Germany* (Oxford: Oxford University Press, 2009)

Gribbohm, G., *The Reichskriegsgericht: The Institution and its Legal Evaluation* (Berlin: Wissenschaftliche Publishing, 2004)

Gruchmann, L., *Justice in the 3rd Reich 1933–1940* (Berlin: Oldenbourg Publishing, 2001)

Grunberger, R., *The 12-Year Reich: A Social History of Nazi Germany, 1933–1945* (New York: Holt, Rinehart and Winston, 1971)

Haase, N., *The Reichskriegsgericht and the Resistance to National Socialist Rule* (Berlin: Memorial to the German Resistance1993)

Hamacher, G., *Against Hitler: Germans in the Resistance, in the Armed Forces of the Anti-Hitler Coalition and the Movement "Free Germany": Short Biographies* (Berlin: Karl Dietz Publishing, 2005)

Handbook on German Military Forces, 1945, TM-30-451, War Department. (Washington D.C.: United States GPO, 1945)

Hermes, O., *500th SS Parachute Battalion* (Saarbrücken Bellum Publishing, 2012)

Hitler, A., and Hugh-Roper, T., (ed.), *Hitler's Table Talk* (Oxford: Enigma Books, 2001)

Hoefer, F., "The Nazi Penal System," I, 35 *Journal of Criminal Law & Criminology* 385 (1944-1945)

Hoefer, F., "The Nazi Penal System," II, 35 *Journal of Criminal Law & Criminology* 385 (1944-1945)

Hoffman, P., *The History of the German Resistance, 1933-1945* (Montreal: McGill-Queen's University Press, 2001)

Horbach, M., *Out of the Night* (London: Vallentine Mitchell, 1967)

Kalmbach, P. L., "Polizeiliche Ermittlungsorgane der Wehrmachtjustiz; www.researchgate.net/publication/259929781_Polizeiliche_Ermittlungsorgane_ der_Wehrmachtjustiz

Kershaw, I., *Hitler 1936–1945: Hubris* (New York: W. W. Norton & Company, 1999)

Kitchen, M., *The Third Reich: Charisma and Community* (Abingdon: Routledge, 2008)

Klausch, H.-P., *Antifascists in SS Uniform: Fate and Resistance of the German Political Concentration Camp Prisoners, Prisoners of Conscience and Wehrmacht Prisoners in the SS Special Formation Dirlewanger* (Bremen: Edition Temmen, 1993); *Die Bewährungstruppe 500* (Bremen: Temmen, 1995); *The 999: from the Brigade "Z" to the Africa Division 999: Probation Battalions and their Share of the Anti-Fascist Resistance* (Frankfurt am Main: Röderberg Publishing, 1986)

Lexicon of the Wehrmacht. www.lexikon-der-Wehrmacht.de

Lo Presti, F., "French Penal Regiment Organization," *www.napoleon-series.org*

MacLean, F. L., *The Cruel Hunters: SS-Sonderkommando Dirlewanger Hitler's Most Notorious Anti-Partisan Unit* (Atglen: Schiffer Publishing, 1998)

Madej, V. W., *German Army Order of Battle 1939–1945*, Volume I (Allentown: Game Marketing, 1981)

Madsen, C., "Victims of Circumstance: the Execution of German Deserters by Surrendered German Troops Under Canadian Control in Amsterdam, May 1945," *Canadian Military History*, Vol. 2, Issue 1, Article 8, 1993.

McNab, C., *Hitler's Elite: The SS 1939–45* (London: Bloomsbury Publishing, 2013)

Messerschmidt, M., and Wüllner, F.*The Military Justice in the Service of National Socialism: Destruction of a Legend* (Baden-Baden: Nomos Publishing, 1987)

Messerschmidt, M., *The Wehrmacht Justice, 1933–1945* (Schöningh: Paderborn, 2005)

Michaelis, R., *Das SS-Sonderkommando Dirlewanger. Ein Beispiel deutscher Besatzungspolitik in Weißrussland* (Berlin, Michaelis Verlag, 1999)

Mitcham, Jr., S. W., *Hitler's Legions* (London: Martin Secker and Warburg Ltd., 1985); *The Tank Legions (Mechanicsburg: Stackpole Books, 2000); German Order of Battle: Panzer, Panzer Grenadier, and Waffen SS divisions in World War II* (Mechanicsburg: Stackpole Books, 2007); *German Order of Battle: 1st–290th Infantry Divisions in World War II* (Mechanicsburg: Stackpole Books, 2007)

Moll, M., *Fuehrer-Erlasse 1939–1945* (Wiesbaden: Franz Steiner Publishing, 1997)

Müller, I., *Hitler's Justice: The Courts of the Third Reich* (Cambridge: Harvard University Press, 1992)

Munoz, A. J., *Forgotten Legions: Obscure Combat Formations of the Waffen-SS* (Boulder: Paladin Press, 1991)

Nipe, G. M., *Decision in the Ukraine: German Tank Operations on the Eastern Front, Summer 1943 (Mechanicsburg: Stackpole Books, 2012)*

Nowak, W., and Kuźniak, A., *My Warsaw Madness: The Other Side of the Warsaw Uprising* (Warsaw: Gazeta Wyborcza, 2004)

O'Kand, R., *Terror, Force and States: The Path from Modernity* (London: Cheltham Publishing, 1996)

O'Reilly, T., *Hitler's Irishmen* (Cork: Mercier Press, 2008)

Oberkommando der Heers, Spione, Verräter und Saboteure (OKH 1938)

Paul, G., *Disobedient Soldiers: Dissent, Refusal and Resistance of German Soldiers (1939–1945)* (Sankt Ingbert: Rohrig University Publishers, 1994)

Päuser, F., *The Rehabilitation of Deserters of the German Wehrmacht under Historical, Juridical and Political Aspects, with Commentary on the Law for the Abolition of National Socialist Judgments* (Munich: University of the German Armed Forces, 2005)

Perrett, B., *At All Companiests: Stories of Impossible Victories (London: Cassell Military Classics, 1998)*

Phillips, P., *The Tragedy of Nazi Germany* (London: Routledge & Kegan Paul PLC, 1969)

Pyl'cyn, A., *Penalty Strike: The Memoirs of a Red Army Penal Company Commander, 1943–45* (Mechanicsburg: Stackpole Books, 2006)

Ricchiardi, E., *The Battalion of Frank Hunters* (The Italian State Archives of Turin, 2014)

Ruffner, K., *Luftwaffe Field Divisions, 1941–45* (Oxford: Osprey, 1997)

Schwinge, E., *The German Military Justice in the Time of National Socialism* (Strasbourg: Elwert Publishing, 1978)

Seidler, F. W., *Prostitution, Homosexuality, Self-Mutilation* (Berlin: K. Vowinckel, 1977); *The Camp of Gdansk-Matzkau Prison in the Waffen-SS* (Königsberg: Bernard & Graefe, 1992)

Senft, W., *From the Holzknecht from the Salzkammergut to the Wilddiebkommando Oranienburg of the Waffen-SS* (Linz: Freya Publishing, 2009)

Sicard, J., "Les Bataillons d'Infanterie Legere d'Afrique et leurs insignes, 1832–1972," *Militaria Magazine*, September 1994

Snyder, D. R., and Patchan, S. C., *Sex Crimes Under the Wehrmacht* (Lincoln: University of Nebraska Press, 2007)

Snyder, T., *Bloodlands: Europe Between Hitler and Stalin* (New York: Basic Books, 2012)

Stargardt, N., *The German War: A Nation Under Arms, 1939–1945: Citizens and Soldiers* (New York: Basic Books, 2015)

Stein, G. H. *The Waffen SS* (Ithaca: Cornell University Press, 1984)

Stoves, R., *The Armoured and Motorised German Divisions and Brigades 1935–45* (Bad Nauheim: Podzun-Pallas Publishing, 1986)

Sulzberger, C. L., *World War II* (Boston: Houghton Mifflin Harcourt, 1985)

Suvorov, V., *Inside The Soviet Army* (London: Hamish Hamilton, 1982)

Tessin, G., *Associations and Troops of the German Wehrmacht and Waffen SS in the Second World War 1939–1945*, Volume IV. (Osnabrück: Biblio, 1976); *Verbände und Truppen der deutschen Wehrmacht und Waffen-SS im Zweiten Weltkrieg, 1939–1945*. Vol. IV: Die Landstreitkräfte 15 -30. (Frankfurt am Main: Mittler, 1970)

Thurston, R., "The Family during the Great Terror 1935–1941," *Soviet Studies*, 43, 3 (1991)

Tieke, W., *Das Ende zwischen Oder und Elbe* (Stuttgart: Motorbuch Publishing, 1995)

Ustinow, D. F., *et al.*, *Geschichte des Zweiten Welt Krieges 1939–1945* (Berlin: Militärverlag der DDR, 1982)

Wachsmann, N., *Hitler's Prison: Legal Terror in Nazi Germany* (New Haven: Yale University Press, 2004)

Wagner, W., *The People's Court in the National Socialist State* (Munich 2011)

Walle, H., (ed.), *Uprising of Conscience: Military Resistance against Hitler and the Nazi Regime 1933–1945*, 4th edition (Mittler, Berlin, 1994)

Watson, B. A., *Exit Rommel: The Tunisian Campaign, 1942–43* (Mechanicsburg Stackpole Books, 2007)

Weale, A., *The SS: A New History* (London: Abacus Publishing, 2010)

Westerlund, L., *German Prison Camps in Finland and in the Border Areas from 1941 to 1944* (Helsinki: Tammi, 2008)

Wette, W., *The Wehrmacht History, Myth, Reality* (Cambridge: Harvard University Press, 2007)

Williamson, G., and Andrew, S., *The Waffen-SS: 24. to 38. Divisions, & Volunteer Legions* (Oxford: Osprey Publishing, 2004)

Wüllner, F., *The Nazi Military Ruling and the Misery of Historiography: A Basic Research Report* (Baden-Baden: Nomos Publishing, 1996)

Ziemke, E. F., *Stalingrad to Berlin: The German Defeat in the East* (Washington D.C.: Center of Military History, US Army, 2002)x